Eucharist and Covenant in John's Last Supper Account

(Jn 12:44-17:26)

Monsignor Anthony A. La Femina, S.T.L., J.C.D.

New Hope Publications

Nihil obstat
Very Rev. Denis Robinson, OSB
St. Meinrad School of Theology
April 2011

Imprimatur (text not inclusive of Appendix 2)
Joseph E. Kurtz, DD
Archbishop of Louisville
May 26, 2011

The *nihil obstat* and *imprimatur* are official declarations that a book or pamphlet is free of doctrinal or moral error. No implication is contained therein that those who have granted the nihil obstat and imprimatur agree with the contents, opinions, or statements expressed.

The Bible text in this publication is from The Holy Bible, Revised Standard Version. Second Catholic Edition, San Francisco: Thomas Nelson Publishing for Ignatius Press, 2006. In certain instances, however, other translations were used and noted.

For additional copies of this book, contact:
St. Martin de Porres Dominican Community
PO Box 10
New Hope, KY 40052
270-325-3061
www.newhope-ky.org

Ask for stock #3278.

ISBN 978-1-892875-56-3

Front cover image: The Footwashing, © 2000 Msgr. Anthony A. La Femina

TABLE OF CONTENTS

Dedication

In homage to St. John the Evangelist,
to my Holy Father St. Dominic,
and to my spiritual mother,
Mrs. Dorothy O'Neill Weimar, O.P.

Preface

This Preface's purpose is to express my deepest gratitude to the many persons who have helped me in so many different ways throughout the many years it has taken to complete this book. So many years have passed that a number of those persons are no longer on this earth. Without committing any person mentioned here to the opinions and interpretations in this book, I thank them for their kindnesses and pray that the Lord bless them, both the living and the dead.

My first debt of gratitude is to the Lord, his Immaculate Mother, and my holy Father St. Dominic, who have granted me so many graces over the span of the years while writing this book. Again, I obviously owe a particular debt of gratitude in the Lord to one of the persons to whom I have dedicated this book and who was responsible for its writing: Mrs. Dorothy O'Neill Weimar, O.P. I also thank my dearest mother and father for all they have done to help me realize this work.

In addition, I would like to thank the following persons: His Eminence Edouard Cardinal Gagnon, p.s.s.; His Eminence Robert J. Cardinal Knox; Most Rev. Fabian W. Bruskewitz, Bishop of Lincoln; Most Rev. Peter Elliott, Auxiliary Bishop of Melbourne; Rev. Msgr. John A. Abruzzese; Rev. Msgr. Hilary C. Franco; Rev. Msgr. Charles Burton Mouton; Rev. Msgr. Robert J. Sarno; Rev. Charles Angell, S.A.; Rev. T. Paul Broadhurst, C.S.B.; Rev. Ignace de la Potterie, S.J; Rev. Michael Dogali; Rev. Roland Fournier, p.s.s.; Rev. Peter Gumpel, S.J.; Rev. Dennis J. McCarthy, S.J.; Rev. Jeremy A. Paretsky, O.P; Rev. Stanley Smolenski, s.p.m.a.; Rev. Deacon Jerome Remkiewicz; Dr. Scott W. Hahn; Mr. Paul R. Lussier; and Dr. Ralph Marcarelli. I owe a special debt of gratitude to Theo Stearns, Hugh Pimentel, Ann Brown and the members of and workers at the St. Martin de Porres Lay Dominican Community, and to Dr. Sebastiano Gattoni-Celli, who have not ceased to encourage my work and who have been so faithful in reviewing my texts and giving their valuable suggestions. Nor could I ever forget all my very dear friends, too numerous to list here, who so faithfully attended for a good number of years my classes in Charleston, South Carolina, during which I both explained and better understood together with them the material I humbly present in this book.

Foreword

The Church calls the Eucharistic Mystery simply the Mystery of Faith. It is the mystery by which Our Lord Jesus Christ makes ever present in the Church the outpouring of His life on the Cross for the salvation of the world. In truth, the entire good of the faith is contained in the Most Holy Eucharist, for it is the Body, Blood, Soul and Divinity of Our Lord Jesus Christ, God the Son made man to save all men. The Second Vatican Ecumenical Council, making reference to the authoritative exposition of the doctrine on the Holy Eucharist by Saint Thomas Aquinas, taught about the Most Blessed Sacrament with these words:

> But the other sacraments, and indeed all ecclesiastical ministries and works of the apostolate, are bound up with the Eucharist and are directed toward it. For in the most blessed Eucharist is contained the whole spiritual good of the Church, namely Christ Himself our Pasch and the living bread which gives life to men through His flesh—that flesh which is given life and gives life in the Holy Spirit. Thus men are invited and led to offer themselves, their works and all creation with Christ.[1]

By the grace of the Eucharistic Sacrifice, men have communion with Our Lord Jesus Christ, God the Son Incarnate, in His supreme act of pure and selfless love, the offering of His Body and Blood for them on the Cross. Participating in the Holy Mass and adoring the Most Blessed Sacrament, they—through, with and in Christ—offer all that they are and have to God the Father with the same pure and selfless love.

In his last Encyclical Letter, *Ecclesia de Eucharistia*, "On the Eucharist and Its Relationship to the Church," Blessed Pope John Paul II reminded the Church that her life has its "foundation and well-spring" in the Sacred Triduum of the Passion, Death and Resurrection of Our Lord Jesus Christ, which is fully contained in the Eucharistic Mystery, the Mystery of Faith.[2]

---

1 "Cetera autem Sacramenta, sicut et omnia ecclesiastica ministeria, et opera apostolatus, cum Sacra Eucharistia cohaerent et ad eam ordinantur. In Sanctissima Eucharistia totum bonum spirituale Ecclesiae continetur, ipse scilicet Christus, Pascha nostrum panisque vivus per Carnem suam Spirituo Sancto vivificatam et vivificantem vitam praestans hominibus, qui ita invitantur et adducuntur ad seipsos, suos labores cunctasque res creatas una cum Ipso offerendos." Sacrosanctum Concilium Oecumenicum Vaticanum II, Decretum de Presbyterorum Ministerio et Vita, *Presbyterorum Ordinis*. 7 decembris 1965, *Acta Apostolicae Sedis* 58 (1966), p. 997, n. 5. English version: Austin Flannery, O.P., ed. *Vatican Council II: The Conciliar and Post Conciliar Documents*, p. 871. Cf. *Summa Theologiae*, III, q. 65, a. 3, ad 1; and *Catechism of the Catholic Church*, n. 1324.
2 "[f]undamentum ... atque origo." Ioannes Paulus PP. II, Litterae Encyclicae *Ecclesia de Eucharistia*, "De Eucharistia eiusque necessitudine cum Ecclesia," 17 Aprilis 2003, *Acta Apostolicae Sedis* 95 (2003), p. 436, n. 5. English translation: Libreria Editrice Vaticana.

The Paschal Triduum, to use his words, "is as it were gathered up, fore-shadowed and 'concentrated' for ever in the gift of the Holy Eucharist."[3] He powerfully reminded the Church that Our Lord Jesus Christ, on the night before He died on the Cross for all men, entrusted to the Church the gift of the Holy Eucharist, "the perennial making present of the paschal mystery."[4]

Continuing his reflection, Blessed Pope John Paul II declared:

> The thought of this leads us to profound amazement and gratitude. In the paschal event and the Eucharist which makes it present throughout the centuries, there is truly enormous "capacity" which embraces all of history as the recipient of the grace of the redemption.[5]

Faithful members of the Church are filled with "profound amazement and gratitude" before the mystery of God's unceasing and immeasurable love of men as it is most perfectly expressed in His gift of the Holy Eucharist. It is a love which indeed embraces all space and all time, the entire world and all of its history.

Saint Paul expressed to the first Christians at Corinth the wonder which must fill the Christian mind and heart in the presence of the Most Blessed Sacrament:

> The cup of blessing which we bless,
> is it not a participation in the blood of Christ?
> The bread which we break,
> is it not a participation in the body of Christ?[6]

Confronting abuses which, already in the first years of the Church's life, had begun to enter into the celebration of the Holy Mass, Saint Paul instructed the Corinthians about the profound reverence and devoted love with which to approach the Eucharistic Sacrifice, recognizing in the Sacred Host the fulfillment of Christ's teaching in the Discourse on the Bread of Life: "I am the living bread which came down from heaven; if any one eats of this

---

[Hereafter, *EE*]. English translation: Pope John Paul II, Encyclical Letter *Ecclesia de Eucharistia*, "On the Eucharist in Its Relationship to the Church," 17 April 2003, Vatican City State: Libreria Editrice Vaticana, nd., p. 7, no. 5. [Hereafter, *EEE*].

3   "quasi colligitur et antecapitur et «consummatur» sempiternum in eucharistico dono...." *EE*, p. 436, n. 5. English translation: *EEE*, p. 7, no. 5.

4   "perpetuam mysterii Paschalis adimpletionem." *EE*, p. 436, n. 5. English translation: *EEE*, p. 7, no. 5.

5   "Haec nos cogitatio ad affectus perducit magni gratique stuporis. Etenim in Paschali eventu atque Eucharistia, quae illum per saecula exsequitur, exsistit re vera immensa «capacitas», qua tota continetur historia uti cui gratia redemptionis destinata est." *EE*, p. 436, n. 5. English translation: *EEE*, pp. 7-8, no. 5

6   *1 Cor* 10:16.

bread, he will live for ever; and the bread which I shall give for the life of the world is my flesh."[7]

Christ's words, in fact, recall the teaching of Moses, at the end of his days, regarding the covenant of all-merciful love, which God the Father had formed with men on Mount Sinai and which He manifested in a most striking way by the gift of manna, "bread which came down from heaven,"[8] which sustained them throughout their forty-year pilgrimage in the desert to reach the Promised Land.[9] Moses reminded them of the profound significance of God's gift, with these words:

> And he humbled you and let you hunger and fed you with manna, which you did not know, nor did your fathers know; that he might make you know that man does not live by bread alone, but that man lives by everything that proceeds out of the mouth of the LORD."[10]

Moses reminded the people that fidelity to the covenant of mercy and love, which God the Father had formed with them, meant total dependence upon God and His Providence, and, therefore, perfect obedience to His law which He has written into creation, has inscribed upon every human heart, and which He teaches us through His holy Word.

How much more should the Church understand that fidelity to the covenant of faithful and enduring love, sealed for us in the Paschal Triduum and fully contained in the Bread of Heaven which is Christ's Body, Blood, Soul and Divinity, means living according to the word of God, especially the Commandments. So central was the significance of the manna that Moses, at the command of the Lord, directed Aaron, the High Priest, to set aside a small portion of the manna to be kept for the succeeding generations, as a sign of the covenant of God with man.[11] In this way, he prefigured the practice of Eucharistic adoration, in order that the members of the Church may grow in knowledge and love of the Mystery of Faith, the Eucharistic Sacrifice and its fruit, Holy Communion.

The manna, the wondrous sign of God's faithful and enduring love, foreshadowed the definitive sign of His love in the sending of His only-begotten Son in human flesh, so that He might purify men of all sin and remain with them always through the Sacrament of His Real Presence, the Heavenly Bread which sustains them on their earthly pilgrimage to the true and lasting Promised Land which is Heaven. Recalling the gift of the manna in the

---

7   *Jn* 6:51.
8   Cf. *Ex* 16:14-15; and *Jn* 6:31-59.
9   Cf. *Ex* 16:35.
10   *Dt* 8:3.
11   Cf. *Ex* 16:31-36.

desert, Christ taught about the immeasurably greater sign, the Mystery of Faith, which is Himself really represent for all men under the species of bread and wine. He declared: "I am the living bread which came down from heaven; if any one eats of this bread, he will live for ever; and the bread which I shall give for the life of the world is my flesh."[12]

Monsignor Anthony A. La Femina, ordained over fifty years ago to offer daily, in the person of Christ, the Eucharistic Sacrifice for the salvation of the world, began some thirty-five years ago to write the book which you now have in your hands. The book, one can rightly say, is the fruit of the many years of his priestly life and ministry, always centered in the offering of the Holy Mass. As he informs the reader in the Introduction, the writing of the book was not his idea. A holy woman, Dorothy O'Neill Weimar, a Dominican oblate, who experienced the Mystery of Faith in a deeply mystical way, whom he was blessed to know from his youth, and who, like him, found in Saint Dominic Guzman a true spiritual master, simply told Father La Femina that the Lord wanted him to write about the Holy Eucharist. She herself had written about the Most Blessed Sacrament as the Passion and Death of the Lord, that is, as the Paschal Triduum, in the words of Pope John Paul II, "as it were gathered up, foreshadowed and 'concentrated' for ever."[13] Recognizing the depth of her mystical participation in the Mystery of Faith, Father La Femina took up the work of writing about the Most Blessed Sacrament, a work which was to span the greater part of his priestly life. Contemplating the great mystery of the Eucharistic Sacrifice, he understandably struggled to know how exactly the Lord wanted him to write about the Holy Eucharist, the most perfect expression of His unceasing and immeasurable love of men.

How fitting that a priest, amidst the great number and variety of his priestly works, should steadfastly pursue writing about the Holy Eucharist. Enjoying the fruits of Monsignor La Femina's persevering study and writing on the Eucharistic Mystery, the reader witnesses the wonder which has filled his mind and heart in the daily offering of the Holy Mass. In a profound way, he reflects the truth that Christ acts through his priestly ministry, uniting Heaven and Earth, making present His glorious Body, Blood, Soul and Divinity for the salvation of the world.

I am reminded of what Blessed Pope John Paul II wrote about the "profound amazement and gratitude" before the reality of the Eucharistic Sacrifice, which should fill the minds and hearts of all the faithful and, especially, of priests:

---

12   *Jn* 6:51.
13   "quasi colligitur et antecapitur et «consummatur» sempiternum ...." *EE*, p. 436, n. 5. English translation: *EEE*, p. 7, no. 5.

The amazement should always fill the Church assembled for the celebration of the Eucharist. But in a special way it should fill the minister of the Eucharist. For it is he who, by the authority given him in the Sacrament of priestly ordination, effects the consecration. It is he who says with the power coming to him from Christ in the Upper Room: "This is my Body which will be given up for you. This is the cup of my blood poured out for you...." The priest says these words, or rather *he puts his voice at the disposal of the One Who spoke these words in the Upper Room* and who desires that they should be repeated in every generation by all those who in the Church ministerially share in His priesthood.[14]

Through Eucharistic faith and devotion, both the priest and the faithful will be always deeply conscious that the priesthood is a gift given by Christ to His Church, so that He might be present, in every time and place, as Head and Shepherd of the flock, giving His life for the flock, above all, through the offering of the Holy Sacrifice of the Mass.

Quoting his Apostolic Letter *Dominicae Cenae*, written to all of the Bishops of the Church, on Holy Thursday of the second year of his pontificate, Blessed Pope John Paul II underlined the essential and central place of the Eucharistic Sacrifice in the life of the priest. He declared:

If the Eucharist is the center and summit of the Church's life, it is likewise the center and summit of priestly ministry. For this reason, with a heart filled with gratitude to our Lord Jesus Christ, I repeat that the Eucharist "is the principal and central *raison d'être* of the sacrament of priesthood, which effectively came into being at the moment of the institution of the Eucharist."[15]

Commenting on the number and variety of the responsibilities of the priest, Blessed Pope John Paul II observed that Eucharistic faith and devotion alone will permit the priest to remain focused in his priestly life, so that every act of his ministry may express the pastoral charity which has its source in the Mystery of Faith.

---

14 "Semper oportet hic stupor Ecclesiam pervadat in eucharistica Celebratione congregatam. Verum comitari debet praecipue Eucharistiae ministrum. Ipse enim, propter facultatem ipsi in sacramento Ordinationis sacerdotalis concessam, peragit consecrationem. Ex potestate, quae a Christo in Cenaculo ei obtingit, ipse pronuntiat voces: «Hoc est enim Corpus meum quod pro vobis tradetur... Hic est enim calix Sanguinis mei novi et aeterni testamenti qui pro vobis et pro multis effundetur...». Enuntiat haec verba sacerdos vel potius *os suum suamque vocem praestat Illi qui in Cenaculo haec vocabula exprompsit*, et qui voluit ut per aetates ab omnibus illis eadem iterarentur qui in Ecclesia ministeriale illius communicant sacerdotium." *EE*, p. 436, n. 5. English translation: *EEE*, p. 8, no. 5.

15 "Si vitae Ecclesiae et media pars et summa est Eucharistia, aequabiliter id valet de ministerio sacerdotali. Qua de causa Nos, gratias Iesu Christo Domino nostro agentes, id iterum inculcamus: Eucharistia «ipsa videlicet princeps summaque ratio est cur omnino sit sacerdotii Sacramentum, quod nempe ortum simul sit instituta Eucharistia unaque cum ea." *EE*, p. 454, n. 31. English translation: *EEE*, pp. 39-40, no. 31.

In his last letter to priests on the occasion of Holy Thursday in 2004, referring to his last Encyclical Letter *Ecclesia de Eucharistia* and to his book, *Gift and Mystery*, written on the occasion of his 50th anniversary of priestly ordination, Blessed Pope John Paul II, wrote:

> We were born from the Eucharist. If we can truly say that the whole Church lives from the Eucharist (*"Ecclesia de Eucharistia vivit"*), as I reaffirmed in my recent Encyclical, we can say the same thing about the ministerial priesthood: it is born, lives, works and bears fruit *"de Eucharistia."* "There can be no Eucharist without the priesthood, just as there can be no priesthood without the Eucharist."[16]

Contemplating the mystery of the ordained priesthood, Blessed Pope John Paul II declared to his brother priests:

> Before this extraordinary reality we find ourselves amazed and overwhelmed, so deep is the humility by which God "stoops" in order to unite himself with man! If we feel moved before the Christmas crib, when we contemplate the Incarnation of the Word, what must we feel before the altar where, by the poor hands of the priest, Christ makes his Sacrifice present in time? We can only fall to our knees and silently adore this supreme mystery of faith.[17]

Studying the fruit of Monsignor La Femina's writing on the Eucharistic Sacrifice, his priestly wonder and humble adoration before the Mystery of Faith, of which he, as a priest, is the minister, are abundantly evident. His book is an offering of deepest love to his Eucharistic Lord, in which he invites us to share by growing in our knowledge and wonder before the Mystery of Faith.

In searching to know how to write about the Holy Eucharist, Monsignor La Femina was led to take up what for many is the cause of some perplexity regarding the institution of the Most Blessed Sacrament. I refer to the account of the Last Supper in the Gospel according to John, which, while it is exceedingly rich in theological content regarding the Mystery of Faith, lacks the account of the institution of the Holy Eucharist, as it is found in Saint Paul's First Letter to the Corinthians[18] and in the Synoptic Gospels.[19] Having studied in depth the Church's canonical discipline, Monsignor La Femina naturally viewed the Evangelist John's Last Supper account with an eye to the juridical structure which underlies every reality in the Church and,

---

16   Ioannes Paulus PP. II, Nuntius, "Presbyteris «in Cena Domini» missus," 28 Martii 2004, *Acta Apostolicae Sedis* 96 (2004), p. 542, no. 2. [The official version of the letter is in English.]

17   *Ibid*, p. 542, no. 2.

18   Cf. *1 Cor* 11:23-26.

19   Cf. *Mt* 26:26-29; *Mk* 14:22-25; and *Lk* 22:17-20.

therefore, in a preeminent way, the most sacred reality, the Eucharistic Sacrifice. His formation as a canon lawyer disposed him to be especially attentive to the right order, the justice, the *ius divinum*, with which the gift of divine love is always given and which safeguards and fosters the gift.

The irreplaceable juridical structure of the relationship of immeasurable and unceasing love of God for men is seen in God's making a covenant with man. The juridical or covenantal structure of God's relationship with man continues to be expressed, but now perfectly, in the Most Blessed Sacrament. The very words of Institution never fail to refer to the Eucharistic Sacrifice as "the new and eternal covenant."[20] In the words of Institution, according to the Extraordinary Form of the Roman Rite, the words, "the new and eternal covenant" are immediately followed by the words, "the mystery of faith."[21]

Monsignor La Femina's canonical eye, which is, by nature, always a fundamentally and deeply theological eye, has uncovered in John the Evangelist's account of the Last Supper, a thorough and rich presentation of the Holy Eucharist as the complete fulfillment of the covenant which God first made with man at Mount Sinai and to which He has remained enduringly faithful in a manner beyond all of man's comprehension. Through his careful and thorough analysis of the juridical structure of the covenant, employing the best research of scholars of the Bible and of the Ancient Near East, Monsignor La Femina uncovers in Saint John's Last Supper account all of the elements of the reality which is alone made present by the Eucharistic Sacrifice.

His juridical eye, in a particular way, has helped him to see how Saint John, through the analogy between the Washing of the Feet and the Eucharistic Sacrifice, expresses the deepest truth of the Mystery of Faith, the immeasurable and unceasing love of God for man, in which man is called to participate, in which man is called to live. The analogical relationship between the Washing of the Feet and the Institution of the Holy Eucharist means that one is not understood without the other, that the deepest meaning of one cannot be plumbed without plumbing the deepest meaning of the other.

20　"novi et aeterni testamenti." *Missale Romanum ex Decreto Sacrosancti Oecumenici Concilii Vaticani II instauratum auctoritate Paul PP. VI promulgatum Ioannis Pauli PP. II cura recognitum*, ed. typica 3ª, Typis Vaticanis, 2002, p. 575, n. 90. English translation: *The Roman Missal Renewed by Decree of the Most Holy Second Ecumenical Council of the Vatican, promulgated by authority of Pope Paul VI and revised at the direction of Pope John Paul II*, 3rd typical edition, Washington, D.C.: United States Conference of Bishops, p. 623, no. 90.

21　"mysterium fidei." *Missale Romanum ex Decreto SS. Concilii Tridentini restitutum Summorum Pontificum cura recognitum*, editio typica 1962, Città del Vaticano: Libreria Editrice Vaticana, 2007, p. 307. English translation by the author.

The study of the analogy makes evident the unmistakable centrality of the Institution of the Holy Eucharist in the Gospel according to John, for the presentation of the analogy is placed within the context of his entire Last Supper account[22] which is clearly the heart, the central content, of the entire Gospel as recounted by Saint John the Evangelist. The account begins with the Washing of the Feet and concludes with the High Priestly Prayer. The interpretative key is found both in the opening and closing verses of the account: "Now before the feast of the Passover, when Jesus knew that his hour had come to depart out of the world to the Father, having loved his own who were in the world, he loved them to the end,"[23] and "I made known to them thy name, and I will make it known, that the love with which thou hast loved me may be in them, and I in them."[24] Through the analogy of the Washing of the Feet and the Institution of the Holy Eucharist, we come to an ever deeper understanding and love of the incomparable and unimaginable reality of the Eucharistic Sacrifice by which men are united to Christ in His love "to the end," so that the eternal love of the Father for the Son and the Son for the Father is "in them."

I cannot conclude without commenting on how, contrary to the antinomian prejudice of a totally secularized culture, the juridical analysis of the Last Supper Account in the Gospel according to John is not only not reductive of the Mystery of Faith but opens the reader to a profound appreciation of the reality of the Redemptive Incarnation, an appreciation which seeks always greater depth. The very structure of Monsignor La Femina's study shows how he, over many years, has plumbed more and more the great reality of our faith, the Mystery of Faith, thanks very much to his lifelong study of the sacred canons of the Church's law. Reading his work, the reader, too, is invited to understand more and more the reality of the covenant of immeasurable and unceasing love which God has formed with man and which has the fullness of its expression in the living reality of the Eucharistic Sacrifice through an appreciation of its rich juridical structure.

In conclusion, I express my heartfelt gratitude to God for the grace of persevering study, over many years, at work in the priestly life of Monsignor Anthony A. La Femina, responding to what he has understood to be God's will that he write about the Eucharistic Sacrifice. By God's grace, Monsignor La Femina has responded, not in a mechanical or solely dutiful way to God's will, but with deepest love, with the desire to give honor and glory to God, according to his best abilities, no matter how long it took him to do so. It is my prayer that many will enter into the study of the Mystery of Faith, guided

---

22   *Jn* 13:1-17:26.
23   *Jn* 13:1.
24   *Jn* 17:26.

by *Eucharist and Covenant in John's Last Supper Account (Jn 12:44-17:26),* and, through their study, under the direction of Monsignor La Femina, grow in their love of Our Lord Jesus Christ Who never fails to make present in the Church, through the Eucharistic Sacrifice, the outpouring of His life for the salvation of all men.

My heartfelt congratulations and gratitude to Monsignor La Femina for the gift to the Church which his book on the Holy Eucharist represents. May God abundantly bless him and you, the reader.

Raymond Leo Cardinal Burke
Prefect of the Supreme Tribunal of the Apostolic Signatura
November 27, 2011 – First Sunday of Advent

Gloria Deo~Pax Hominibus

PICTORIAL SUMMARY OF THE BOOK

The Eucharistic Sacrifice (**Chalice and Host**) makes present in a mysterical manner (**white cross**) the shedding of Jesus' blood (**red background**). This establishes the Royal Enthronement Covenant of Jesus Messiah. By this covenant is formed **"the true vine"**—the Church, who is Jesus Messiah, one with his faithful people (**chi ro cross/vine bearing fruit**). This vine grows by the light of the sevenfold gifts of the Holy Spirit coming through Mary (**blue seven-pointed star with gold rays**). Because of the Royal Enthronement Covenant established by the Eucharistic Sacrifice of Holy Thursday, John the Evangelist likens "the true vine" to the vassal king (**small gold crown over the vine**) of God the Father, who is in the position of the "Great King" of the ancient Near Eastern Vassal Treaties (**large gold crown on ermine background**). The Eucharistic Sacrifice brings glory to God and peace to men (**Gloria Deo—Pax Hominibus**).

Introduction

It has been most puzzling throughout the centuries that the Johannine Last Supper Account (JLSA) makes no mention of the institution of the Eucharist. The present study proposes an answer to this enigma. Consequently the very title of this book, *Eucharist and Covenant in John's Last Supper Account (Jn 12:44-17:26)*, should spark interest and provoke discussion.

This book is divided into two parts. Part I deals with the sacrificial nature of the Eucharist and its implications from the time of its institution at the Last Supper. Part II discusses the elements and nature of the Eucharistic Covenant.

How did this study come about? It owes its origin to the woman to whom I dedicated this book, Mrs. Dorothy O'Neill Weimar, OP. I came to know her personally during my teenage years and have solid reasons to believe that she was the recipient of many extraordinary graces. Her life was centered upon the Mass, and in obedience to her spiritual director she wrote a short account about her experiences during Mass which she called: "The Mass is the Passion and Death of Our Lord."[1] During the Mass up until the Consecration she lived through the passion and death of the Lord. In giving her these graces the Lord told her: **"They may deny you experience what you say, but they cannot deny that what you say is true."**

Shortly before her death in 1974, Dorothy informed me that the Lord wanted me to write about the Mass. He gave no further specifications. For approximately five years I tried to write about the Mass, but came up with nothing new. Then in desperation, because Dorothy spoke of St. John together with Mary on the road to Calvary, I decided to investigate St. John's Last Supper Account (JLSA) despite the fact that he makes no mention there of the Eucharistic institution. I began studying this account while already studying G.E. Mendenhall's contribution on "Covenant" in *The Interpreter's Dictionary of the Bible*.[2] On December 2, 1980, the two matters came together when I realized that John was using in his Last Supper account the elements of the Hittite treaty about which Mendenhall wrote. It was my training in Canon Law that enabled me to recognize the use of those legal elements. I mentioned what I had found to a friend, the Rev. T. Paul Broadhurst, C.S.B., who was studying at the Biblicum. He told me that this was done in the Book of Deuteronomy and that I should speak to his professor at the Pontifical Biblical Institute in Rome, the Rev. Dennis J. McCarthy, S.J., who was teaching about and wrote a book on this matter.[3]

---

1   See Appendix 2.

2   IDB, Vol. 1, pp. 714-723.

3   McCarthy, Dennis J., S.J. *Treaty and Covenant: A Study in Form in the Ancient Oriental*

Since I was residing in Rome and working in the Roman Curia, I was able to meet personally with Fr. McCarthy to discuss my findings. He said that though he was not an expert in John, my proposal seemed very reasonable. He was most encouraging. I had other meetings with him, but he unexpectedly passed away while working in Avila during the summer. Subsequently I discovered that the Rev. Aelred Lacomara, C.P., writing about what he calls "the Farewell Discourse," had also noticed the use in John of elements of the Vassal Treaty.[4] However, our research did not cover all the same Scripture texts and had different objectives.

In my subsequent studies I found other OT covenantal elements besides those of the Vassal Treaty in the JLSA. I examined these elements and explained their significance for the Eucharistic Covenant. John used the Hittite Vassal Treaty and the other OT covenantal elements to explain in words rather than ritual the nature of the covenant established by the Eucharist on Holy Thursday. I found that this covenant is specifically one of Royal Enthronement, establishing Jesus as Messiah of God's new Israel. John's treatment of the stipulation clause of the New Covenant revealed an astounding insight into the nature of the New Commandment as a rephrasing of the Apostolic Commission for evangelization in Mt 28:18-20.[5] With John's use of the ancient Vassal Treaty and certain OT covenantal elements, many other amazing and unexpected aspects of the New Covenant came to light. John's motives for his use of the Hittite treaty and the other covenantal elements are both significant and instructive. These new insights on the various aspects of the Eucharistic Covenant should profoundly influence Christian spirituality in hitherto unforeseen ways.

However, John's treatment of the New Covenant in his Last Supper account did not seem to link it to the Mass. There were, nonetheless, two mystifying verses in the JLSA: Jn 13:1[6] and Jn 13:31.[7] Jn 13:1 introduces the Footwashing and literally indicates that the Lord's death would be present during the supper since it states that during the supper Jesus would show

---

Documents and in the Old Testament. 2d ed., "Analecta Biblica, Investigationes Scientificae In Res Biblicas" 21 A. Rome: Biblical Institute Press, 1978.

4   Lacomara, A. "Deuteronomy and the Farewell Discourse (Jn 13:31-16:33)," *CBQ*, 36 (January 1974), pp. 65-84.

5   "All authority in heaven and on earth has been given to me. Go therefore and make disciples of all nations, baptizing them in the name of the Father and of the Son and of the Holy Spirit, teaching them to observe all that I have commanded you, and behold, I am with you always, to the close of the age.'"

6   "Now before the feast of the Passover, when Jesus knew that his hour had come to depart out of this world to the Father, having loved his own who were in the world, he loved them to the end."

7   "When he (Judas Iscariot) had gone out, Jesus said, 'Now is the Son of man glorified, and in him God is glorified.'"

"to the end" his love for "his own." The other verse, Jn 13:31, understood in the light of the program for "the hour" (Jn 12:23, 28, 31-33), comes right after the Footwashing and literally indicates that the Lord had just accomplished his glorification and that of the Father, concluding in this way his final earthly mission. Why? Because that program, specifically in Jn 12:33, required the Lord's death for this twofold glorification. Are these verses to be taken literally or metaphorically? Until now they have been understood only metaphorically. Reading the JLSA, John signals that Jesus' sacrifice was accomplished by the Footwashing since the only action of the Lord during the supper is the Footwashing which, in fact, is sandwiched by the above two verses. But we know from the teaching of the Church that this could not be so, even though, in introducing the Footwashing, John explicitly speaks of a supernatural power given Jesus by the Father that could theoretically have empowered him to use the Footwashing to accomplish what the Fourth Gospel states in the two verses in question regarding the Footwashing. I then found that John had devised an analogy between the Footwashing and the Eucharist so that whenever he speaks about the Footwashing he is actually speaking expressly but implicitly about the Eucharist. John was very careful in his analogy to make the Footwashing accomplish all that the program for "the hour" stipulated.

There was just one more matter to be investigated and about which the program only speaks implicitly, in that the matter of the bestowal of the Holy Spirit at the glorification of the Son of man was previously mentioned in Jn 7:39.[8] Thus, John does mention that the Spirit had already been bestowed at the time of the Last Supper when Jesus declared that his glorification had just taken place. There is, therefore, no lacuna in the JLSA because John devoted his whole Last Supper account to the Eucharist. Jn 13:1 and 13:31 are to be taken literally: the death of Jesus on the cross was truly made present at the Last Supper. This indicates that John is affirming the Eucharist's sacrificial character. Then, of course, the fact that the death of Jesus was present on Holy Thursday means that the Church is essentially Eucharistic by reason of her very origin. She was born from the side of the sleeping Christ on Calvary[9] because the High Priest made his unique death on Calvary pre-exist ontologically on Holy Thursday through the Eucharist.

Looking back on the whole study, I could very honestly say that I never expected to find what I found. I was astounded when I saw that St. John was

---

8   "Now this he said about the Spirit, which those who believed in him were to receive, for as yet the Spirit had not been given, because Jesus was not yet glorified."

9   Just as Eve was formed from the side of the sleeping Adam, so the Church was born from the pierced heart of Christ hanging dead on the cross. See: St. Ambrose, *In Luc,* J.P. Migne, ed., *Patrologiae Cursus Completus, Series Latina,* Paris: Migne, 1844-1864, 2, 85-89; PL 15, pp. 1666-1668.

using the Vassal Treaty and the other OT covenantal elements to explain the New Covenant, much like what was done in Deuteronomy for the Mosaic Covenant. However, I was truly awestruck by how St. John reveals the sacrificial aspect of the Eucharist in his Last Supper account through his analogy of the Footwashing. I see now the direction I was being pointed towards in being told to write about the Mass. It is truly wondrous now to behold St. John teaching in his Last Supper account precisely what the Lord showed Dorothy Weimar in her mystical experience, that *"the Mass is the Passion and Death of the Lord."* [10]

---

10   See Appendix 2.

Abbreviations

Books and Reviews

AGLR *The Analytical Greek Lexicon Revised,* ed. Harold K. Moulton (Grand Rapids, Michigan: Zondervan Publishing House, 1978).

CBQ *The Catholic Biblical Quarterly.*

CCHS *A Catholic Commentary on Holy Scripture,* edd. Bernard Orchard, Edmund F. Sutcliffe, Reginald C. Fuller, Ralph Russell (New York: Thomas Nelson & Sons, 1953).

DOB *Dictionary of the Bible,* John L. McKenzie, S.J. (New York: Macmillan Publishing Co., Inc., 1977).

IDB *The Interpreter's Dictionary of the Bible: An Illustrated Encyclopedia,* edd. George Arthur Buttrick, Thomas Samuel Kepler, John Knox, Herbert Gordon May, Samuel Terrien, Emory Stevens Bucke. 4 vols. and supplement (Nashville: Abingdon Press, 1962-1976).

JBC *The Jerome Biblical Commentary,* edd. Raymond E. Brown, Joseph A. Fitzmyer, Roland E. Murphy 2 vols. (Englewood Cliffs, New Jersey: Prentice-Hall, Inc., 1968).

VT *Vetus Testamentum*

Pontifical and Conciliar Documents

CCC *The Catechism of the Catholic Church*, 1994.

D *Enchiridion Symbolorum Definitionum et Declarationum de Rebus Fidei et Morum*, edd. Henricus Denzinger, Adolfus Schonmetzer, editio XXXIII (Barcinone: Herder, MCMLXV).

DV Encyclical Letter, *Dominum et vivificantem*, John Paul II, May 18, 1986.

EM Instruction, *Eucharisticum mysterium*, Sacred Congregation of Rites, May 25, 1967.

GS Pastoral Constitution on the Church in the Modern World, *Gaudium et spes*, December 7, 1965.

LG Dogmatic Constitution on the Church, *Lumen gentium*, Vatican II, November 21, 1964.

PO Decree on the Ministry and Life of Priests, *Presbyterium ordinis*, Vatican II, December 7, 1965.

RH Encyclical Letter, *Redemptor hominis*, John Paul II, March 4, 1979.

RM Encyclical Letter, *Redemptoris missio*, John Paul II, December 7, 1990.

SC Constitution on the Sacred Liturgy, *Sacrosanctum concilium*, Vatican II, December 4, 1963.

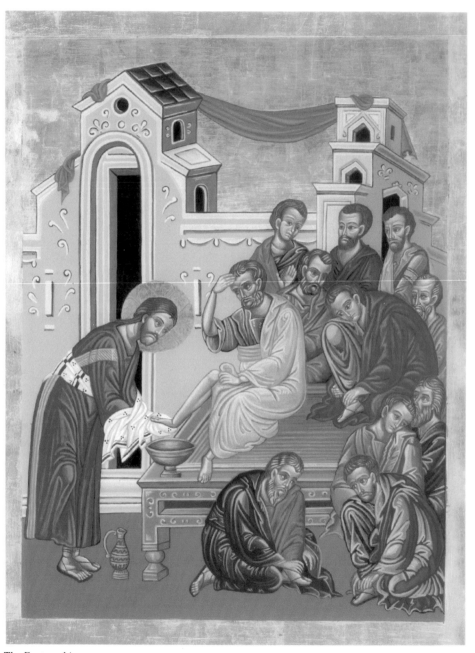

The Footwashing

© 2000, Msgr. Anthony La Femina

Part I

The Footwashing
and the Eucharist

CHAPTER 1

The Eucharist in the JLSA[1]

1.1. The Fundamental Problem

The Synoptic and Pauline Last Supper accounts are brief, with Matthew devoting to his account 11 verses;[2] Mark, 10 verses;[3] Luke, 25 verses;[4] and Paul, 4 verses.[5] The central action in all these accounts is the institution of the Eucharist, to which specifically Matthew devoted 4 verses;[6] Mark, 4 verses;[7] Luke, 2 verses;[8] and Paul, 4 verses.[9]

Compared to the above accounts, the Last Supper account in the Fourth Gospel is truly monumental, being made up of 5 chapters and 7 verses, comprising nearly one quarter of the entire gospel. The JLSA's central action, however, is the Footwashing, not the institution of the Eucharist. John's entire Last Supper account starts with and flows from this mysterious action that is omitted by the Synoptics and Paul in their Last Supper accounts.

Rudolph Bultmann asserts that John's reason for omitting the Eucharist in his Last Supper account is due to the fact that he considered the Eucharist to be irrelevant, superfluous and even suspicious.[10]

The Jerome Biblical Commentary has this to say: "A striking omission, in view of John's sacramental interests, is the Syn's account of the institution of the Eucharist. However, what needed to be said on this score had already been said in ch. 6, and in point of fact the discourse to the disciples is wholly concerned with the divine life that is the explanation of all the sacraments."[11]

Commenting on the Eucharistic teaching in Jn 6, John F. O'Grady says that one would have expected the institution of the Eucharist to have been

1 JLSA stands for the "Johannine Last Supper Account" (Jn 12:44 -17) and will henceforth be written as such in the text. The seven verses of Chapter 12 are added to what is considered to be the complete Last Supper account of John. The reason for this addition will be explained in Part II.
2 Mt 26:20-30.
3 Mk 14:17-26.
4 Lk 22:14-38.
5 1 Cor 11:23-26.
6 Mt 26:26-29.
7 Mk 14:22-25.
8 Lk 22:19, 20.
9 1 Cor 11:23-26.
10 Bultmann, Rudolf, *The Gospel of John,* pp. 472, 485, 486.
11 *The Jerome Biblical Commentary*, p. 450, n. 137 A.

placed in the farewell discourses at the Last Supper. He writes: "The question appears more baffling when the reader recalls that the Fourth Gospel has the longest section on the Last Supper and makes no mention of the institution of the eucharist."[12]

Reflecting a general frustration at the absence of any clear reference to the Eucharist in the JLSA, Schnackenburg writes, "It is both extremely surprising and very irritating that one evangelist should pass over in silence the institution of the Eucharist that is handed down by the others in their account of the Last Supper."[13] Schnackenburg's observation summarizes the sentiments of many persons throughout the centuries who, despite the various explanations about this omission, still remain dissatisfied and perplexed by this apparent lacuna in the Fourth Gospel.

Attempting to explain John's omission of the Eucharist in his Last Supper account, Schnackenburg suggests that John might be using the Footwashing to reveal the real meaning of the Eucharist as "the lasting revelation of Jesus' love for his own, the commemoration of his death and a share in his life."[14] However, despite attributing a possible Eucharistic significance to the Footwashing, Schnackenburg concludes that there can never be absolute certainty that John did, in fact, treat of the Eucharist in his Last Supper account. Moreover, Schnackenburg says that he is in agreement with John Chrysostom, Cyril of Alexandria, Ammonius Saccas, W. Bauer, R. Bultmann and Grossouw in stating that John's possible use of the Footwashing to teach what the Eucharist signifies "does not reduce the washing of the feet to a symbol for the Eucharist."[15]

In addition to the above observations, one might also wonder why the Footwashing has been passed over by the Synoptics and Paul in their own Last Supper reports, when this action is so essential to John's account. But above all, given the Eucharist's vital importance and John's special treatment of its promise in the sixth chapter of his Gospel, the even more fundamental question remains: Why would John omit speaking of the Eucharist at the precise time of its institution at the Last Supper?

1.2. Proposed Solution

The present study proposes a solution to the general frustration and puzzlement created both by the apparent lacuna regarding the Eucharist in

---

12   O'Grady, John F. *According to John, The Witness of the Beloved Disciple*, p. 77.
13   Schnackenburg, Rudolf. *The Gospel According to St. John,* 3 vols. (New York: Crossroad, 1982), III, p. 42.
14   *Ibid.,* III, p. 46; see also III, pp. 42-47 for Schnackenburg's complete treatment of John's silence about the Eucharist in his Last Supper account.
15   *Ibid.,* and the relative footnote 27 on p. 398.

the JLSA as well as by the omission of the Footwashing in the Synoptic and Pauline Last Supper accounts.

This proposal is based on two statements in the JLSA that bracket the Footwashing. The first, just preceding the Footwashing, is Jn 13:1: **"Now, before the feast of the Passover, when Jesus knew that his hour had come to depart out of this world to the Father, having loved his own who were in the world, he loved them to the end."** The second statement closely following the Footwashing is Jesus' declaration in Jn 13:31: **"Now is the Son of man glorified, and in him God is glorified."**

John wrote these verses to give meaning to the Footwashing. The literal meaning of Jn 13:1 is that Jesus would complete his final earthly mission at the Last Supper by an act of the greatest love for his own, a love unto death. This act is presented by John to be the Footwashing. Jn 13:31, following the Footwashing, is Jesus' declaration of having just accomplished his final earthly work. In fact, following this declaration of work accomplished, the title "the Son of man" is never used again.[16]

According to the Fourth Gospel Jesus' final work was to take place during "the hour," that special period of Jesus' life which was to witness the completion of his earthly task and his departure from this world.[17] Therefore Jn 13:1 and Jn 13:31 can only be properly understood in the light of the Fourth Gospel's program for "the hour." In the following verses is the program for the Son of man's final earthly work.

Jn 12:23   *And Jesus answered them, "The hour has come for the Son of man to be glorified."*

28   *"Father, glorify thy name."*

31   *"Now is the judgment of this world, now shall the ruler of this world be cast out;*

32   *and I, when I am lifted up from the earth, will draw all men to myself."*

33   *He said this to show by what death he was to die.*

This program will be dealt with in detail in Chapter 4. However, it is important to emphasize here that the purpose of the Son of man's work in the hour is his glorification and that of God as Father, and the *sine qua non* **requirement** for the completion of Jesus' mission is specified by the words *"when I am lifted up from the earth."* This phrase alludes to Jesus' death on the cross, and John confirms this in the next verse.

---

16   This point will become more significant when discussing Jesus' title of "the Son of man."

17   "The hour" is treated in more detail in Chapter 5 when dealing specifically with the introduction to the Footwashing.

Jn 13:1 states literally that during the supper Jesus would love his own "to the end," meaning to his death; and in Jn 13:31 Jesus declares that he had just accomplished the purpose of his final work—his glorification and that of God—a work that required his death. When examined in the light of the Johannine program for the completion of the Son of man's earthly mission, the literal meaning of the above two verses bracketing the Footwashing forces the logical conclusion that John is stating that Jesus' death was indeed present at the Last Supper through the Footwashing, being the only action that Jesus performed.

However, despite the literal meaning of Jn 13:1 and Jn 13:31, the Footwashing is generally interpreted as a prophetic or parabolic action about the significance of what Jesus would accomplish by his death on the cross the following day.[18] Salvatore Alberto Panimolle expresses this generally accepted view: "It is about a prophetic gesture that symbolically pre-announces Jesus' supreme service of love for his people by his passion and death on the cross."[19] He calls the Footwashing a *"gesto profetico del sacrificio della vita sul calvario."*[20] Brown is in agreement: "The simplest explanation of the footwashing, then, remains that Jesus performed this servile task to prophesy symbolically that he was about to be humiliated in death."[21] He further states: "… the footwashing is something that makes it possible for the disciples to have eternal life with Jesus. Such emphasis is intelligible if we understand the footwashing as a symbol for Jesus' salvific death."[22] Taylor calls the Footwashing "the symbol that encases Jesus' death" and says that in the Footwashing Jesus *acts out* the ultimate and full love of his "hour" before it takes place.[23] Barrett says the Footwashing is a symbolic narrative that prefigures the crucifixion and is a divine action that releases men from sin and gives them an example they must imitate.[24]

---

18   A prophetic or parabolic action is a symbolic action meant to convey some truth. An example of such is found in Ek 12:1-16 where the prophet is commanded to perform actions that portray the future flight of the exiles at the time of the destruction of Jerusalem by the Babylonians. Other examples may be found in Is 20:2-4; Jer 13:1-11; 19:1-13; Ek 4:1-5:17; 37:15-28. In the opinion of most scholars the Footwashing is simply a prophetic or parabolic action that prefigures and interprets the crucifixion.

19   Panimolle, Salvatore Alberto, *Lettura Pastorale del Vangelo di Giovanni*, III, p. 178: "… si tratta di un gesto profetico che preannunzia simbolicamente il servizio supremo di amore, reso da Gesù al suo popolo con la passione e la morte in croce."

20   Panimolle, Salvatore Alberto, *Lettura Pastorale del Vangelo di Giovanni*, III, p. 171. Translation: *A prophetic gesture of the sacrifice of his life on Calvary.*

21   Brown, *The Gospel According to John*, II, p. 568.

22   *Ibid.*, p. 566.

23   Michael J. Taylor, *John, The Different Gospel, A Reflective Commentary* (New York: Alba House, 1983), pp. 156-158. Emphasis mine.

24   Barrett, *The Gospel According to St. John*, p. 436.

How is the Footwashing to be correctly interpreted? The first principle of interpretation is to examine thoroughly the *literal meaning* of a statement or text. This principle is based upon a common-sense presumption that one normally says or writes exactly what one means. Therefore the literal sense must first be carefully examined for the possibilities of its being accepted on face value; even considering, if such be the case in dealing with Holy Scriptures, any supernatural aspects that might be involved. Only when a literal interpretation proves unacceptable is it justifiable to resort to a figurative one.

This study proposes that John links the Footwashing to the Eucharist by creating an analogy between them[25] and through this analogy teaches that Jesus made his death ontologically "pre-exist" at the Last Supper.[26] This means that John teaches specifically about the sacrificial nature of the Eucharist of the Last Supper as well as of all later Eucharistic celebrations. In seeking to understand the Footwashing it is imperative to keep in mind that it is a ***mysterious action***. In its regard Jesus said: "What I am doing you do not know now, but afterward you will understand."[27]

This study's proposal is consistent with the observation that John, who is called "The Theologian" in the Byzantine tradition, often teaches points of revelation in his Gospel through analogy.[28] An analogy is a type of comparison, and one example of an analogy made by John is his comparison of the union of Jesus and his disciples to a vine and its branches.[29] The proposal of

---

25   The historicity of the Footwashing does not fall within the scope of this study. Brown does discuss this problem (*The Gospel According to John*, II, p. 568). He does not seem to think that John invented this "highly symbolic action." Schnackenburg also discusses the origin and historicity of the Footwashing (cf. Schnackenburg, *The Gospel According to St. John*, III, pp. 39-42). While he says that the washing is not an historically proven event, he thinks that John followed an earlier tradition in which Jesus' serving at the Last Supper was reported. On the other hand, Barrett (*The Gospel According to St. John: An Introduction with Commentary and Notes on the Greek Text*, [2d ed.: Philadelphia: The Westminster Press, 1978], p. 463) says that the Footwashing is a symbolic narrative prefiguring the crucifixion and thus indicates how it is to be interpreted. He says that the Footwashing is probably to be regarded as a Johannine construction based on the Lucan Last Supper account: "But I am among you as one who serves" (Lk 22:27).

26   In fact, the Church teaches that the Eucharist makes Jesus' death "post-exist" in the Mass. Cf. The Catechism of the Catholic Church, nn. 1366, 1367. These essentially state: "The Eucharist is thus a sacrifice because it *re-presents* (makes present) the sacrifice of the cross.... The sacrifice of Christ and the sacrifice of the Eucharist are *one single sacrifice*...." (italics are in the *CCC*).

27   Jn 13:7.

28   Symbolism is the use of analogy. A work dedicated to symbolism in John's Gospel is: Koester, Craig R., *Symbolism in the Fourth Gospel, Meaning, Mystery, Community*, 2d ed. (Minneapolis: Fortress Press, 2003).

29   Jn 15:1-5.

this study is that in his presentation of the Footwashing, John uses the tool of analogy to convey truths about the Eucharist that are not evident in the other Last Supper accounts.

If John wished to speak *expressly* about the Eucharist in his Last Supper account, he could have done so in two ways. Firstly, he could have spoken of the Eucharist *explicitly* by using the institution narrative, just like the Synoptics and Paul. He would thus be speaking of the Eucharist distinctly and specifically, but he did not do this. Secondly, John could have spoken of the Eucharist *implicitly* by analogy in such a way that this could be deduced from the circumstances, attributes, and effects he described when speaking about the Footwashing. Thus, for example, one speaks expressly and explicitly of a lion when using the word "lion." However, one could speak of a lion expressly but in an implicit manner by referring to it as "the king of beasts." Both these designations *expressly* refer to the identical reality. The first one speaks *explicitly* of the lion, whereas the second speaks *implicitly* of it.

It logically follows from the above that if the Footwashing is truly an analogical figure of the Eucharist, then John is referring *expressly* but *implicitly* to the Eucharist when speaking of the Footwashing. And since the Footwashing is central to the JLSA, this would mean that the entire JLSA is really about the Eucharist in one way or another.

In the effort to discover the correct interpretation of Jn 13:1 and Jn 13:31, close attention must be given to the proposed analogy between the Footwashing and the Eucharist. This analogy will be specifically examined in Chapter 2; however, it is first necessary to consider the general nature of analogy that underlies this study's proposal.

1.3. The Concept of Analogy

Analogy is basically a comparison between entities that, while different from each other, do have a certain similarity. The entities being compared are called *analogues*. The major analogue is the one to which the minor analogue(s) is (are) compared. Their similarity may be based upon circumstances, attributes and effects. There are different kinds of analogy according to how the things being compared possess the characteristics of the major analogue.

When the circumstances, attributes and effects of each of the analogues are part of their integral or essential makeup—i.e., belonging to each of the analogues properly, intrinsically and formally—then the comparison between them is called an **analogy of proper proportionality**. An example of such an analogy is the comparison of God and man as beings. Existence is an integral and essential part of the makeup of both God and man. But while their existences are proportionately similar, they are absolutely different. God's existence is identified with his essence. Existence *is* God's very nature. God cannot be defined without existence because God's essence IS existence. God is a necessary and supreme being; he must always exist because he is without beginning or end. On the other hand, nothing outside of God must necessarily exist. Like all other creatures, man's existence is separate and distinct from his essence. Man is therefore a contingent being whose existence is conditional and dependent. Nonetheless, both God, the supreme being, and man, a contingent being, do truly exist. And precisely because of this inherent similarity as beings, the comparison between God and man is an analogy of *proper* proportionality.

On the other hand one may compare things that are not similar in any way by their makeup. This type of comparison is based upon some consideration which is independent of the nature of the things being compared. For this reason the comparison is an *extrinsic* analogy.

The first type of extrinsic analogy is based only upon an *alleged* similarity between the things being compared. This comparison is called an **analogy of improper proportionality** and is simply a **metaphor**. In this analogy the similarities said of both the analogues really exist only in **one** of them. In the other analogue those similarities do not exist in the analogue itself, but only in the *consideration* of the person who is making the comparison. An example of this analogy is the comparison of Christ with a lion because of its strength. The nature of the lion's strength is found only in the beast while this strength is *attributed* extrinsically and accidentally to Christ. Christ is called a lion because of a resemblance that exists only in the consideration of the person who makes the comparison. Thus, in this analogy Christ is called a lion only *figuratively* or *metaphorically*.

The second type of extrinsic comparison is called an **analogy of attribution**. This comparison is based upon a certain connection of causality between the things being compared: either (a) of one or more analogues to another as when food, animals and/or color are said to be "healthy;" or (b) of two or more analogues related among themselves to a third analogue, as when food and color are said to be similar because they both indicate health.

Having considered above the nature of analogy in general, the next chapter will investigate this study's proposal that an analogy exists in the JLSA between the Footwashing and the Eucharist, and the specific kind of analogy it is.

CHAPTER 2

The Analogy

This study proposes that John speaks *expressly* but *implicitly* in his Last Supper account about the Eucharist through an analogy he devised between the Footwashing and the Eucharist.

2.1. The Elements of the Analogy

In his Last Supper account John constructed his analogy by attributing to the Footwashing the identical circumstances, attributes and effects that the Eucharist possesses in the Synoptic and Pauline Last Supper Accounts.[30] What follows is a brief explanation of each of the Eucharist's characteristics attributed to the Footwashing in the JLSA.

2.1.1. Similarity in Circumstances

From the texts of the Fourth Gospel it is evident that the Footwashing shares three identical circumstances that the Eucharist possesses. To verify these circumstances, the scriptural texts regarding the Eucharist in the Synoptic and Pauline Last Supper Accounts may be consulted.[31] Like the Eucharist, the Footwashing in the Fourth Gospel is:

1) the principal event of its Last Supper account,
2) linked to Jesus' betrayal by Judas Iscariot,[32]
3) the object of the Lord's command to repeat what he had just done.[33]

2.1.2. Similarity in Attributes and Effects

The Footwashing also shares the following Eucharistic attributes and effects: it

1) signifies the death of Jesus,
2) establishes a covenant,
3) purifies from sin.

These three attributes and effects of the Footwashing need explanation and will now be individually examined.

---

30   This analogy will be treated in more detail later in this chapter.
31   Mt 26:20-30; Mk 14:17-26; Lk 22:14-38; 1 Cor 11:23-26.
32   Cf. Jn.13:2, 10, 11, 18, 19, 21-31. John even mentions the betrayal of Judas when treating the Eucharist in Jn 6:70, 71.
33   Jn 13:14, 15.

2.1.2.1. Similarity as a Sign of the Death of Jesus

The eucharistic ritual signifies the death of Jesus. The Synoptics and Paul speak of Jesus' body *"being given"*[34] under the appearance of bread, and his blood *"being shed"* [35] under the appearance of wine. These expressions sacramentally signify the sacrificial separation of Jesus' body and blood and hence symbolize his death on the cross in a ritualistic manner. Paul explicitly states that the Eucharist is a memorial of the Lord's death: *"For as often as you eat this bread and drink the cup, you proclaim the Lord's death until he comes."*[36]

It is indeed amazing to see how John's carefully-chosen words and phrases present the Footwashing, like the Eucharist in the Synoptic and Pauline Last Supper Accounts, as a sign of the death of Jesus. [37]

Firstly, the JLSA introduces the Footwashing as Jesus' *final act* that entails his death during the supper. John immediately associates the Footwashing with "the hour" and says that Jesus knew he *"was going to God."* The hour is the time when Jesus is *"to depart out of this world to the Father."* The introduction specifies that during the supper, *Jesus ...having loved his own who were in the world, loved them* to the end. Here John distinguishes between Jesus' loving actions in the past and this final act which was to be accomplished by the Footwashing. The Greek active aorist participle translated *"having loved"* signifies Jesus' past loving actions which were the motivating reason for his final and consummate act of love *"during supper."*[38] To introduce the Footwashing as Jesus' final act, the Greek uses the active indicative aorist verb translated *"he loved."* This use of the aorist expresses a punctiliar or single action in the past and is equivalent to the English simple past tense. By this action Jesus loved his disciples *"to the end"* (Greek: *eis telos*). The Greek word used for "end" (*telos*) has the same stem as the Greek word used in Jn 19:30 for the last word of Jesus on the cross: "It is finished" (*tetelestai*). By choosing this word John relates the Footwashing to Jesus' death on the cross.

Secondly, John in Jn 13:4 presents the Footwashing as a sign of Jesus' death by his choice of the Greek word stating that Jesus *"laid aside"* (*tithenai*) his garments as part of the Footwashing. This verb is the same one used in Jn 10:11, 15, 17, 18, where Jesus speaks of *"laying down"* his life. Thus,

---

34   Lk 22:19; I Cor 11:24.
35   Mt 26:28; Mk 14:24; Lk 22:20; I Cor 11:24.
36   1 Cor 11:26.
37   Here in Chapter 2 it is shown how Jn 13:1-4 presents the Footwashing as a sign of Jesus' death. On the other hand, because the same texts are dealt with in Chapter 5 to explain the theological setting of the Footwashing, there will be some necessary repetition in Chapter 5.
38   See Nolli, Gianfranco, *Il Vangelo Secondo Giovanni*, p. 500.

John implies that Jesus' action of "laying down" his garments signifies *"laying down"* his life on the cross.[39]

2.1.2.2. Similarity as a Covenantal Action

The Synoptic and Pauline Last Supper Accounts expressly and explicitly attest to the fact that the Eucharist of the Last Supper established a covenant.[40] This is clear in all the Eucharistic institution narratives.

Nowhere does the JLSA or the rest of the Fourth Gospel use a word for *covenant*. In this regard Dennis J. McCarthy's statement is pertinent: "Israel never worked out a definition for covenant or insisted on a single word for it."[41] Israel's understanding of covenant was based upon how covenant was established and what it brought about. Therefore there may be different ways of speaking about the dynamic reality of covenant. McCarthy appropriately observes that "covenant was an action and a state, not a word."[42] This study will show that John, though he does not use the word, does speak of the action and state in his Last Supper account. To appreciate this fact an understanding of the origin and nature of covenant are necessary.

In the Ancient Near East, covenant and contract were both considered agreements. However, a brief comparison of covenant and contract will illustrate their significant differences.

A contract was established either in writing or by solemnizing it before a civil court as its proper forum. The contractual relationship was impersonal and depended upon the fulfillment of the stipulations which were concerned with business negotiations. Failure to observe those stipulations made one liable to legal action to enforce their observance or to definitively terminate the contract.

Covenant was an ancient institution that came about from the necessity to provide society with relationships for trustworthy negotiations outside the family circle. A covenant ensured those moral dispositions of trust,

---

39   While the Footwashing is a sign of the death of Jesus, John alludes to Jesus' resurrection *after* the Footwashing is completed. The "laying down" of Jesus' garments before the Footwashing (Jn 13:5a) establishes the Footwashing as a sign of Jesus' death. But following the Footwashing Jesus *once again takes up* his garments. This signifies the resurrection (Jn 13:12). Jesus' death and resurrection are parts of the same Paschal Mystery, but they are completely distinct parts of that Mystery.

40   Mt 26:28; Mk 14:24; Lk 22:20; 1 Cor 11:25.

41   McCarthy, Dennis J., S.J. *Treaty and Covenant: A Study in Form in the Ancient Oriental Documents and in the Old Testament* (2d ed.. Analecta Biblica, Investigationes Scientificae In Res Biblicas 21 A. Rome: Biblical Institute Press, 1978), p. 21.

42   McCarthy, *Treaty and Covenant,* p. 14.

reliability and stability by forging a "family-like" relationship.[43] The deity confirmed, witnessed, guaranteed and sanctioned the covenantal agreement and its special relationship. Covenant eventually came to regulate not only social and religious behavior, but also political behavior as is evident in the ancient treaties between the rulers of nations.

Because covenant was concerned with the establishment and preservation of a permanent personal relationship, the ancient covenants bound the parties to love and respect each other.[44] Thus, viewing covenant's cause (oath) by its effect (family-like kinship), McCarthy logically states that the basic meaning of covenant is "union."[45]

Covenant essentially consisted of an oath pledging personal commitment. The oath is understood as a covenant in its constitutive, causal and active sense (covenant *in fieri*). This is to say that the oath was the transitory action by which covenant was established. The oath was expressed either explicitly by word and/or implicitly by ritual actions. Covenant had a sacred character because it was a pledge sworn to the deity as judge and guarantor of the agreement. The oath was always accompanied by curses for infidelity. The deity was personally involved in covenant and was believed to punish whoever was unfaithful to it. Sometimes blessings were also expressed as a reward for fidelity. It is interesting to note that in making covenants the blessings were not considered as important to mention as the curses.[46] A covenant was a relationship sanctioned by the deity after the likeness of family. The importance of curses in covenant came from the fact that since a covenantal relationship was like that of family, the covenant relation could only be dissolved by death. That is why death was invoked as the principal curse for infidelity.

---

43   McCarthy writes: "As for the general concept of covenant or treaty, it remained connected with the idea of kinship even late in the history of old Israel. Even a purely political treaty with Assyria was thought to produce a kind of dependent kinship so that in 2 Kgs 16,7 Ahaz could call himself the son even of his tyrannical overlord." See "Notes on the Love of God in Deuteronomy and the Father-Son Relationship Between Yahweh and Israel," *CBQ*, 27 (1965), p. 147. Again, to illustrate the quasi-familial bond created by covenant, King Hiram of Tyre made a covenant with Solomon, whereby King Hiram called Solomon "my brother" (Am 9:13; see also 5:15-30). And it was precisely because of this covenant that the prophet Amos announced God's judgment upon Tyre because it had not respected its "pact of brotherhood" (Am 1:9), which is to say the "covenant" that was made by its king. Hahan, *Kinship By Covenant*, pp. 28-31.

44   In his book, Hahan identifies three types of covenant according to various ways of distributing their obligations. This study deals with covenant as it creates kinship between its parties, and this all covenants do. Hahn, Scott W., *Kinship by Covenant: A Canonical Approach to the Fulfillment of God's Saving Promises* (New Haven & London: Yale University Press, 2009).

45   McCarthy, *Treaty and Covenant*, pp. 21, 297.

46   Cf. McCarthy, *Treaty and Covenant*, p. 76.

Covenant in its formal and passive sense (covenant *in facto esse*) was the stable family-like union resulting from the oath. It is imperative to note that the covenant bond did not depend for its continued existence upon the parties' fidelity to the covenantal stipulations as in the case of contractual stipulations. The stipulations of the covenant had the purpose of setting explicit guidelines for living out the family-like union, not to be conditions *sine qua non* for its continued existence. In fact, death alone could terminate covenant union.

Because covenant was established by solemn oath, the deity was the sole judge, witness and guarantor of the covenant union. Consequently, the covenant's unique forum was divine. Because it was sanctioned by the deity, the covenant created a "personal union pledged by symbol and/or oath."[47] McCarthy explains the nature of this union as "close and quasi-familial."[48] This intimate covenantal relationship confirmed and perpetuated an already-existing personal relationship between the parties. Together with the family-like union, a covenant created a juridical bond which made the covenant relationship as permanent as that of the family.

Like the family relationship, covenant kinship was based upon mutual love and respect. The Hebrew word *hesed*, signifying the sentiments within the natural family,[49] was also used to signify the family-like quality of affection and loyalty proper to covenant.[50]

The Fourth Gospel presents the Footwashing as an action establishing covenant (covenant *in fieri*) because by that action Jesus gives his disciples a share in his unique heritage:[51] *"If I do not wash you, you have no part with me."*[52] The Greek word *meros* normally signifies a part, portion, share or division of a whole, a partnership or fellowship. *Meros* is used in the Septuagint translation of Psalm 15 (14):5 together with the genitive of the word for "inheritance" to designate the Lord as the choice portion of

---

47   McCarthy, *Treaty and Covenant*, p. 297. See also Tucker, Gene M., *"Covenant Forms and Contract Forms,"* VT, 15 (1965), pp. 487-503.
48   *Ibid.,* p. 21; see also McKenzie, *Dictionary of the Bible* (New York: Macmillan Publishing Co., Inc., 1977), p. 154.
49   For example, between father and son in Gn 22:2; 37:3; 44:20; 47:29; Pr 13:24; or between parents and their children in Prv 15:17; Ho 9:16.
50   See McKenzie, John L., Dictionary of the Bible, p. 154; Good, E.M., "Love in the OT," *BID*, III, p. 167.
51   Because the disciples in the Johannine Last Supper Account are never called "the twelve," and any explicit mention of such a term appears to be consciously avoided, Bultmann concludes that the disciples present at the Last Supper represent the whole Christian community, those referred to in 13:1 as "his own." See Bultmann, *The Gospel of John*, pp. 458, 459.
52   Jn 13:8.

the psalmist's inheritance: *"The Lord is the portion of mine inheritance."*[53] Brown further explains that *meros* is used in the Septuagint to translate the Hebrew word *heleq* which describes the heritage given to Israel by God.[54] Thus Num 18:20 and Dt 12:12 and 14:27, 29 indicate that the tribe of Levi has no "portion"—understood as "heritage"—with the other tribes in the Promised Land. In accord with this understanding of *meros*, that word in Jn 13:8b should be understood as signifying Jesus' heritage. Brown notes that the idea of Jesus' sharing his heritage with his disciples is reinforced by the phrase "with me" (Gr *met emou*).[55]

A heritage consists in what one receives or will receive as a birthright from a parent or predecessor within a family. And what is Jesus' heritage? In his discourse following the Footwashing, Jesus speaks of his heritage that consists in two gifts he received from his Father. However, these gifts are, in fact, one and the same but spoken of under different aspects.[56] In Jn 17:11, 12, Jesus speaks of the *gift of God's name* (i.e. Father). In Jn 17:22, Jesus speaks of the *gift of glory*, which he specifies in Jn 17:24 as the glory which makes Jesus the man to be the only-begotten Son of God: *"… my glory that you gave me, because you loved me before the foundation of the world*." In theological terms this glory is called the "grace of union" or hypostatic union by which the divine and human natures are united in the one Person of Jesus Christ. Because of this union Jesus Christ is the God-man.[57] This greatest of all graces makes the man Jesus, from the very moment of his conception in Mary's womb, to be the Son of God by nature. Jesus' unique gift, called in the JLSA in two ways, is the divine Sonship. This is Jesus' heritage, and it is precisely his divine Sonship that Jesus shares with his disciples by the Footwashing.

Through grace Jesus gives his disciples the *"power to become children of God"*[58] by giving them a share in his birthright: the divine life that belongs to him as the only-begotten Son of God. In fact, Jesus affirms this in his prayer to the Father after the Footwashing: *"The glory which you have given me I have given to them, that they may be one even as we are one… and (you) have loved them even as you have loved me."*[59] Thus Jesus reveals

---

53   Translation from Brenton, Lancelot C.L., *The Septuagint Version: Greek and English,* p. 705.

54   Cf. Brown, *The Gospel According to John,* II, pp. 565, 566. See also Panimolle, *Lettura Pastorale del Vangelo di Giovanni,* III, pp. 171, 172.

55   Cf. Brown, *The Gospel According to John,* II, pp. 565, 566.

56   The nature of the gift of glory/divine name that Jesus received and shared with his disciples will be examined in detail in Chapter 12 of this study when treating the nature of Jesus' covenant.

57   The grace of union is also called the *hypostatic union.*

58   Jn 1:12.

59   Jn 17:6.

God his Father to men as their Father in accord with what is said of him in the Prologue: *"No one has ever seen God; the only-begotten Son, who is in the bosom of the Father, he has made him known."*[60]

Israel already addressed Yahweh as Father,[61] but in Jesus' covenant God's fatherhood is very different. Jesus spoke about sharing his gift of glory that reveals God's name of Father to his disciples. By accepting this covenant offered through the Footwashing, the disciples enter into a family-like union with Jesus, the only-begotten Son. This incorporation into Jesus gives his disciples a filial relationship with his Father. Thus, after the Footwashing Jesus stated that God loved his disciples as a true father because he loved them with the very love that belongs *by right* solely to the only-begotten Son of God. The fact that the Father loved Jesus' disciples with his unique paternal love is again an implicit affirmation that a covenant was made by the Footwashing. It is clear that Jesus speaks here about covenant by the Footwashing's effect of creating a kinship likened to that of family. In his covenant Jesus draws men to himself.

The Footwashing's covenantal character is also discernible in the conversation between Jesus and Peter when Jesus approached to wash Peter's feet. At first Peter adamantly refused Jesus' service, saying to him: *"You shall never wash my feet!"*[62] Peter's refusal of the Footwashing amounts to a refusal to accept Jesus' greatest act of love for his own "to the end."[63] Brown notes that this statement has the force of oath because of the Greek words (*ou me*) translated as *"never."*[64] This point is of *capital importance* since the act of making a covenant was precisely by an oath, either explicitly in words and/or implicitly by symbolic actions that pledged personal commitment. Jesus answers Peter that if he does not accept the Footwashing, he can have no share in his heritage. Just as Peter's refusal was tantamount to an oath and was absolute, so his exaggerated response was an ardent and total acceptance of Jesus' proposal: *"Lord, not my feet only but also my hands and my head."*[65] Parallel to Peter's refusal, therefore, his acceptance has the force of swearing an oath of personal commitment. Peter's response thus amounts to his complete and unreserved acceptance of the covenant. It is evident, moreover, that Jesus considered Peter's answer as counting for all the other disciples, because in Jn 13:10, Jesus responds to Peter with "you" in the plural form.[66]

---

60   Jn 1:18.
61   *E.g.* Dt 1:31; 8:5; 14:1; 32:5, 6, 19; Is 30:1; 63:16, 64:7; Jer 31:9; Mal 1:6.
62   Jn 13:8a.
63   Jn 13:1 presents the Footwashing as Jesus' greatest act of love for his own "to the end."
64   Brown, *The Gospel According to John*, II, p. 552.
65   Jn 13:8b.
66   Bultmann notes: "The plural ... shows that Peter had spoken as the disciples' representative,

John indeed presents the Footwashing as a covenant action that establishes a family-like union between the disciples with Jesus and his Father. John gives this covenantal characteristic to the Footwashing so that through this similarity with the Eucharist he might teach in his Last Supper account about the Eucharist itself and, as will be seen in Part Two of this study, the nature of the covenant it established.

2.1.2.3. Similarity as a Purificatory Action

Matthew explicitly indicates the Eucharist's purificatory character by stating that the specific purpose of Jesus' death is *"for the forgiveness of sins."* [67] This sacrificially purifying character is implicit in the other Synoptics and Paul when they state that Jesus' body is given *"for you,"*[68] and his blood is shed *"for you"* (plural)[69] and *"for many."*[70]

Like the Eucharist, John presents the Footwashing as a sacrificial action that purifies from sin. The Footwashing's nature as a purificatory action is immediately evident because Jesus tells his disciples that they were cleansed of their sins through his washing their feet: *"Jesus said to him* (Peter), *'He who has bathed does not need to wash, except for his feet, but he is clean all over; and you are clean, but not all of you.' For he knew who was to betray him; that was why he said, 'You are not all clean.'"*[71] By affirming the exception of Judas' retention of guilt because of his persistence in betraying Jesus, Jesus stresses the purificatory character of the Footwashing. The exception of Judas' case proves the rule that all were cleansed of sin. It is imperative to note how John studiously connects the betrayal of the Lord by Judas to the Footwashing. Here John follows the ancient Eucharistic tradition found in the Synoptics and Paul in which the Eucharist is linked to this betrayal.[72] John follows this tradition in the JLSA when speaking of the Footwashing. [73]

John 15 opens with the Lord's description of the disciples' union with himself and his Father: Jesus is the true vine, his disciples are the branches

---

and if we take the farewell discourses as a whole, it is clear that the disciples represent the Christian community as such." (Cf. Bultmann, *The Gospel of John*, p. 473.) Brown is not certain that Peter was a spokesman here for the other disciples. (See Brown, *The Gospel According to John*, II, p. 565.) However, whatever Peter's intention, Jesus himself regarded Peter as spokesman for the others since in his response to Peter he uses the plural form for "you."

67   Mt 26:28.
68   Cf. 1 Cor 11:24.
69   Lk 22:19, 20; I Cor 11:24.
70   Mk 14:24.
71   Jn 13:10, 11.
72   Brown notes the connection of the Footwashing with the betrayal as a possible association with the ancient Eucharistic tradition. Brown, *The Gospel According to John*, II, p. 571.
73   Cf. Jn 13:2, 10, 11, 18, 19, 21-31.

and his Father is the vinedresser.[74] This simile used by Jesus refers to ancient Israel which was spoken of in the OT as God's chosen vine, but, alas, a sterile one.[75] Because Jesus purified his disciples and made covenant with them, Jesus tells them in Jn 15:3 that they are now ready to bear fruit: *"You are already made clean by the word which I have spoken to you."*[76] The Greek word for "clean" here is the same one the Lord previously used in Jn 13:10, 11 when he declared his disciples clean from the Footwashing.[77] For this reason this, declaration refers to the cleansing effected by the Footwashing which enables them in union with Jesus to bear fruit that is pleasing to the Father. However, here in Jn 15:3, Jesus attributes this cleansing to his word rather than to the Footwashing. Is there a contradiction here? In answer to this, Brown states: "A dichotomy between the salvific action of Jesus and his salvific word is not true to John." In fact the Prologue identifies Jesus as the Word, and the Johannine Jesus said in Jn 12:49 that his word will be the judge on the last day of those who reject him. Brown notes that Bultmann uses Jn 15:3 to interpret the Footwashing as a symbol of the cleansing power of Jesus' word.[78] Bultmann states: "While the service Jesus performs is symbolized by the footwashing, its essential nature is not expressly defined; and yet basically it is self-evident, as 15:3 expresses it: 'Already you are clean, because of the word I have spoken to you.' Thus the *word* has cleansed them. His service is accomplished in the word which he speaks and which by speaking it, he himself is. For his word is not a doctrine that could be separated from his person, a complex of ideas with general validity. Rather he is himself encountered as the word in all the separate things he says....."[79]

2.2. The Nature of the Analogy

Having examined all the eucharistic circumstances, attributes and effects that John attributed to the Footwashing, the question arises as to what kind of analogy John used for these two actions so different in themselves. The answer depends upon whether these Eucharistic characteristics truly belong to the essential makeup of the Footwashing. The answer is that those eucharistic characteristics alleged by John about the Footwashing really belong *intrinsically and formally* only to the Eucharist. Therefore the analogy constructed by John is the ***analogy of improper proportionality***.

---

74   Speaking about Jn 15:1-6, Brown says: "The disciples are already in union with Jesus, and the emphasis is on remaining in that union."

75   Vg. Ps 80 (79):8-16; Isa 3:14; 5:1-7; Jer 2:21; 12:10; Ezek 17:8; 19:10-14; Hos 10:1; Nahum 2:3.

76   Cf. Brown, *The Gospel According to John*, II, pp. 676, 677.

77   Cf. Lightfoot, R.H., *St. John's Gospel, A Commentary*, p. 282.

78   Cf. Brown, *The Gospel According to John*, II, p. 677.

79   Bultmann, *The Gospel of John*, pp. 470, 471.

It is clear from the belief and practice of the Church that the eucharistic characteristics attributed to the Footwashing do not belong to its essential makeup. The Church has never understood the command to repeat the Footwashing in the same way as it has for the Eucharist. The command for washing feet has not been rigorously observed despite the fact that the liturgical observance of that command is called by the Latin word *mandatum*, meaning "command." In fact, the Mandatum had long fallen into disuse and was only restored to the Liturgy in 1955 by Pope Pius XII as a part of the reform of Holy Week. Moreover, the faith of the Church has always professed that the Eucharist, not the Footwashing, is the action that established the Christian covenant for the forgiveness of sins at the Last Supper. Therefore the only logical conclusion is that John made his analogy knowing well that his analogy is simply a metaphor for teaching purposes.

John's analogy is similar to the one made in 2 Sam 12:1-11 by the prophet Nathan when confronting David about the slaying of Uriah the Hittite, husband of Bathsheba. The prophet asked David to pass judgment on a case he described of a rich man who, to feed a visitor, took a poor man's dearly prized ewe lamb because he did not want to take any animal from his own flocks. David condemned the rich man. Nathan then told David that he was that rich man. The rich man was simply an allegorical figure used by Nathan to illustrate David's culpability and to impose sentence upon him. Nathan attributed to this fictitious rich man the situation of King David. In speaking about the rich man, Nathan was actually speaking about David, just like John, speaking about the Footwashing, is, in reality, speaking about the Eucharist. However, Nathan and John present their analogies differently. Nathan, in his conclusion, openly affirms his analogical presentation to David when he told him: "You are the man." Unlike Nathan, John does not explain his allegory. John leaves his readers to deduce his allegoric presentation of the Eucharist from those things he ascribed to the Footwashing. He seems to have assumed that, given the well-known eucharistic context of the Last Supper and the Eucharist's special characteristics, his analogy did not need explicit identification. Unfortunately this was not the case; the dots were not connected.

2.3. Motive for the Analogy

Alfred Loisy correctly understood the Footwashing as an analogue of the Eucharist: "The real meaning of the washing of the feet is the Eucharist itself, a life sacrificed out of love, a charity lasting until death." But Loisy, not pursuing his insight any further, continues: "What makes difficult understanding this symbolism (i.e. of the Eucharist) is the flawed choice of the symbol itself (i.e. the Footwashing), and this difficulty constantly surfaces .... The washing of the feet could have been substituted by the simple narrative of the supper, which, however, the author did not wish to employ, and the absence of which remains very noticeable."[80] This remark about the poor choice of the Footwashing for the Eucharist suggests that Loisy missed the pedagogical reason for John's choice.

The JLSA presents the Footwashing as the means by which Jesus literally completed his final earthly messianic mission. John's motive for the Footwashing analogy was to deepen the understanding of the Eucharistic Sacrifice and its covenant. Through his analogy John was able to present the Eucharist and its covenant on the dynamic level of an exchange in word rather than at the level of the symbolic ritual of the institution narratives. The ritual's symbolic character makes the Eucharist more prone to misinterpretation and superstition[81] than does a covenant expressed, accepted, and explained in an explicit manner through word as in the ancient vassal treaty.[82] It was precisely for this reason that the central portion of Deuteronomy verbalized the Sinai covenant by employing the formulary of the ancient vassal treaty.[83] Through the Footwashing analogy and its ensuing discourses, John was able to explain the Eucharist and its covenant at the level of word by following Deuteronomy's example. By the Footwashing John explained and verbalized the ritual on a different level so as to teach in a more detailed manner about the rite's nature, the covenant it established, and the commitment necessary to be party to the Eucharistic Covenant.

Aside from John's desire to teach more profoundly about the Eucharist, one might also assume that he may have wished to address some particular difficulties regarding the Eucharist. Even before John wrote his gospel there were problems with the Eucharist in the community at Corinth. In 1 Corinthians, 11:17-34, St. Paul upbraids the Corinthians because of their flagrant abuses in the celebration of the Lord's Supper and the unworthy reception of the body and blood of Jesus Christ in the Eucharist.

Contrary to Bultmann's views, this study maintains that John certainly did write about the Eucharist in his Last Supper account. His motives for devising the Footwashing analogy were never to diminish the importance of the Eucharist as the foundation ceremony of the Christian Covenant. Instead,

---

80   Loisy, Alfred, *Le Quatrième Évangile*, p. 389: "La signification proper du lavement des pieds est celle de l'eucharistie, de la vie sacrifiée par amour, de la charité servante jusqu'à la mort. C'est le choix défectueux du symbole qui en rend l'intelligence difficile, et cet inconvénient se fera sentir jusqu'au bout.... Le lavement des pieds a pu être substitué à un récit de la cêne qu'on n'a pas voulu garder, et don't l'absence demeure sensible." (Translation is by the author of this work.)

81   The Eucharist is seen by many as magic par excellence. In fact, the phrase "*hocus pocus*" is coined from the consecratory words over the bread.

82   The ancient vassal treaty will be treated in Part II.

83   The word "treaty" is generally used when referring to non-biblical covenants.

John wished to explain in a more profound way the nature of the Eucharist for the worship of God "in spirit and truth"[84] as well as the nature of the Eucharistic Covenant, its obligations and consequences.

2.4. Conclusion

There are many meanings attributed to the Footwashing and to the various verses of the JLSA, but the discussion of these matters goes beyond the scope of the present study. The real problem is that the meaning of the Footwashing has not been understood as an analogue of the Eucharist.

This study concentrates on showing that John created this analogy and what he is teaching by it. **Following the above explanation there can no longer be any doubt about the existence of an analogy between the Footwashing and the Eucharist.** Necessarily, therefore, whenever the JLSA speaks of the Footwashing, it expressly but implicitly speaks of the Eucharist. Understanding this fact opens a new avenue for interpreting the JLSA and even the Fourth Gospel as a whole.

John is not always understood because of his way of expressing himself. He is sometimes characterized as a "mystic" who speaks in prophetic and mysterious language. But through this study it should become apparent that while John does speak analogically in his Last Supper Account, he has both feet very much on the ground and says exactly what he means about the most profound mystery of the Eucharist.

The analogy between the Footwashing and the Eucharist of the Synoptic and Pauline Last Supper Accounts is schematically illustrated on the next page.

---

84   Jn 4:23, 24.

THE ANALOGY CREATED BY JOHN BETWEEN:
The <u>EUCHARIST</u> & The <u>FOOTWASHING</u>:

<u>THEY EACH HAVE *IDENTICAL CIRCUMSTANCES*</u>:

1. MAIN EVENT OF LAST SUPPER:

MT 26:20-30; MK 14:17-26; LK 22:14-38;   JN 13-17
        1 COR 11:23-26

2. CONNECTED WITH JUDAS' BETRAYAL:

MT 26:21-25; MK 14:18-21; LK 22:21-23;   (JN 6:70, 71) JN 13:2, 10, 11, 18, 19, 21-31
        1 COR 11:23

3. COMMAND TO REPEAT ACTION:

LK 22:19; 1 COR 11:24, 25   JN 13:14, 15

<u>THEY EACH HAVE *IDENTICAL ATTRIBUTES AND EFFECTS*</u>:

1. SIGN OF DEATH OF JESUS:

-body *"given"*   LK 22:19; 1 COR 11:24   - show love *"to the end"* JN 13:1
                                                        (JN 19:30)

- blood *"poured out"* MT 26:2; MK 14:24;   - *"laid down his garments"* JN 13:4
        LK 22:20; 1 COR 11:24   (JN 10:17. 18)

-*"the Lord's death"*   1 COR 11:26

2. COVENANTAL ACTION (creates a family-like relationship):

-*"blood of the covenant"* MT 26:28;   - *"no <u>part</u> with me"* (i.e. HERITAGE) JN 13:8a
MK 14:24   Jesus' heritage is the revelation of
- *"new covenant in my blood"* LK 22:20;   God as Father, which consists in the
COR 11:23   Father's gift of:
                                                    - the Father's Name JN 17:12
                                                    - the glory of divine Sonship
                                                    (Hypostatic Union) JN 17:14
                                                    (given by covenant JN 17:22, 23)

                            -*"never"* (oath) JN 13:8b / *"not my feet only"*
                                        JN 13:9

3. PURIFICATORY ACTION   (i.e. CLEANSE FROM SIN)

- body given *"for you"* 1 COR 11:4   - *"you are clean"* JN 13:10, 11
- blood shed *"for you"* LK 22:19, 20; MK 14:24 - *"you are already made clean"* JN 15:3
- *"for the forgiveness of sins"* MT 26:28

CHAPTER 3

The Footwasher

The main event of the JLSA is the Footwashing, and the Footwasher is Jesus. The Fourth Gospel must now be examined regarding its teachings about: (1) who Jesus is, and (2) the nature of his final earthly mission that was accomplished by the Footwashing.

3.1. Who Jesus Is

Eternal life is the gift of God through Jesus Christ[85] who is himself this life[86] and its source.[87]

John states that his gospel's purpose is *"that you may believe that Jesus is the Christ, the Son of God, and that believing you may have life in his name."*[88] To obtain the life that Jesus is and offers, one must believe: (1) in the man Jesus' divine origin as the Son of God, and (2) in his royal status as the Christ. These two specifications define who Jesus is.

3.1.1. Jesus' Divine Origin: Pre-existent Word, Son of God

Jesus' divine origin is clearly stated in the Fourth Gospel's Prologue.[89] He is the pre-existing Word, who is of God and is God; he is Yahweh's only-begotten Son. All was created through him. The Word became flesh and in his human identity took the name of Jesus. He is the God-man: a divine Person having both divine and human natures.

Jn 1:14 declares that Jesus is *"full of grace and truth"* (Gr. *pleres charitos kai aletheias*) and Jn 1:17 states *"the law was given through Moses; grace and truth came through Jesus Christ."* The Mosaic Covenant's law offered life to God's chosen people through the faithful observance of the law.[90] By proclaiming himself *"the way, and the truth, and the life,"*[91] Jesus presents himself as the fulfillment of the law.[92] The law offered long life on the Promised Land;[93] Jesus offers eternal life in his Father's house.[94]

---

85 Jn 6:27, 54; 10:28; 17:2, 3.
86 Jn 11:25; 14:6; 1 Jn 1, 2.
87 Jn 1:4; 5:26, 40; 6:35; 17:2, 3.
88 Jn 20:31; see also Jn 10:10.
89 Jn 1:1-3, 14, 18.
90 See Dt. 4:1; 5:33; 6:20; 30:6, 15, 19, 20; 32:45-47.
91 Jn 14:6.
92 See Mt 5:17; Rm 10:4.
93 See Dt 4:40; 5:33; 6:2, 24; 11:9.
94 See Jn 10:10; 12:50; 14:2, 3; 17:2, 3.

The OT often expressed Yahweh's covenant love by pairing the Hebrew words for "love" and "truth" (*hesed we'emet*). *Hesed* signifies family love,[95] but it is also used for the love that "presupposes the relationship of covenant and operates within it."[96] *Emet* is the Hebrew word for "truth." These words used together signify Yahweh's enduring, steadfast and faithful covenant love.[97] In Jn 1:14, 17, John adopts the OT practice by pairing *charis* and *alethia*. *Charis* is the Greek word for "grace" or "loving-kindness," and *alethia* is the Greek word for "truth." John uses the Greek word *charis* as the counterpart of the Hebrew word *hesed*.[98] After the Prologue, the Fourth Gospel no longer uses the word *charis*.

The Prologue teaches that Jesus communicates Yahweh's steadfast covenant love with which he is filled.[99] While Jesus' covenant love is in continuity with Yahweh's OT covenant love,[100] its specific nature is different because of who Jesus is, and because of the nature of his messianic mission. Yahweh's faithful loving-kindness that Jesus communicates is intimately connected to the nature of his covenant. Jn 1:12 alludes to it when it states that Jesus would give to those who believe in him the power to become the *"children of God."* Jesus' covenant establishes a new relationship with God because it confers a sharing in his own life, the divine filial life of the Son of God incarnate. As the only-begotten Son of God, Jesus alone is able to share his unique filial life.

Jn 1:17 explicitly identifies the Word-made-flesh by his personal name of "Jesus" together with his royal messianic title of "Christ." John presents Jesus, the incarnate Son of God, as the Messiah king of God's people whom he makes children of God. Brown states that in Jn 1:17 the Prologue "comes

---

95   The OT often expressed the love of Yahweh for his people by two different words. The first word, *ahab*, regards the initial stage of Yahweh's loving relationship with Israel. It expresses the love whereby Yahweh elects or chooses Israel to be his own. (For example: Dt 4:37; 7:8; 10:15; Hos 3:1) The other verb, *hesed*, primarily expresses the love of Yahweh that perpetuates his loving choice through covenant. However, the distinction between the two words – *hesed* and *ahab* – is subtle since the love of election and covenant love are both related to and rooted in the identical loving relationship. (See Good, E.M., *"Love in the OT,"* *BID*, III, pp. 166, 167.)
96   Good, E.M., *"Love in the OT,"* *BID*, III, p. 167.
97   See Gn 24:27; 32:11; 2 Sam 2:6; 15:20; Ps 40:11; 61:8; 89:25; 98:3; 115:1; 138:2.
98   See Vine, W.E., et al, Vine's Complete Expository Dictionary of Old and New Testament Words, pp. 142, 143.
99   Jn 1:14, 17.
100   Brown, referring to Jn 1:14, 16ss, says that Jesus serves as the Tabernacle of God and that the glory of Jesus, likened to the *shekinah* of the OT, is the visible and powerful manifestation of God. Jesus, as the manifestation of God's glory, is full of God's faithful loving-kindness, which is to say covenant love, and we have received this loving-kindness from Jesus in place of the OT covenant love that was given through Moses. See: Brown, *The Gospel According to John*, I, pp. 34, 35.

to an end with the triumphant proclamation of a new covenant replacing the Sinai covenant."[101]

Since Jesus establishes his new covenant in continuity with the Mosaic one, the Fourth Gospel also presents Jesus as the "prophet like Moses" who is spoken of in Dt 18:15: *"The LORD your God will raise up for you a prophet like me from among you, from your brethren—him you shall heed."*

Jn 1:18, the last verse of the Prologue, indicates the specific nature of the new covenant that Jesus will establish. Since by that covenant Jesus is to make those who accept him become "children of God," it is a covenant that will reveal God's name of Father. Jesus alone is able to reveal his Father's name since he is God's only-begotten Son.

3.1.2. Jesus' Royal Status: Messiah, Christ, the Son of Man

Messiah, Christ and the Son of man are titles assigned to Jesus that indicate him to be Yahweh's choice as sovereign for his people.

Messiah is the transliterated form of the Aramaic and Hebrew words signifying "the anointed one." *Christ* is the Greek translation of that title. In the OT, Messiah was the title of the king of ancient Israel.[102] Of all NT authors, John is most conscious of the Jewish concepts associated with the title of Messiah and puts the greatest emphasis on Jesus' kingship.[103] John uses the name Jesus together with his title of Christ twice in his Gospel. He does this the first time in concluding his Prologue in Jn 1:17, when speaking of Jesus as establishing the New Covenant. The second time is in Jn 17:3, where Jesus uses the title with his name when speaking of the necessity of accepting himself as Messiah in order to gain eternal life. Since belief in Jesus' kingship is necessary for receiving eternal life, the title of Christ or Messiah and his messianic mission is obviously of capital importance in the Fourth Gospel.

It was common Jewish belief that the expected Messiah would be a victorious political leader like David. John's teaching, however, differed from the generally accepted messianic concepts and terms. Jesus' kingship is *"not of this world."*[104] In order to avoid any confusion between the political and the authentic concepts of Messiah, John teaches just who the long-awaited Messiah is under the title *"the Son of man."* [105]

101   Brown, *The Gospel According to John*, I, p. 35.
102   In most cases this title indicates the sovereign of God's people. After the Exile it was also used for the high priest who had some functions of the king. Cf. *BID*, Vol. 3, p. 360.
103   See Dodd, *The Interpretation of the Fourth Gospel*, pp. 228, 229.
104   Jn 18:35.
105   Cf. Sanders, J.N., Mastin, B.A., *A Commentary on the Gospel According to St. John*, p. 106.

Commenting on the Fourth Gospel's use of the title "the Son of man," Moloney states: "Behind the title stands the conviction, taken from Dan. 7, that the Son of Man must suffer many things. This theme was first used to correct the strictly Jewish categories of an all-conquering Davidic messiah, but at a later stage its connection with the Cross took it along the uniquely Johannine path of a Son of Man 'lifted up' on a Cross to reveal God among men. Thus, the Son of Man is now the unique revealer of God among men, and the place where men can come to life or death in their acceptance or refusal of that revelation."[106]

Immediately following the Prologue, John develops his presentation of Jesus as Messiah. He indicates through the prophetic testimony of the Baptist that Jesus is the bearer of the Spirit.[107] The Spirit descended and remained upon Jesus[108] in fulfillment of the prophecies of Isaiah about the Messiah.[109] By the bestowal of the Spirit Jesus would complete his earthly messianic mission of revealing God's name of Father.[110] The Prologue states that Jesus gives power to those who believe in him to become the children of God, but it is through the operation of his Spirit that they become God's children.[111] The permanency of the Spirit in Jesus also alludes to David, the only king in Israel about whom this affirmation was made.[112] John, therefore, presents Jesus as the new David in accordance with the prophecy of Ezekiel: "And I will set up over them one shepherd, my servant David, and he shall feed them: he shall feed them and be their shepherd. And I, the LORD, will be their God, and my servant David shall be prince among them: I, the LORD, have spoken."[113]

For the first time the Fourth Gospel uses Jesus' messianic title in the transliterated form (*ton Messian*) when Andrew informs Simon Peter that he has found "the Messiah." The title is then immediately translated into Greek as *Christos*.[114] In presenting Jesus as Messiah to the Samaritan woman,[115] the Fourth Gospel again follows the same procedure as when Jesus is introduced to Peter.[116] The Fourth Gospel uses the Aramaic title for Jesus only in these two instances in which Peter represents the faithful people of ancient

106　Moloney, *The Johannine Son of Man*, p. 256.
107　Cf. Jn 1:32, 33.
108　Cf. Jn 1:33; 3:5-8.
109　See Is 11:1-9; 42:1-9; 61:1-3.
110　See Jn 1:33; 3:5-8; 7:37-39.
111　See Jn 3:3-8.
112　Cf. 1 Sam 16:13.
113　Ezk 34:23, 24.
114　Cf. Jn 1:41.
115　Cf. Jn 4:4-42.
116　Cf. Jn 4:25, 26.

Israel and the Samaritan woman represents the Gentile world. Thus does the Fourth Gospel indicate that Jesus is to hold his kingly office over the New Israel, which is a universal kingdom, composed of both Jews and Gentiles.[117] This universal kingship is what the Johannine Jesus himself claims for himself at the Last Supper in Jn 17:2,3, when he unites his royal title with his proper name: "Jesus Christ."

The Fourth Gospel refers both to Jesus' divine origin and to his royal status in Nathaniel's profession of faith in Jn 1:49: *"Rabbi, you are the Son of God! You are the King of Israel."* This twofold profession embraces exactly what the Fourth Gospel speaks of in Jn 20:31 about what must be believed concerning Jesus. In Nathaniel's profession the Johannine Gospel makes it clear, by using "King of Israel" for the title "Messiah," that Jesus' messianic authority is regal like that of David, and extends over all God's people, theologically designated as "Israel."[118]

Jesus responds to Nathaniel's profession of faith: *"Truly, truly, I say to you, you will see heaven opened, and the angels of God ascending and descending upon the Son of man."*[119] These words refer to the narrative about Jacob's dream in which he saw a stairway reaching up to heaven with angels ascending and descending on it.[120] Jacob, after wrestling an angel,[121] was given the name "Israel," the name by which his descendants became known. Jacob's new name of Israel is related to the passage where Jesus says that he is "the true vine"[122] and his followers are the branches of that vine.[123] The vine and vineyard were often used in the OT as ancient biblical figures of Israel.[124] By calling himself "the true vine" Jesus alludes to himself as the new Israel, who is alone able to bring forth fruit pleasing to his Father.[125] In his statement about being "the true vine," Jesus also affirms the special nature of his kingship because he is one with his people by much more than a mere moral union.

In his response to Nathaniel Jesus affirmed his royal status as king of Israel while indicating at the same time his special role as Messiah. He presented himself as the true Israel[126] who is the revealer of the mysteries of

---

117   Cf. Jn 12:34.
118   Cf. also Jn 7:42.
119   Jn 1:51.
120   Gn 28:11-17.
121   Cf. Hos 12:5.
122   Jn 15:1.
123   Jn 15:5.
124   V.g. Ps 80 (79):8; Is 3:14; 5:1-7; Jer 2:21; 12:10; Ez 17:8; Hos 10:1; Nahum 2:3.
125   This matter will be dealt with in more detail in Part II.
126   Cf. Sanders, J.N., Mastin, B.A., *A Commentary on the Gospel According to St. John*, p. 105.

God. The ministering angels from heaven indicate the Son of man's continuous contact with God. The Messiah is the revealer of God, recalling the words of the Prologue: *"No one has ever seen God; the only-begotten Son, who is in the bosom of the Father, he has made him known."*[127] For this reason the Son of man *"descended from heaven.*[128]

Nathaniel calls Jesus the King of Israel. Jesus answers by calling himself "the Son of man." This specific title may be expressed in Greek in either of two ways: (1) *without* the definite article before "man" (*ho huios anthropou*), or (2) *with* the definite article (*ho huios tou anthropou*), which would literally be translated as "the Son of **the** man." Normally, there would be no difference in the translation since both could correctly be understood as "the Son of man." However, it is intriguing that John uses the title **without** the definite article twelve times,[129] and only once **with** the definite article in Jn 5:27. Could there be a special reason why John makes an exception in one case? Is there a subtle difference in John's meaning by his inclusion of the definite article in Jn 5:27?

Firstly, consider the Fourth Gospel's use of the title twelve times ***without*** the definite article: *ho huios anthropou*. This expression resembles the title given to the mysterious figure in the Septuagint's account in Dan 7:13. Here "the son of man" (without the article) is seen "coming on the clouds of heaven." This phrase alludes to the divine origin of that mysterious figure. The Jerome Biblical Commentary states that in Dan 7:13, "the son of man is a figure of the kingdom of 'the holy ones of the Most High' (v. 18)."[130] However, the Commentary adds: "… because in Dan the thought of 'kingdom' often shifts imperceptibly into that of 'king,' the concept of the 'son of man' eventually shifted from a figure of speech for the theocratic kingdom into a term for the messianic king himself."[131] In the Fourth Gospel the Messiah is not an ordinary king of Israel. He is rather a figure whose origin is more than human. The expression without the article alludes to Jesus as a royal figure whose origin is more than human. In fact, the extraordinary nature of Jesus as king is brought out in Jn 15:1-5, where Jesus uses the allegorical figure of "the true vine" to refer to himself as the entire kingdom of Israel and his disciples as branches of the vine. This sense is parallel to what is often understood about "the son of man" in Dan 7:13. Therefore it seems that by its use of "the son of man" **without** the definite article, the Fourth Gospel alludes to the divine origin of Jesus as the Messiah king of Israel.

---

127   Jn 1:18.
128   Jn 3:13.
129   Jn 1:51; 3:13, 14; 6:27, 53, 62; 8:28; 9:35; 12:23, 34 (twice); 13:31.
130   *JBC*, n. 28, p. 456.
131   *Ibid.*

Secondly, consider the Fourth Gospel's only use of the title "the Son of man" **with** the definite article in Jn 5:25-27: *ho huios **tou** anthropou. "Truly, truly, I say to you, the hour is coming and now is, when the dead will hear the voice of the Son of God, and those who hear will live. For as the Father has life in himself, so he has granted the Son also to have life in himself, and has given him authority to execute judgment, because he is the Son of* (**the**) *man. "*[132]

In the book of Genesis the Hebrew word for "man" in the generic sense is *adam*. However, the word is also used as the proper name of the first man: *Adam*.[133] The association of the proper name of the first man with the generic word for "man" is because Adam was the first man and, therefore, the original father of men who was made by God to be the sovereign over the visible creation.[134] Thus, the use of the title "the Son of *the* man" could well indicate Jesus' *human origins* as the *son of the original man*, Adam, who was sovereign over visible creation. This sense would be in conformity with the Fourth Gospel's perspective of Jesus as the new Adam who comes to complete creation by bringing a new life, i.e. eternal life, to the human race. The Fourth Gospel conceives the mission of Jesus Messiah as completing the Father's plan for creation and taking back the kingdom usurped by Satan, whom Jesus called "the ruler of this world."[135] This fundamental mission of Jesus is demonstrated by the fact that the Fourth Gospel opens like the book of Genesis: *"In the beginning."* In the beginning creation was brought about through God's Word.[136] It is to be perfected through Jesus, God's Incarnate Word.[137]

This being said, Jesus, as the Son of *the* man, openly claims in the three verses quoted above (Jn 5:25-27), two uniquely divine prerogatives: (1) giving life, and (2) rendering judgment.[138] Jesus claims these prerogatives precisely because he is "the Son of *the* man." As this title is written with the article in Jn 5:27, it stresses the fact that Jesus as Messiah is the **second Adam** who comes to bring new life and judgment precisely because he is also the eternal Son of God. The two prerogatives of giving eternal life and

---

132   Jn 5:25-27.

133   In the Hebrew Bible the first time it appears as a proper name for the first man is Gn 4:25 (see McKenzie, John L., *Dictionary of the Bible*, p.12). However, the Greek translation of the OT (Septuagint) begins the use of the word as the proper name for Adam in Gn 3:16.

134   See Gn 1:27-29; 2:19.

135   Jn 12:31; 14:30; 16:11.

136   Jn 1:3

137   See Jn 3:12, 16, 36; 5:24; 40; 6:40, 47; 10:10, 28; 11:25; 12:50; 14:6; 13:8; 17:2; 20:31.

138   Jn 9:39 states that Jesus Christ came into this world for the purpose of judgment. Jn 12:48 states that his word will judge those who reject him. According to Jn 12:31, Jesus' final mission was to execute judgment upon this world.

rendering judgment are precisely the mission that Jesus must accomplish as Messiah. In this way he completes his Father's plan for creation and restores the kingdom of God usurped by Satan. He fulfilled the messianic mission of the revelation of God's name of "Father" by a work of judgment upon this world, a judgment about which he spoke when announcing the arrival of his "hour" and revealing his program in Jn 12:23, 28, 31-33.[139]

In Jn 6:27, Jesus, having miraculously fed the crowds, affirms his royal status as the new Adam, a status confirmed by God his Father. Jesus states: *"Do not labor for the food that perishes, but for the food which endures to eternal life, which the Son of man will give to you; for on him has God the Father set his seal."* Here, when Jesus speaks of himself as the Son of man, he states that it was on him that *"God the Father set his seal."* Commenting on this verse Nolli mentions that the verb "setting seal" is in the aorist tense, which indicates here that the action is definitive, accomplished once and for all.[140] Thus the seal of which Jesus speaks in Jn 6:27 is precisely the Spirit. John the Baptist states that he saw the Spirit descend from the sky and rest upon Jesus, and that the one who sent him to baptize told him that the person upon whom he would see the Spirit descend would be the one who is to baptize with the Holy Spirit.[141] When discussing Jn 6:27, Brown states that "John clearly understands the impact of the Spirit's descent on Jesus ... that it marks him out as God's unique instrument, and in particular as the Messiah and the servant of the Lord. In Isa xi 2 we are told that the spirit of Yahweh shall rest ... on the shoot from the stump of Jesse who is the Davidic king."[142]

In Jn 6:27 Jesus implicitly affirms his royal status as the new Adam, the King who has been sealed by God with the Spirit.[143] This is particularly important because it is precisely through the bestowal of the Spirit that Jesus accomplishes his final earthly messianic mission of revealing the Father's name to those who accept him and thus is glorified as the Son of man, which is to say, the Messiah King of Israel.[144]

The title, "the Son of man," is used in the Fourth Gospel to communicate the genuine meaning of Jesus' messianic kingship and personality.[145] The purpose of Jesus' title of "the Son of man" in the Fourth Gospel is to present

---

139   This matter will be treated in the following chapter.
140   Nolli, *Evangelo Secondo Giovanni*, p. 213.
141   Jn 1:29-34.
142   Brown, *The Gospel According to John*, I, p. 66.
143   Cf. Jn 1:32.
144   This matter will be discussed further in Chapter 6.
145   See Moloney, Francis J., *The Johannine Son of Man* (2nd ed.: Biblioteca di Scienze Religiose, vol. 14; Roma: Libreria Ateneo Salesiano, 1978), p. 206.

Jesus as the authentic and long-awaited Messiah king, whose origin is both human and divine. He comes as the new Adam to restore the fallen creation and retake the sovereignty lost by the first Adam to the devil, who then became "the ruler of this world." It is important to note that the title "the Son of man" focuses on Jesus as the *incarnate* Son of God; it concentrates upon his *human* figure and his *earthly* messianic mission. By the term "earthly" this study refers to the part of the mission that Jesus Messiah had to accomplish up to and including his death on the cross. In fact, Moloney observes that the title, "the Son of man," "*seems to be strictly limited to the historical life and death of Jesus.*"[146] It is important to note that the last time this title is used in the Fourth Gospel is at the Last Supper where Jesus declares that the Son of man has just been glorified, which is to say that he had just completed his final earthly messianic mission.[147]

3.2. The Nature of Jesus' Final Earthly Mission

John teaches that the culminating point of the Son of man's earthly messianic mission was to be "lifted up."

In the Septuagint text Isaiah was the first to employ that term with reference to the Servant of Yahweh.[148] He writes: "Behold, my servant shall understand and be lifted up and glorified exceedingly."[149] This Servant, who had undergone untold sufferings in fulfilling the task entrusted to him by Yahweh, would be "lifted up." This phrase is also translated as "exalted." The Servant would not only restore Israel, but he would also be the instrument for bringing Yahweh's salvation to the ends of the earth, i.e. to both Jews and Gentiles. However, the Servant effectively accomplished his saving work through his sufferings. North writes about the Servant of the Lord in Isaiah: "… it is agreed that whoever was the original of the Servant, none except Christ was its fulfillment."[150]

The Fourth Gospel speaks three times of the Son of man's being "lifted up." This Greek word (*hypsothenai*) has the meaning of exaltation. De la Potterie significantly points out that this word was used in ancient documents, both profane and biblical,[151] to signify royal power.[152] The king was "lifted up" by ruling over his people. In using this word the Fourth Gospel refers to the royal status of the Son of man. He is to be "lifted up" in his royal

---

146   Moloney, *The Johannine Son of Man*, p. 201. Italics ours.
147   Jn 13:31.
148   Is 52:13.
149   This is a translation from the Septuagint.
150   North, C.R., *IDB*, vol. 4, p. 294.
151   E.g. 1 Mc 8:13; 11:16.
152   See de la Potterie, Ignace, *The Hour of Jesus: The Passion and the Resurrection of Jesus According to John* (New York: Alba House, 1997), p. 7.

enthronement. However, the Fourth Gospel gives an additional meaning to the expression. The phrase also signifies the kind of death Jesus would have to endure in fulfilling his final mission for his glorification as Messiah.[153] The incarnate Son of God's earthly mission as the Son of man concerned both his royal status and the death whereby he would effectively be enthroned as Messiah. Jesus Christ is king by reason of his nature as well as by his conquest of Satan through the judgment he brought upon this world.[154]

The Fourth Gospel speaks for the first time about the "lifting up" of the Son of man during Jesus' conversation with Nicodemus. Jesus tells him: *"And as Moses lifted up the serpent in the wilderness, so must the Son of man be lifted up, that whoever believes in him may have eternal life."* [155] Jesus indicates here that he must be lifted up like Moses lifted up the bronze serpent in the desert (Nm 21:4-9). The Israelites rebelled against God and Moses and consequently God sent fiery serpents that bit and killed many as punishment. The people expressed their repentance to Moses and he prayed for them. Then, at God's command, Moses made a bronze serpent and mounted it on a pole so that whoever looked upon it might be healed. Jesus thus intimated that he as Messiah would be lifted up on the cross and would be effective in giving life like the bronze serpent. Schnackenburg's statement is pertinent here: "The bringer of revelation, come in the flesh, the Son of God, is the bringer of life for mankind who has succumbed to death, and he is, in this sense, the Messiah."[156]

While the Fourth Gospel's first statement about the lifting up of the Son of man indicates the eventual success of Jesus' messianic mission, it has a twofold meaning: (a) his royal glorification as the messiah, who brings salvation and life to his people, and, at the same time, (b) his death upon the cross.

The Fourth Gospel speaks for the second time of the Son of man being "lifted up" during Jesus' conversation with the Jews who refused to accept his and his Father's testimony regarding his messianic mission. Jesus tells them: *"When you have lifted up the Son of man, then you will know that I am he, and that I do nothing on my own authority but speak thus as the Father taught me."*[157] Jesus' prophetic words signify that once the Jews crucified him they will see that he is God's Son and that his activity was faithful to his messianic mission. Here Jesus' being "lifted up" indicates the eventual vindication of his claim to divine origin and of the success of his mission.

---

153   Cf. Jn 12:32, 33.
154   Jn 12:31.
155   Jn 3:14,15.
156   Schnackenburg, *The Gospel According to St. John*, III, 339.
157   Jn 8:28.

However, this statement adds another element: the Jews who do not accept his divinity and messianic mission will be instrumental in his being lifted up and in his glorification.

The Fourth Gospel's third and final declaration about the Son of man's being "lifted up" is made when Jesus announces the beginning of "the hour." On this occasion the Fourth Gospel specifies the program for the hour that the Father had set aside for the fulfillment of Jesus' messianic mission.[158] This program will be analyzed in the next chapter, but it is important to note here that the expression "lifted up" refers to "the sort of death he (the Son of man) had to die." The lifting up of the Son of man takes place during "the hour." [159]

The "hour" is alluded to from the beginning of the Fourth Gospel. This hour was mentioned in Chapter 1 of this work when briefly examining the program for the final work of Jesus. "The hour" is that particular time to which Jesus' life and mission are directed. For the Synoptics "the hour" is a time of capture, darkness, terribly humiliating suffering and death. But for John, though the hour of the lifting up of the Son of man is the hour of his death and the departure of the light from this world, it is the time of the Son of man's glorification and the glorification of God's name of Father. The mention of the glorification of the Son of man recalls Isaiah's Servant of Yahweh who, through his suffering, was "lifted up and glorified exceedingly."[160]

The notion of "glory" as understood in the Fourth Gospel is of fundamental importance for understanding the nature of Jesus' earthly messianic mission. As mentioned in Chapter 1, the Hebrew word for glory is *kabod*. Its basic meaning is "weight," "consideration," and "importance." The glory of a person or thing is that which gives him or it importance. This glory may be essential qualities or the external manifestation of inner worth, dignity or status. The visible manifestations of God's glory consisted in his saving works of righteousness and fidelity for the deliverance of Israel. These works were "the splendor of the divine presence."[161] On the other hand, one gave glory to God by submissive recognition of his holiness.[162] Creation itself gives glory to God, and in this sense God's glory is found in the perfection of his creation.

For the Fourth Gospel, the greatest visible manifestations of God's glory are the Incarnate Word himself and what he did.[163] Of the thirteen times that

---

158   Jn 12:23, 28, 31-33.
159   This special time will be treated later in more detail.
160   Is 52:13. This is a translation from the Septuagint.
161   See Mateos, J., and Barreto, J., *Il Vangelo di Giovanni*, p. 63.
162   E.g. Ps 66:2; 79:9; 96:7; 115:1.
163   Jn 1:14.

John uses the title of "the Son of man," five of these refer to Jesus' death and the manifestation of his glory.[164] *Jesus' death and glorification are to take place contemporaneously.* **At his death the Son of man will be glorified by his royal enthronement as Messiah of God's people.** Jesus, by reason of his human and divine natures, is sovereign king of all creation. However, Jesus was, in a way, "pretender" to the messianic throne that he would finally occupy as "the true vine" when he would establish the new covenant. At that time Jesus would be glorified by his royal enthronement as Messiah king of God's New Israel.

The glorification of God was to take place by and in his Son's glorification since it is the task of the Son to reveal his Father (cf Jn 1:18). Jesus accomplished this by transmitting to his messianic people God's paternal love, who is the Holy Spirit. Through the Spirit's operation the people are incorporated into Jesus so that they become the children of God.[165] Thus Jesus, by his own glorification as Messiah King of the New Israel, also glorifies his Father by giving him a multitude of new children and becoming the "first-born among many brethren."[166]

The completion of Jesus' earthly messianic mission would take place with his death upon the cross. At that time Jesus would bestow the Spirit.[167] For this reason after Jesus' second messianic discourse the Fourth Gospel remarks about the Spirit: *"... for as yet the Spirit had not been given, because Jesus was not yet glorified"* (Jn 7:39b).[168] Commenting on this discourse Brown states: "At the moment of his death Jesus will hand over the Spirit (xix 30), even as water will come from his side (xix 34)."[169]

---

164   See Jn 3:14; 8:28; 12:23, 24.

165   Cf Jn 1: 12, 13. The matter of the identification of the Holy Spirit with the Love of God will be treated later in this study.

166   Rom 8:29.

167   The precise role of the Spirit in the completion of the earthly messianic mission of Jesus will be treated later in this study. There is also the giving of the Spirit in the post-resurrection appearance of Jesus in Jn 20:22. According to the findings of this study the Spirit has different covenantal roles in the Johannine Gospel and these will be discussed later in this study.

168   Commenting on this verse Senior says: "It is certainly compatible with Johannine theology to link the donation of the Spirit with the death of Jesus (7:39)." However, he adds that since the Fourth Gospel also refers to the giving of the Spirit on two other occasions (Jn 19:34; 20:22) he does not feel that by the phrase in Jn 19:30, "hand over his spirit," the evangelist intends to describe the donation of the Spirit at that point. See Senior, Donald, *The Passion of Jesus in the Gospel of John* (Collegeville, Minnesota: The Liturgical Press, 1991), p. 119. It is hoped that the findings of this study on John's treatment of the new covenant in his Last Supper Account might offer an acceptable solution regarding the different roles and communications of the Spirit within the covenant. This should clarify what Senior speaks about regarding the Spirit's bestowal.

169   Brown, *The Gospel According to John*, I, p. 328.

3.3. The Priestly Character of Jesus and of His Mission

Correlative with the concept of priest are the concepts of mediator and sacrifice. Not every mediator is a priest, but a priest is always a mediator. Offering sacrifice to God on behalf of men is the principal task of the priest, and all his other functions flow from it.

Both the knowledge of who Jesus is and the nature of his final earthly mission of being "lifted up" facilitate seeing how the priestly office is intimately connected with Jesus' person and work. The office of high priest belongs to Jesus by reason of the hypostatic union, which is to say that the priestly office belongs to him by nature as the only-begotten Son of God incarnate. He is substantially, by reason of the union of his two natures, both God's mediator and priest. While none of the gospels calls Jesus a priest, specific words are not always necessary since there are other ways of expressing the identical reality.

The Footwashing, having the same circumstances, attributes and effects as the Eucharist, is an action that makes present the sacrifice of Jesus' life for the forgiveness of sin and establishes a covenant. Consequently the Footwashing requires the exercise of Jesus' priestly office as Footwasher.

While the JLSA literally attributes the accomplishment of Jesus' final earthly messianic mission to the Footwashing, one of the purposes of this study is to determine whether the JLSA's assertion is to be taken literally or figuratively.

CHAPTER 4

Program for the Completion of the Son of Man's Final Mission

The program of Jesus' final earthly work will now be examined with specific focus upon the possibility that Jn 13:1 and Jn 13:31 are literally true because of John's teaching that Jesus truly accomplished his final work at the Last Supper through the Eucharist under the analogical figure of the Footwashing.

Jn 13:1-4 and Jn 13:31 bracket the Footwashing. Jn 13:1-4 explains its meaning and gives pertinent information about it while Jn 13:31 declares its consequence: the completion of the Son of man's earthly mission. In order to understand these verses and their interpretation correctly, they must be viewed in the light of the Fourth Gospel's program for "the hour."

4.1. Program for "the Hour"

The following program for Jesus' final earthly work will now be carefully analyzed.

Jn 12:23   *And Jesus answered them, "The hour has come for the Son of man to be glorified."*

28   *"Father, glorify thy name."*

31   *"Now is the judgment of this world, now shall the ruler of this world be cast out;*

32   *and I, when I am lifted up from the earth, will draw all men to myself."*

33   *He said this to show by what death he was to die.*

The above verses specify the program's five elements: its (1) **time**, (2) **nature**, (3) **purpose**, (4) **object**, (5) *sine-qua-non* **requirement**.

The **time** for this program is "the hour," which is that special and terminating period of Jesus' life in which he will accomplish his final earthly messianic mission and return to the Father.

The **nature** of Jesus' final earthly mission is one of judgment. Jesus stated in Jn 9:39: "For judgment I came into this world, that those who do not see may see, and those who see may become blind." Mateos and Barreto point out the meaning of this verse: that Jesus came to open a judicial process and pass sentence on the present governance of this world, resulting in the liberation of the oppressed and the definitive exclusion of those who propose a false ideology that denies the patent evidence of facts.[170] This judgment of the world follows upon the sentence pronounced over the serpent in Gn 3:15.

The **purpose** of the judgment is to obtain the glorification of Jesus as "the Son of man" and the glorification of God by the revelation of his name of Father.

The **object** of this judgment is "this world." The judgment is twofold. By this judgment Jesus must:

(1) cast out Satan, the Messiah's rival sovereign: *"now shall the ruler of this world be cast out"* (Jn 12:31). The judgment's first task is the defeat of the devil who is presented as the usurping sovereign of this world.

(2) establish a covenant: *"I … will draw all men to myself"* (Jn 12:32). The judgment's second task is the establishment of a universal covenant.

The *sine-qua-non* **requirement** is the death of Jesus on the cross: *"…when I am lifted up from the earth …. He said this to show by what death he was to die"* (Jn 12:32, 33). This death is the true, ontological, unique death of Jesus on Calvary.

The above two tasks and the *sine-qua-non* requirement will now be individually examined with regard to their relationship to the Footwashing/Eucharist for the realization of the twofold glorification.

4.2. The Program's First Task

The program's first task consists in casting out Satan and involves the program's **purificatory character**. Since the devil usurped his dominion through sin, Jesus vanquishes the ruler of this world through the forgiveness of sin. For this reason John the Baptist calls Jesus *"the Lamb of God who takes away the sin of the world"* (Jn 1:29). The forgiveness of sin breaks the devil's power, dispossesses him of his subjects and allows them to become worthy candidates for Jesus' covenant.

4.3. The Program's Second Task

The program's second task involves the program's **covenantal charac-ter** and consists in the establishment of a covenant union with Jesus. It is a covenant open to all men without distinction: between Jew and Gentile. Having been incorporated into Jesus these persons are also united with Jesus' Father. By this covenant Jesus is glorified as Messiah and God is glorified as

---

170   Mateos, Juan, and Barreto, Juan, *Dizionario Teologico del Vangelo di Giovanni*, p.158.

Father. Thus through this covenant the Incarnate Son of God reveals God's name of Father to men.[171] By making men become "sons in the Son"[172] Jesus becomes "the first-born among many brethren."[173]

4.4. The Program's *Sine-Qua-Non* Requirement

Jn 12:32 places the necessary condition for the fulfillment of Jesus' program and Jn 12:33 immediately clarifies the meaning of this phrase. The death of Jesus is the logical consequence of the program's purificatory task because men cannot become members of Jesus' covenant unless they are first freed from Satan's dominion. This task requires expiation and, therefore, Jesus' death on the cross. The Footwashing, like the Eucharist, is a sign of the death of Jesus. The necessity of Jesus' death is clear from the Letter to the Hebrews: *"Without the shedding of blood there is no forgiveness of sins."*[174]

4.5. The Relationship Between the Program and the Footwashing/ Eucharist

The Footwashing is an analogical figure of the Eucharist. Consequently, what the Footwashing is said to accomplish should be understood as being accomplished by the Eucharist. Remembering this, the relationship of the Footwashing/Eucharist to the two tasks of the above program and its necessary requisite must now be investigated. This relationship should shed light on: (1) whether Jesus' death was present at the Last Supper as is literally affirmed in Jn 13:1, and (2) whether Jesus' declaration in Jn 13:31 about the completion of his work and the realization of his glorification and that of God was literally true.

It bears repeating that once Jesus made his declaration that "the Son of man" was glorified, that title is never more used in the Fourth Gospel. From that point on the Fourth Gospel openly refers to Jesus as messiah[175] and king.[176] The title "the Son of man" was used in the Fourth Gospel to explain the authentic meaning of messiah, but since the explanation was completed with Jesus' glorification as messiah, the use of that title no longer made sense.

It has been shown that the Footwashing is presented as a mysterious action signifying the death of Jesus and possessing the purificatory and cov-

---

171   Jn 1:18; see also Lk 10:22.
172   Vatican II, *Pastoral Constitution on the Church in the Modern World, Gaudium et spes*, n. 22.
173   Rom. 8:29.
174   Heb. 9:22.
175   Cf. Jn 20:31.
176   Cf. Jn 18:36, 37; 19:14, 15.

enantal characters that the program indicates as essential for the completion of the Son of man's final messianic mission. Moreover, Jn 13:1 expressly but implicitly asserts that "during the supper" Jesus would die for his own by loving them "to the end." That complete and final act of love was to be accomplished by the Footwashing.

Precisely because the Footwashing is John's presentation of the Eucharist, he certainly had no intention of ascribing the presence of Jesus' death at the Last Supper to the instrumentality of the Footwashing as such. Precisely because of his analogy, John speaks about, not what the Footwashing accomplished at the Last Supper, but rather about what the Eucharist accomplished at that time. The Footwashing should be seen as representing expressly but implicitly the instrumentality of the Eucharist in the accomplishment of Jesus' final earthly mission.

4.6. The Dilemma

Therefore the dilemma regarding Jn 13:1 and Jn 13:31 must be resolved: was the Son of man's death ontologically present **at the Last Supper** so that he literally completed his final earthly mission **at that time**?

Brown sees the JLSA as an account in which Jesus—about to *begin* his passion and death—made the oblation of his life to the Father at the Last Supper. Brown says: "The 'lifting up' begins with the crucifixion and ends with the resurrection and ascension."[177] Brown even questions why the Last Supper with Jesus' discourse was ever included in the Book of Glory.[178] He answers by stating: "In the Book of Glory the Last Supper and the Discourse that precede the action of glorification serve to interpret that action."[179] Brown therefore understands Jn 13:1 and Jn 13:31 in a *figurative* manner.

In agreement with Dodd, Brown further states that there is a problem of time perspective in the JLSA beginning with the first verse of Chapter 13.[180] According to Dodd, Jesus uses the past tense in reference to the two-fold glorification in Jn 13:31 because he is "in effect already accomplishing His Passion.... In all that follows it is Christ crucified who speaks, the living Christ who has already passed through death, although dramatically He speaks on the eve of death."[181]

---

177   Brown, *The Gospel According to John*, II, p. 542.
178   Brown, *The Gospel According to John*, I, CXXXVIII. Here Brown explains the title "Book of Glory." This division of the Johannine Gospel (13:1-20:31) has this title because in it Jesus shows his glory to those who accept him "by returning to the Father in 'the hour' of his crucifixion, resurrection, and ascension. Fully glorified, he communicates the Spirit of life."
179   Brown, *The Gospel According to John*, I, CXXXVIII.
180   Brown, *The Gospel According to John*, 29A, p. 585.
181   Dodd, C. H., *The Interpretation of the Fourth Gospel*, p. 403.

Along the same lines, with regard to Jn 13:31, the *Catholic Commentary on Holy Scripture* states: "Separated from the traitor and thereby set on the way to his Passion the Man Christ regards his glorification, soon to be accomplished on the cross, as *virtually realized.*"[182]

Barrett also interprets Jesus' declaration of Jn 13:31 in a figurative way, saying it signifies that "the passion is regarded as already worked out (it has been visibly expressed in the feet-washing), and the glory of Jesus has thereby been revealed (cf. 12:23)."[183]

Beasley-Murray sees Jesus' statement as a reaction to the departure of Judas. In this departure Jesus sees "the beginning of the end."[184] McPolin sees Judas' departure as heralding for Jesus the beginning of his hour and his glorification.[185]

In addition to the above opinions there are others that hypothesize disarray in the text of the Fourth Gospel due either to its author or to a supposed redactor. These commentators suggest various rearrangements of the text.[186] This study, however, finds no problems with the various tenses used in the JLSA text nor any lack of textual unity. Consequently, it finds no reason to look beyond the evangelist himself for the composition of the JLSA.[187] This study is in complete agreement with Dodd's observation: "And after all it is still not proven that the evangelist himself was not his own redactor."[188]

It is imperative to recall here that the first principle of interpretation requires the literal interpretation of a text unless such an interpretation would not make sense. Jn 13:1 and Jn 13:31 literally affirm, respectively, that Jesus' true death was present at the Last Supper and that he therefore completed his final earthly mission at that time. If these texts may be literally true then they cannot be cavalierly dismissed as having a figurative sense before serious examination. Because other arguments remain to be investigated before a definitive judgment can be reached, a further investigation of the JLSA text is necessary for solving the dilemma regarding the interpretation of these two verses. With this solution in mind the introduction to the JLSA must now be closely examined.

---

182   ACCHS, p. 1005, n. 803a (emphasis mine).
183   Barrett, *The Gospel According to St. John*, p. 450.
184   Beasley-Murray, George R., *Word Biblical Commentary*, Vol. 36 John, p. 246.
185   McPolin, James, *John,* New Testament Message 6, p. 194.
186   A well-known example is Rudolf Bultmann, *The Gospel of John*, (Oxford: Basil Blackwell, 1971). Among the many authors, the following may be consulted: Brown, *The Gospel According to John*, 29A, pp. 583-586; Beasley-Murray, George R., *John*, (Word Biblical Commentary, Vol. 36, Waco, Texas, Word Books, Publisher: 1987), pp. lxvi-lxxv; Schnackenburg, Rudolf, *The Gospel According to St. John*, Vol. 1, pp. 44-54, 75-104, 173-191.
187   The reason for this will become more evident as this study develops.
188   Dodd, C.H., *The Interpretation of the Fourth Gospel*, p. 407.

CHAPTER 5

The JLSA Introduction

John 13:1-4 constitutes the JLSA introduction. And since this account begins with and is about the Footwashing, Jn 13:1-4 introduces the Footwashing. A careful examination of these verses is necessary.

5.1. Status of the Footwashing

Jesus refers to the Footwashing as a *mysterious* action: *"What I am doing you do not know now, but afterward you will understand."*[189]

John's Footwashing/Eucharist analogy that was established in Chapter 2 of this work clarifies the Footwashing's meaning as well as that of the JLSA as a whole. For this reason it is imperative to keep in mind when examining the introductory verses to the Footwashing that because of the Footwashing/Eucharist analogy, whenever John speaks of the Footwashing he is speaking expressly but implicitly about the Eucharist.

The Footwashing's central role in the JLSA is immediately evident in the meticulous care with which the Evangelist introduces it.

5.2. Analysis of the Introduction

In Jn 13:1-4 John carefully introduces the Footwashing by specifying its: (a) **time:** both chronological and theological in Jn 13:1a and (b) **setting:** both physical and theological in Jn 13:2-4.

5.2.1. Time

Jn 13:1a fixes the time of the Footwashing: *"Now before the feast of the Passover, when Jesus knew that his hour had come to depart out of this world to the Father...."* Two kinds of time are indicated in this verse: **chronological** and **theological**.

5.2.1.1 Chronological Time

The Footwashing's chronological time is *"before the feast of the Passover."*[190] The Passover is the Mosaic Covenant's celebration of the lib-

---

189   Jn 13:7.

190   For the Synoptics the Last Supper was celebrated on the feast of Passover (cf. Mt 26:17; Mk 16:12; Lk 22:7). For John the Last Supper took place on the day before the Passover feast (cf. Jn 18:28; 13:1; 19:14; 19:31). The historicity of the date of the Last Supper is impossible to determine and certainly does not pertain to the scope of this study. Brown states

eration of Israel from slavery in Egypt. According to John the Last Supper took place before this feast. But the fact that he indicates the time of the Last Supper within the context of the Passover means that the Footwashing is in some way related to that celebration. Therefore as protagonist of the Footwashing, Jesus is presented as the new Moses (see Dt 18:15) who leads God's people of the new Israel to true freedom, i.e., freedom from bondage to sin and "the ruler of this world."[191]

5.2.1.2 Theological Time

The Footwashing's theological time is ***"his hour."*** Jesus often spoke of "the hour" in the Fourth Gospel.[192] He had already announced its beginning in Jn 12:23: *"The hour has come for the Son of man to be glorified."*

"The hour" is a very special time; it is Jesus' final period when he will complete his earthly messianic mission. This time necessarily involves his death. It is a time of special darkness because it marks the light's departure from the world.[193] "The hour" does not depend upon the will of men but solely upon the Father's will.[194] It is that period in which Jesus, obedient to his Father's command, freely laid down his life so as to take it up again.[195] Jesus says of this time: "Now is my soul troubled. And what shall I say? 'Father, save me from this hour?' No, for this purpose I have come to this hour."[196] It is the time for Jesus *"to depart out of this world to the Father."*[197] While "the hour" is the time of Jesus' death, it is also the time of his glorification and for that reason Dodd calls "the hour" Jesus' "supreme moment of fulfillment."[198]

5.2.2. Setting

The second part of the introduction is found in Jn 13:2-4: ***"Having loved his own who were in the world, he loved them to the end. And during supper, when the devil had already put it into the heart of Judas Iscariot, Simon's son, to betray him, Jesus, knowing that the Father had given all things into his hands...."*** In these verses the JLSA establishes the Footwashing's dual setting: physical and theological.

---

that this is "perhaps the most disputed calendric question in the NT" (*The Gospel According to John*, II, p. 555). The present work focuses uniquely on the Johannine Gospel's report about the Last Supper.

191   Cf. Jn 12:31, 14:30, 16:11.
192   See Jn 2:4; 7:30; 8:20; 12:23, 27; 13:1; 17:1.
193   See Jn 12:35. See also Brown, *The Gospel According to John*, I, p. 516.
194   See Schnackenburg, *The Gospel According to St. John*, I, p. 330 and II, p. 140; Brown, *The Gospel According to John*, I, p. 518; Mateos and Barreto, *Il Vangelo di Giovanni*, p. 239.
195   See Jn 10:17, 18.
196   Jn 12:27.
197   Jn 13:1.
198   Dodd, *The Interpretation of the Fourth Gospel*, p. 417.

5.2.2.1 Physical Setting

The Footwashing's physical setting is indicated by the words *"during supper."* The physical setting of the Footwashing was an ordinary supper since its chronological time is "before the feast of the Passover." Bultmann is very adamant on this point, and from the gospel text he has every reason to be so.[199] If John did make a change by making the Last Supper an ordinary meal—and it is not certain that he did—his motive could well have been to correct some misinterpretation, superstition or abuse which arose from connecting the celebration of the Last Supper with the celebration of the Jewish Passover Seder.[200] At any rate one may presume that John, if he set aside historical accuracy, had his own good reasons for establishing the chronological time of the Footwashing as before the Feast of Passover and its physical setting an ordinary meal. If John did change the historical time of the Last Supper he certainly would have done so only for an important teaching purpose.

5.2.2.2 Theological Setting

The Footwashing's **theological setting** is found in the following three verses:

Jn 13:1   *"...having loved his own who were in the world, he loved them to the end.*

Jn 13:2   *The devil had already put it into the heart of Judas Iscariot, Simon's son, to betray him.*

Jn 13:3   *Jesus, knowing that the Father had given all things into his hands...."*

The theological setting of the supper and the Footwashing is Jesus' final act of love for "his own," and this final act is the Footwashing itself. The theological setting also recalls Jesus' past love for "his own." The Greek active aorist participle, translated *"having loved,"* signifies that Jesus' loving actions in the past were the motivating reason for his final act of love *"during supper."*[201]

The words *"his own"* allude to the Footwashing's covenantal character. The expression recalls those texts of the OT where Israel was considered to be

---

199   "The meal in question is an ordinary one; as is shown by v. 30, it is in fact the customary main meal in the evening, and not the Passover meal, as in the synoptic account; for it is the 13th Nisan, and there is no mention at all of a Passover meal." Rudolf Bultmann, *The Gospel of John, A Commentary*, trans. G.R. Beasley-Murray (Oxford: Basil Blackwell, 1971), p. 465. Cf. also Lindars, *The Gospel of John*, pp. 444-446.

200   John could have had his reasons for separating the Last Supper from the Jewish Passover Seder like Paul wanted to separate the Eucharist and ordinary meals (see Chenderlin, Fritz, *"Do This As My Memorial,"* n. 387, p. 183).

201   See Nolli, Gianfranco, *Il Vangelo Secondo Giovanni*, p. 500.

Yahweh's own possession because he chose Israel and perpetuated his choice through covenant. Thus the OT writers referred to Israel as Yahweh's own people[202] and Yahweh himself spoke of Israel as "my own,"[203] "my own people,"[204] "my own special possession,"[205] "my people."[206] As Israel was Yahweh's covenanted people in the OT, so Jesus and his Father chose Jesus' disciples as their own and perpetuated their love for them by the family-like union of covenant.

Jn 13:1-3 presents the Footwashing as the final action by which Jesus would love his own. The Greek word translated as *"he loved"* is in the indicative aorist tense. Nolli notes that the verb indicates, not by its nature but rather by its use, a priority in respect to the action of the principal verb.[207] Here the aorist expresses a punctiliar or single action in the past and is equivalent to the English simple past tense.[208] The introduction goes on to say that by his loving action of the Footwashing, Jesus loved his disciples *"to the end"* (Greek: *eis telos*). These words should be seen as connecting the Footwashing—Jesus' final act of love—with the last words of Jesus on the cross in Jn 19:30, *"It is finished"* (Gr: *telelestai*). Because of the use of the same Greek root (*tel*) in Jn 13:1 and Jn 19:30, both verses should be seen in relationship to the Septuagint's use of the same expression in Dt 31:24 which refers to Moses having completed his final earthly work by writing out the law *"to the end."* Thus Jesus the Footwasher is like Moses who led the chosen people to freedom from slavery.

The introduction therefore presents the Footwashing as the final and consummate act of Jesus' saving love. While this act continues Jesus' past love, it is that love's supreme culmination both from the aspect of time and from the aspect of intensity or measure.[209]

---

202   For example: Ex 32:11; 33:13; 34:9; Dt 4:20; 7:6; 14:2; 32:9; 1 Chr 17:22; Pss 33:12; 74:2; 94:5, 14; 106:40; Sir 17:4; Jer 10:16.

203   Lv 20:26.

204   Ex 6:7.

205   Mal 3:17.

206   For example: Ex 3:7, 10, 12; 5:1; 7:4, 16, 26; 8:16, 17, 18, 19; 9:1, 13, 17; 10:3, 4; 22:24; Lv 26:12; 1 Sam 2:29; 9:16, 17; 2 Sam 3:18, 52; 7:7, 8; 7:10, 11; 22:44; 1 Kgs 8:16; 14:7; 16:2; 20:5; 1 Chr 11:20; 17:6, 7, 9, 10; 2 Chr 1:11; 6:5, 6; 7:13, 14; Pss 50:7; 81:12, 14; Is 1:3; 3:15; 10:24; 19:25; 40:1; 47:6; 51:4, 16; 52:4, 5, 6; 57:14; 58:1; 63:8; 65:10, 19, 22; Jer 2:11, 13, 31, 32; 4:11, 22; 5:26, 31; 6:14, 26, 27; 7:12, 7:23; 8:7, 11, 19; 11:4; 12:14, 16; 13:11; 15:7; 18:15; 23:2, 13, 22, 27, 32; 24:7; 30:3, 22; 31:1, 14, 33; 32:38; 33:24; 50:6; 51:45; Bar 2:35; Ezk 11:20; 13:9, 23, 18, 19, 21; 14:8, 9, 11; 21:17; 25:14; 33:31; 34:30; 36:8, 12, 28; 37:12, 13, 23; 37:27; 38:14, 16; 39:7; 44:23; 45:8, 9; 46:18; Ho 1:9; 2:25; 4:6, 8, 11; 7:1; Jl 2:7; 4:2,3; Am 7:8, 15; 8:2; 9:10, 14; Ob 1:13; Mi 1:9; 2:4, 8, 9; 3:3, 5; 6:3, 5; Zeph 2:8, 9; Zech 8:7, 8; 13:9.

207   Nolli, Gianfranco, *Il Vangelo Secondo Giovanni*, p. 500.

208   Cf. Nunn, H.P.V., *A Short Syntax of New Testament Greek*, p. 68, #92, Jay, Eric G., *New Testament Greek*, p. 43.

209   Mateos & Barreto, *Il Vangelo di Giovanni*, p. 549.

John gives the devil an active role in the theological setting of the Footwashing by placing the Footwashing within the context of the devil's inducement of Judas Iscariot to betray Jesus. Thus the Footwashing's setting places Jesus in his final act of love as engaging in a mortal battle, a *battle between two rival sovereigns*: the devil, or Satan the usurper who is "ruler of this world,"[210] and Jesus, God's Messiah.[211] In this battle Jesus will conquer Satan by his consummate act of love which is the Footwashing. This battle recalls the fall of the first man and woman and the divine promise of the victory of the seed of the woman over the serpent in Gn 3:15.

The theological setting in Jn 13:3 also links the Footwashing to a **supernatural power** given to Jesus by the Father: *"the Father had given all things into his hands."* The Greek text does not use a word for power or authority; instead here John uses a Semitic expression for giving something to another. Nolli remarks that the phrase means that Jesus received a **sovereign power not limited to the laws of nature** and that these words are an allusion to that supernatural power to produce the Eucharist.[212] It is extremely important to note that John speaks of this signal power of Jesus *precisely when introducing the Footwashing*. Since the Footwashing is an analogical figure of the Eucharist, John should be seen as implying that this supernatural power was used in the Footwashing so that the Footwashing should be seen as accomplishing all that he (i.e. John) attributed to it, just as that power did for the Eucharist in the Synoptics and Paul (viz. making the death of Jesus present). This supernatural power belongs to Jesus the High Priest by reason of the hypostatic union.

Chapter 2 indicated how the Footwashing/Eucharist analogy is further corroborated by the frequent connections John makes between the Footwashing and the betrayal by Judas, both before and after the Footwashing action.[213] The importance of this connection is based upon the ancient eucharistic tradition of the Synoptics and Paul of associating the betrayal of Judas with the Eucharist.[214] Thus the introduction connects the Footwashing to the Eucharist in the Synoptic and Pauline accounts.

---

210   See Jn 12:31; 14:30; 16:11.

211   The Johannine Gospel refers to Jesus as "Messiah" 2 times, "Christ" 19 times, and "king" 15 times.

212   Nolli, Gianfranco, *Evangelo Secondo Giovanni*, p. 502: "...esprime una potenza sovrana, che non è limitata dalle leggi della natura." This special power is also mentioned in Jn 3:35. This power is also alluded to in Jn 16:15. Jesus possesses this power because he and the Father are One: cf. Jn 10:30; 17:22.

213   cf. Jn 13:2, 10, 11, 18, 19, 21-31.

214   See Mt 26:21-25; Mk 14:18-21; Lk 22:21-23; 1 Cor 11:23; Jn 6:70, 71. Cf. Brown, *The Gospel According to John*, II, p. 571.

To sum up, the theological setting presents the Footwashing as the final act of Jesus' love by which Jesus Messiah engages in mortal battle with the devil, "the ruler of this world." John connects the Footwashing with the supernatural power Jesus received from his Father.

5.3. Significance of the Introduction

The introduction to the Footwashing places the reader before the mortal battle between Jesus, the Son of man, and Satan, the ruler of this world. Therefore, the Footwashing is that action of Jesus whereby he accomplished his final earthly messianic mission. In fact, following the Footwashing, Jesus confirmed the completion of his final mission by declaring in Jn 13:31: "Now is the Son of man glorified ...." It is of capital importance to note that John significantly links the Footwashing to Jesus' supernatural power and through this he connects the battle waged by the Footwashing to the Eucharistic Synoptic and Pauline Tradition.

The JLSA's introduction is astutely written. It presents the Footwashing as an analogical figure of the Eucharist and, as such, an action that is absolutely capable of winning the victory in the mortal battle between Jesus and the devil. The JLSA introduction, therefore, contributes greatly to solving the dilemma expressed in Chapter 4 of the present study about the correct interpretation of Jn 13:1 and Jn 13:31 regarding the completion of the Son of man's final earthly work at the Last Supper.

It was noted in Chapter 4 that the literal meaning of Jn 13:1 is that the death of the Son of Man would be present at the Last Supper. In that same chapter were noted the contrary opinions of commentators who are in favor of a figurative interpretation or of textual disarray. But these opinions only serve to confirm the literal meaning of the verse that those commentators were unable to see.

Having examined the introductory verses to the Footwashing, there remains but to definitively resolve the dilemma regarding the correct interpretation of Jn 13:1 and 13:31.

CHAPTER 6

Resolution of the Dilemma

There is no doubt that the program for "the hour" requires Jesus' death on the cross. The present chapter seeks to resolve the dilemma that depends upon whether that program was, in fact, completed at the Last Supper with the death of the Lord. The outcome will determine whether Jn 13:1 and Jn 13:31 are to be literally or figuratively interpreted.

John attributed to the Footwashing the identical circumstances, attributes and effects predicated of the Eucharist in the Synoptic and Pauline Last Supper Accounts and thus made the Footwashing an analogue of the Eucharist. Consequently what John attributes to the Footwashing he is attributing to the Eucharist. It is imperative to recall that in his introduction to the Footwashing John speaks about a supernatural power that the Father gave Jesus. This power is another allusion to the Eucharist. By connecting this Eucharistic power to the Footwashing, John made the Footwashing capable, analogically speaking, of completing the final work of the Son of man in accord with the above-mentioned program for judgment upon this world. The present study proposes that the literal meaning of the JLSA text is that Jesus, through the Footwashing at the Last Supper, made his death present and therefore fully accomplished his final earthly mission at that time.

Jn 13:1-4 and Jn 13:31 frame the Footwashing and respectively explain its meaning and announce its consequence. Jn 13:1 and Jn 13:31 expressly but implicitly affirm the literal meaning of the program's completion at the Last Supper. According to their context Jesus accomplished this through the Footwashing because it is the only action that intervenes. But one last investigation remains to resolve the dilemma of the correct interpretation.

6.1 Necessity of the Communication of the Spirit

Jn 7:39 teaches that at the time of his death Jesus, who is bearer of the Spirit, would be glorified and communicate his Spirit: *"Now this he said about the Spirit, which those who believed in him were to receive; **for as yet the Sprit had not been given, because Jesus was not yet glorified.**"*

From the above verse it may be concluded that in his being "lifted up" in death on the cross, Jesus gives up the Spirit (Jn 19:30).[215] Brown states: "At the moment of his death Jesus will hand over the Spirit (xix 30), even as

---

215   See O'Grady, John F., *According to John, The Witness of the Beloved Disciple*, p. 71.

water will come from his side (xix 34)."[216] Moloney explains: "The perfection of the messianic promise, the gift of the Spirit, and the glorification of Jesus are linked to Jesus' death by crucifixion."[217] Moloney comments that it is "in the moment of elevation on the cross that the fullness of revelation will come ...."[218] Again Moloney states: "The hour of glorification and the giving of the Spirit are intimately linked. This will take place when Jesus bows his head on the cross and *paredoken to pneuma* [219] (19:30). It is, therefore, on the cross that Jesus will be glorified, and it is as the Son of Man that he receives this glory (see Jn 3:13-14; 8:28; 12:23-28; 13:31)." [220]

Viewing Jn 7:39 within the context of the program for judgment upon this world, Jesus' death and bestowal of the Spirit are interconnected and are **both necessary for the completion of Jesus' earthly messianic mission**. Therefore, if John does not treat the communication of the Spirit at the Last Supper, then a figurative interpretation of Jn 13:1 and Jn 13:31 is justified. However, if John does speak of the bestowal of the Spirit at the Last Supper, then: (1) the judgment upon this world took place at that time; (2) the nature and function of the Footwashing become certain; and (3) the dilemma is resolved with the conclusion that Jn 13:1 and Jn 13:31 must be literally interpreted.

6.2. The Communication of the Spirit

The introduction to the JLSA, Jn 13:1, literally declares that Jesus would show his love for his own by his death at the Last Supper, and in Jn 13:31 Jesus expressly and explicitly declares that he had just been glorified. And the confirmation of the literal truth of these verses lies in the fact that John mentions in the JLSA after the Footwashing took place that **the Spirit had been communicated**. This is expressly and explicitly noted in Jn 14:17 where Jesus speaks about the Spirit of truth[221] and declares to his disciples: ***"You <u>know</u> him, because he <u>remains</u> with you, and <u>is</u> within you."*** [222]

---

216   Brown, *The Gospel According to John*, I, p. 328.
217   Moloney, *The Gospel of John*, p. 253.
218   Moloney, *The Johannine Son of Man*, p. 190.
219   "Hands over the Spirit" (Jn 19:30).
220   Moloney, *The Johannine Son of Man*, p. 178.
221   Here the Spirit is not spoken of in his role as "another Paraclete" (Jn 14:16). "The Spirit of truth" and the "other Paraclete" designate the same Person. However, the Fourth Gospel presents the Spirit in different roles or missions. His first mission is to be the mediator of the new divine filial life to be bestowed by the New Covenant. But the Spirit's role as "another Paraclete" (Jn 14:16) refers to his future mission as the blessing of Jesus' covenant. The matter of this future role of the Spirit specifically as Paraclete will be taken up in the second part of this study.
222   This translation is that of this study's author. It is imperative to note that the present tenses of the three verbs in this verse are in agreement with those found in the editions of *The Jerusalem Bible*.

Many translations of the last part of the above verse render the text as *"**will be** within you*," using the future instead of the present tense. Moloney's comments about Jn 14:17 are interesting. His attention is focused on the second and third verbs. He explains that the use of the present tense "remains" and the future "will be" causes some interpreters "notorious difficulty."[223] It is only right that such a contradiction should cause "notorious difficulty"!

The declaration of Jn 14:17 is essential for the resolution of the dilemma regarding the correct interpretation of Jn 13:1 and Jn 13:31. The first two Greek verbs in Jn 14:17—"know" and "remain"—are in the present tense, and there is no discussion about this fact. For the third verb "to be," however, two translations are offered, one with the future form, "will be" (Gr. *estai*), the other with the present form, "is" (Gr. *estin*). Brown says that "the textual witnesses are divided on whether to read a present or future form of the verb."[224] However, **Brown, Barrett, Bernard and Lindars are all in agreement that the present tense is the authentic one**, even though, as Lindars says, it is more difficult to explain.[225] It has already been noted that *The Jerusalem Bible* uses the present tense of the verb.

If the first part of Jn 14:17 declares that the disciples ***know*** the Spirit because he already ***abides*** (Gr. *menei*) in them, then it would not make sense to say that the Spirit *will be* with them! If the disciples know the Spirit because he already abides with them, then he *is* with them. However, the present tense of the verb "to be" causes the commentators "notorious difficulty" precisely because they think that the communication of the Spirit before Calvary would contradict Jn 7:39, which requires the death of Jesus. These interpreters simply made various attempts to explain away the possibility of the communication of the Spirit before Jesus' death on Calvary and changed the tense of the last verb.[226]

This study, however, is in complete agreement with the generally accepted authentic version of Jn 14:17 that reads all three verbs in the present tense. Jn 14:17 teaches that the Spirit was indeed communicated at the Last Supper.[227] This means that the introduction of the Footwashing in Jn 13:1

223 Moloney, *The Gospel of John*, pp. 406, 407.

224 Brown, *The Gospel According to John*, II, p. 640.

225 See Brown, *The Gospel According to John*, II, pp. 637, 639, 640; Barrett, *The Gospel According to St. John*, p. 463; Bernard, *The International Critical Commentary on the Gospel According to St. John*, II, p. 546; Lindars, *The Gospel of John*, p. 480.

226 Since this study encounters no problems with 14:17 as it stands, it is beyond the scope of this study to explain these various interpretations. They may be seen in Moloney, *The Gospel of John*, pp. 406, 407.

227 The present chapter considers the fact of the Spirit's communication at the Last Supper. While this is sufficient for the present, Part II of this study will go into more detail about the Spirit's communication.

and Jesus' declaration after the Footwashing in Jn 13:31 are to be literally understood. Thus is the dilemma resolved.

6.3. Conclusion

The confirmation of the Spirit's communication at the Last Supper validates the conclusion that the Footwashing truly has a vital and profoundly mysterious role to play in the JLSA. It is much more than a mere prophetic or symbolic action. Since John affirms the presence of the Spirit in the disciples at the Last Supper, then it is clear that all the requirements for the literal interpretation of Jn 13:1 and Jn 13:31 have been met. Consequently Jesus did indeed complete his final earthly messianic mission with the bestowal of the Spirit at the Last Supper through the eucharistic action which John presents in the analogical figure of the Footwashing.

The Sacrificial Nature of the Eucharist

Jn 13:1 and Jn 13:31 take on new significance with the resolution of the dilemma since these two verses must now be understood literally. This constitutes a new insight into the eucharistic mystery in general, and specifically into the nature of the Eucharist of the Last Supper. It was precisely through this particular Eucharist that Jesus accomplished his final earthly mission before Good Friday. Consequently, the sacrificial nature of the Eucharist should be studied and contemplated within the specific context of the **Eucharist of the Last Supper.**

7.1 The Sacrificial Nature of the Eucharist of the Last Supper in the JLSA

The examination of the Eucharist's sacrificial nature must first focus upon the generic nature of sacrifice. A sacrificial action is essentially made up of two elements: (1) **oblation** of the victim and (2) the **immolation** of the victim. The *oblation* is the offering of the victim to God by the priest; and its *immolation* consists in its removal from human use by its destruction. Oblation is the heart of sacrifice because it directs the immolation of the victim to God, but the immolation of the victim is required for the completeness of the sacrificial action.

In the Council of Trent's discussion about the Eucharist's sacrificial nature, certain of its Fathers held that Jesus could not have offered a complete sacrifice at the time of the Last Supper since Jesus' immolation on the cross had not yet taken place.[228] Consequently, that Council simply stated that to leave his Church a visible sacrifice, the Lord at the Last Supper "*offered (obtulit)* his body and blood to the Eternal Father under the appearances of bread and wine."[229] The key word here is "offered."

---

228   Cf. Kilmartin, E.J., "Eucharist (As Sacrifice)," *NCE*, V, pp. 611, 612; Brodie Brosnan, *The Sacrifice of the New Law* (New York: Benzinger Brothers, 1926), p. 104.

229   D 1740: "... corpus et sanguinem suum sub speciebus panis et vini Deo Patri obtulit ...." Waterworth writes the following about the decree of Trent on the Holy Sacrifice of the Mass. "A third party among the Fathers recommended that the decree should indeed declare that Christ offered Himself to the Father, under the species of bread and wine, but that no mention should be made of the nature of that offering, seeing that the opinions of the prelates did not agree regarding it. This suggestion, as may be seen, by the decree in question, in the first chapter on doctrine was eventually accepted, and it is with only two dissentients."

This word refers to the oblation of Jesus' sacrifice as distinguished from its immolation.

Because of the divided opinion among the Council Fathers, Trent made the following distinction: the title of "Mass" was used for all the Eucharists offered **after** the Eucharist of the Last Supper, while the matter of the Eucharist celebrated at the Last Supper was left in abeyance by simply re-ferring to it as "the Eucharist of the Last Supper."[230] Trent then solemnly defined the Mass as a complete sacrifice in which Jesus offers the sacrificial action as priest and is immolated as its victim.[231] Thus the Council of Trent passed over the matter of the sacrificial completeness of "the Eucharist of the Last Supper." [232]

F.J. Wengier presents the opinion of those Fathers of Trent who did not admit the completeness of the sacrificial nature of the Eucharist of the Last Supper.[233] According to this opinion, that particular Eucharist was related to the sacrifice of Calvary as a complementary part of numerically one sacrifice. Wengier speaks of "two correlative elements of one and the same Sacrifice: the passion and the Last Supper." This is to say that the Eucharist of the Last Supper was the oblation of Jesus' sacrificial death, while his death on Calvary was the immolation of that oblation. Wengier states that Jesus, after celebrating the Eucharist of the Last Supper, went immediately to the garden "to substantiate His words, to materialize the symbol of the Cenacle, to re-deem His pictorial pledge." Wengier summarizes his opinion in saying that

---

Waterworth, Rev. J., *The Canons and Decrees of the Council of Trent*, (London: Dolman, 1948), p. 189.

230   Cf. Brosnan, J. Brodie, *The Sacrifice of the New Law* (New York: Benzinger Brothers, 1926), p. 104.

231   Cf. D. 1743, 1751, 1753, 1754.

232   Cardinal Lepicier agrees with the opinion of those Fathers of the Council of Trent who held that the Eucharist of the Last Supper did not posses the complete sacrificial nature as does the Mass. He explains: "… [the Mass] is something more than what Jesus Christ did at the Last Supper. This is because the Last Supper preceded the death of the Redeemer in time, while the sacrifice of the Mass is celebrated after the sacrifice of the cross had already been completed. For this reason we say that our Eucharistic Sacrifice, that is to say the Mass, is not, properly speaking, the same thing as the Last Supper. It is something more excellent than the latter." Cardinal Lepicier continues: "But if we consider the Last Supper in its real relation-ship to the sacrifice of the cross—inasmuch as the Last Supper was ordered to pre-announce this great sacrifice—we already have at the time of the Last Supper, not a sacrifice in bread and wine, but the very sacrifice of the cross, though still not yet physically actualized, but only sketched out and, therefore, morally signified and pictured." Cf. Cardinal Alessio Enrico M. Lepicier, O.S.M., *In Che Cosa Consista l'Essenza del Sacrificio Eucaristico* (Roma: Officina Poligrafica Laziale, 1934-XII), pp. 9, 11. (Translation from the Italian made by the author of this study)

233   Cf. Francis J. Wengier, *The Eucharist-Sacrifice* (Milwaukee: Bruce Publishing Com-pany, 1955), pp. 27, 30, 34.

"the Last Supper, therefore, was the beginning of Calvary and Calvary was the end of the Last Supper."

Jesus did indeed accomplish his final earthly mission at the Last Supper because his death was made present through the Eucharist. Therefore that Eucharist could hardly have been a mere "symbol of the Cenacle" or the "pictorial pledge" of Calvary. It was not *part* of the bloody sacrifice of Calvary; it was, rather, that very sacrifice: a true and complete sacrifice *unto itself* because by it Jesus was both sacramentally offered and immolated. The Eucharist of the Last Supper was a complete and true realization of the unique sacrifice of Calvary, while numerically distinct from it in the *manner* of its offering.[234] The conclusion of this study regarding the completeness of the Eucharist of the Last Supper is far from the opinion of Lepicier and others that views the Mass as something more than what Jesus Christ did at the Last Supper.

This study maintains that, according to John's teaching, Calvary ontologically *"pre-existed"* in a sacramental manner in the Eucharist of the Last Supper.[235] By his presentation of the Eucharist of the Last Supper in this manner, John puts the whole doctrine of the sacrificial nature of the Eucharist into its proper perspective. **It is specifically within the context of "the Eucharist of the Last Supper" that the sacrificial nature of the Eucharist must be examined and contemplated. This particular Eucharist is consequently the basis for understanding the Eucharist's sacrificial nature.** In the same way that Calvary *"pre-existed"* at the Last Supper, so Calvary *"post-exists"* in every subsequent Eucharist.

---

234   This is to say that on Calvary Jesus' sacrifice was offered in a bloody manner while at the Last Supper the identical complete sacrifice was offered in a sacramental and, therefore, non-bloody manner.

235   It is most interesting to read the account of St. Mary Faustina, the first canonized saint of this millennium, about a vision she was given of the Last Supper. She wrote: *"Jesus allowed me to enter the Cenacle, and I was a witness to what happened there. However, I was most deeply moved when, before the Consecration, Jesus raised his eyes to heaven and entered into a mysterious conversation with His Father. It is only in eternity that we shall really understand that moment. His eyes were like two flames; His face was radiant, white as snow; His whole personage full of majesty, His soul full of longing. At the moment of Consecration,* **love rested satiated***—the sacrifice was fully consummated. Now only the external ceremony of death will be carried out—external destruction;* **the essence of the sacrifice is in the Cenacle***. Never in my whole life had I understood this mystery so profoundly as during that hour of adoration. Oh, how ardently I desire that the whole world would come to know this unfathomable mystery!"* (*Diary*, Notebook II, #684, emphasis added)

St. Faustina tells us in the passage above that the death of Our Lord indeed mystically and sacramentally preceded the bloody scene on Calvary. She tells us that just as we know the Mass to be the re-presentation (i.e. making present again or *post-existing* in time) of the Sacrifice of Calvary, the first Eucharist in the Cenacle was the pre-presentation (i.e. making present beforehand – or *pre-existing* in time) of that identical saving act.

7.2. The Sacramental Presence of the Historical Death of Jesus

The pre-existence of Jesus' death on Calvary at the celebration of the Eucharist of the Last Supper amounts to the affirmation of the presence of the historical death of Jesus at that time.

James T. O'Connor points out that subsequent to the Council of Trent various theories were proposed to explain how the Eucharist is a sacrifice.[236] Kilmartin further notes: "From the early part of the twentieth century, beginning with the research of the German monk Dom Odo Casel, O.S.B., a new approach to the subject of the relationship of the eucharistic sacrifice to the historical sacrifice of the cross was undertaken in the Western Church."[237] However, the present study does not deal with these theories. It deals with the JLSA, and the findings expounded in this study are new. The scope of this study is solely to present these new findings and explain them.

The sacrificial nature of the Eucharist as a sacramental memorial of the passion and death of Jesus necessarily and completely depends upon its relationship to the historical death of Jesus. This death is the unique sacrifice of the New Covenant.

The Eucharist as a memorial presentation of the unique death of Jesus on Calvary derives from Jesus' command to celebrate the eucharistic action. In his *Do This As My Memorial,* Fritz Chenderlin discusses the various possible types of memorial that the Eucharist could be.[238] However, precisely in this regard, The Catechism of the Catholic Church presents the Eucharist as a memorial in this way: "The Eucharist is ... a sacrifice because it *re-presents* (makes present) the sacrifice of the cross....,"[239] and "the sacrifice of Christ and the sacrifice of the Eucharist are *one single sacrifice.*"[240]

---

236   James T. O'Connor, *The Hidden Manna,* pp. 236-245. See also: Journet, Charles, *La Messe,* pp. 343-361; Piolanti, Antonio, *The Holy Eucharist,* pp. 92-111; Kilmartin, *The Eucharist in the West,* pp. 244, 245; 267-337, 352.

237   Kilmartin, *The Eucharist in the West,* pp. 244, 245. Dom Odo Casel, O.S.B., in his book *The Mystery of Christian Worship,* proposes that the historical mysteries in the life of Jesus are made present through the Liturgy of the Church. With regard to the celebration of the Eucharist Casel proposes that it makes present the historical sacrifice of Calvary. However, he makes no particular mention of the Eucharist of the Last Supper. He approaches the matter in a very different way from this study and reaches his conclusions by proceeding from factors extraneous to the present work. The present study concentrates only on conclusions drawn from the study of the Johannine Last Supper Account. The discussion and examination of Casel's proposal, therefore, do not pertain to the scope of this work.

238   See Chenderlin, Fritz, S.J., *"Do This As My Memorial"* ("Analecta Biblica, Investigationes Scientificae in Res Biblicas" 99. Rome: Biblical Institute Press, 1982), nn. 140-178, pp. 71-87.

239   Cf. CCC, n. 1366 (italics theirs).

240   Cf. CCC, n.1367 (italics theirs).

The Eucharist is not a virtual sacrifice, which it would be if it depended solely upon the presence of its priest and victim (*Christus passus*). Instead, the Eucharist is a true memorial of Calvary because it makes sacramentally present the unique historical death of Jesus in its ontological reality.[241] It makes present the priest and victim of the sacrifice *in the very act* by which Jesus offered himself in his unique death. If the Eucharistic Sacrifice were other than the very Sacrifice of Calvary, then it could not be the unique sacrifice of Jesus accomplished approximately two thousand years ago on Calvary.

The sacrifice of Calvary is nothing more or less than the historical death of Jesus. Therefore, since the Eucharist is a sacramental memorial of that very death, the first question is whether it is possible for an historical event that did not yet exist before Calvary and no longer exists after Calvary to be made present for persons living in time and space either before it took place (at the Last Supper) or after it took place (at Holy Mass).[242] In other words, is it possible for God to make Calvary "*pre-exist*" or "*post-exist*" in its ontological reality through the Eucharist?

If the Eucharist depended upon human possibilities it could be nothing more than a mere ritual commemoration of Calvary. This, however, is not what the Eucharist is. In the context of the Footwashing/Eucharist, the JLSA speaks of a special power above the forces of nature—a supernatural power—that was given to Jesus by his Father.[243] This is the very power by which Jesus Christ the High Priest instituted the Eucharist at the Last Supper.

Because the Eucharist is a supernatural reality, it is the "ineffable Sacrament."[244] It can never be exhaustively understood. But while the Eucharist transcends created intelligence, it is not incomprehensible. The Eucharist has been given to humans who naturally seek to understand it. But in order to do this one must call to mind that the Eucharist is a *mystery of faith*. And precisely because it pertains to the realm of faith, it is necessary for one to *change perspective*. One cannot view the eucharistic mystery in a solely human fashion as if it were limited by the categories of time and space. At the same time it is also imperative to recall what is known from reason about how those categories exist in God's presence as well as what is known by faith regarding Jesus Christ who, while possessing a human nature, is always a divine Person.

---

241   Rm 6:9 states: "For we know that Christ being raised from the dead will never die again; death no longer has dominion over him."

242   This matter has been discussed by many theologians. It is beyond the scope of this study to give an overview of these opinions. However, for an extended discussion one may consult the work of Kilmartin, *The Eucharist in the West*, pp. 294-299, 311.

243   Cf. Jn 13:3.

244   RH, n. 91.

In human understanding, to be present in time and space means to be located at a certain moment and in a certain place situated in the past, present, or future. While this understanding is correct, it is insufficient to answer the question of how time and space exist *before God*.

Eternity is the duration of God: it is the duration of a being that is immutable in its existence and operation. Eternity is without beginning or end because it has no succession. In God all the past, present, and future of our time and space, from beginning to end, are simultaneously present within the unique *now* of eternity. Therefore, to God, our human past, present and future are *present reality*. Naturally, God knows all places and events in relation to each other as past, present, or future. However, in relation to God himself, all places and all events of human history are simultaneously present because in God there is all-encompassing presence and vision. This presence/vision excludes remembrance of the past or conjecture about the future. Before God all the ages of time and space are simultaneously present in their *ontological reality* and not as frames of a motion picture film. The eternity of God indubitably transcends our human understanding because it is part of the mystery that is God himself. However, eternity is not incompatible with time and space any more than God is incompatible with humans or faith is incompatible with created intelligence.

Human dimensions do not limit God in his dealing with humans. In the Eucharist, God acts within human dimensions while transcending them. At the Consecration, Jesus, the God-man, through the operation of the Holy Spirit, makes his sacrifice on Calvary really and truly present in a sacramental manner. But what does this mean?

The High Priest Jesus Christ opens the window on eternity to share with persons in time and space the saving presence of his sacrifice on the cross of Calvary, a sacrifice that, according to our human mode of reckoning time, is past. In the Eucharist that sacrifice's ontological reality, irretrievable according to human possibilities, is truly made present because Jesus makes present at the Consecration *what is present to himself as the God-Man*. **Jesus Christ is the Pontiff**[245] **who bridges the gap between God and humans, between eternity and time.** Could he do this? He certainly could, and he did at the Last Supper and he does at every subsequent Eucharist.[246]**Jesus is the God-Man to whom every moment of time was**

245 Etymologically, the title "pontiff" comes from two Latin words: *pons, pontis*, bridge + *facere*, to do or make. The chief priests of pagan Rome were given this title because they were considered to bridge the gap between the gods and humanity. The title was later attributed to Christ, our mediator, and is used in the official title of the Pope as Supreme Pontiff.

246 This recalls the basic argument of John Duns Scotus against those who opposed the Immaculate Conception: *Deus potuit plane. Si igitur voluit, fecit* ("God surely could. Therefore, if he willed it, he did it").

ontologically present from the very first moment of his Incarnation. Therefore he made his "future" death present at the Consecration of the Last Supper; and ever since he is in a risen and glorious state, he makes his "past" death present at the Consecrations of all subsequent Eucharists. This does not contradict but transcends our notions of time and space. One must avoid such an anthropomorphic view of God that it would exclude this power from Jesus Christ, God incarnate, who is "the same yesterday, today and forever."[247]

In the Eucharistic Sacrifice the earthly Church's union with the heavenly Church is perfectly realized in God's sole mediator, Jesus Christ, Head of the Mystical Body. The Church on earth is united through and in Jesus Christ with the eternal adoration of the heavenly Church in the unique sacrificial action of the Eternal High Priest.[248]

7.3. The Institution Formulas of the Synoptic and Pauline Last Supper Accounts

Through its analogous presentation of the Footwashing, the JLSA indicates both in Jn 13:1 and Jn 13:13 that the Eucharist of the Last Supper is a complete sacrifice. It affirms *before* the Calvary event that Jesus completed his final earthly mission and accomplished the twofold glorification of himself as Messiah and of God as Father. This could only happen because the Eucharist of the Last Supper made ontologically present in a sacramental manner the unique historical reality of Jesus' sacrificial death on Calvary. However, the institution formulas of the Synoptics and Paul are not clear as to the precise time they were to have their effect…. immediately at the Last Supper or only at future celebrations. This could be one of the reasons for John's JLSA teaching.

While all the institution formulas signify the sacrifice of Calvary by force of their words indicating the separation of the Lord's blood from his body, the question is whether the formulas themselves indicate *at what specific time* the Lord's body was actually given and his blood was actually shed. If they use the present tense (*i.e.* "is being given" and "is being shed"), then the formulas would seem to indicate the completeness of the sacrificial nature of the Eucharist at the time they were spoken. However, if they use the future tense (*i.e.* "will be given" and "will be shed"), then the Eucharist of the Last Supper could be understood as the offering or oblation of the sacrifice that was to be immolated on the next day. In this latter case the Eucharist of the Last Supper would constitute only the first part (*i.e.*, the oblation) of the sacrifice of Good Friday and thus would not be a complete sacrifice unto

---

247   Heb 13:8.
248   Cf. LG, n. 50.

itself. This would mean that the Mass is "more excellent" [249] than what the Lord did at the Last Supper.

In 1 Cor 11:23-25, Paul gives only the bare liturgical essentials of the eucharistic institution. The Pauline institution formula over the bread and the wine simply signify the saving sacrifice of Christ without any specific reference as to when it was taking place.

Of all the Synoptic institution formulas over the bread, only the Lucan formula modifies the Greek word for "body" (*soma*) with the present passive participle "being given" (*didomenon*). On the other hand, all of the Synoptic words of institution over the wine modify the Greek word for "blood" (Mt and Mk: *aima*; Lk *aimati*) with the identical present passive participle "being shed" (*ekchunnomenon*).

The Synoptic institution formulas, because of their use of the present participle, could be interpreted on face value as indicating the time of the Last Supper as the time of Jesus' body actually being given and his blood actually being shed. However, the Greek is open to two interpretations. It is possible to use the present participle as in Hebrew and Aramaic in place of a future participle where the context indicates a future sense.[250] Maximilian Zerwick, S.J., brings this point up with regard to interpreting the Synoptic institution formulas and says that the participles may be understood "atemporally."[251] However, in concluding, he states: "A theological argument in favour of the sacrificial character of the Last Supper cannot be based on the mere fact that the participles are present ones (on the grounds that if the reference were to the sacrifice of the cross the future would have been used)."[252]

Thus, the use of the present participle in the institution formulas regarding the completeness of the sacrificial nature of the Eucharist of the Last Supper remains inconclusive. However, the Footwashing, as an analogous presentation of the Eucharist of the Last Supper, clarifies the ambiguity of the Synoptic Accounts and settles the matter regarding the sacrificial nature of the Eucharist of the Last Supper. **For John, the historical death of Jesus was present at the Last Supper.**

---

249   Again, these are the words of Cardinal Lepicier who was quoted in a previous footnote in this chapter.
250   Such examples are found in Mt 25:14; 26:25; Lk 1:35; 2:34; 14:31; Acts 21:2f; 26:17. Cf. Zerwick, Maximilian, *Biblical Greek Illustrated by Examples*, (2nd ed.; Rome, Scripta Pontificii Instituti Biblici, 1983), p. 95, n. 283. However, the whole problem is precisely whether the context of the Eucharistic Sacrifice is about the present or the future.
251   Zerwick, Maximilian, *Biblical Greek Illustrated by Examples*, pp. 95, 96, n. 283. "Atemporally" means independent of time and, thus, without any reference to a particular time.
252   *Ibid.*

Only in accepting the completeness of the sacrificial nature of the Eucharist of the Last Supper as explained in the JLSA does one see more clearly how the Eucharist is a true sacrifice. It seems that John, through his analogical presentation of the Eucharist, wished to dispel any confusion that might be found in the Synoptic Last Supper Accounts regarding the sacrificial nature of the Eucharist. John forces the acceptance of the presence of the historical sacrifice of the cross as the reality of the Eucharistic Action of the Last Supper and, consequently, of all other eucharistic celebrations.

7.4. Conclusion

The matter of the ontological presence of Jesus' unique death at the Last Supper cannot be definitively resolved from the words of the institution formulas in the Pauline and Synoptic Last Supper Accounts.

However, John means literally what he wrote in Jn 13:1 and Jn 13:31. The sacrifice of Calvary was truly present at the Last Supper in its two component parts: the oblation and the immolation of the victim. In teaching the ontological presence of Calvary at the Last Supper, John affirms the completeness of the sacrificial nature of the Eucharist at that Supper. The Last Supper is precisely where the eucharistic mystery should be contemplated. Calvary *"post-exists"* in the Mass by the identical power by which it *"pre-existed"* at the Last Supper.

The completeness of the sacrifice of the Eucharist of the Last Supper has not been given the necessary attention it deserves. Certain Fathers of the Council of Trent, judging in too human a fashion, could not get over the hurdle of the human categories of time and space and God's power to transcend them. This has definitely been an obstacle to a more profound appreciation of both the Eucharist and of the Church.

John's clarification of the sacrificial nature of the Eucharist of the Last Supper is most important for at least three reasons. Firstly, it explains the nature of the Eucharistic Sacrifice by showing that it is indeed a true sacrifice because it is the pre-existent presence of the very death of Jesus on Calvary. This is to say that the JLSA shows in a different way than in other Scriptures the relationship of the Eucharist to Calvary. Secondly, since the Eucharist of the Last Supper was the complete sacrifice of Calvary, it was the instrumental cause of the Church's very origin. The Church was not born on Pentecost but from the side of Jesus on the cross through the Eucharist of the Last Supper. This is why the Church is **essentially** a Eucharistic People. The origin of the Church seems to be the principal reason for the Lord's institution of the Eucharist *before* he suffered and died rather than after his Resurrection, the reason for his special desire to celebrate the Supper *before he died*: "*And he*

*said to them, 'I have earnestly desired to eat this Passover with you **before I*
suffer....'"*[253] Thirdly, since the Lord used the Eucharist to establish his covenant, the Eucharist is the formal basis of the covenanted relationship between
God and the Christian and between Christians among themselves.

---

253   See Lk 22:15. This matter of the origin of the Church is treated in more detail below
in Chapter 8, 8, 2.

CHAPTER 8

Implications of the Eucharist
of the Last Supper

From the JLSA's teaching about the Eucharist of the Last Supper, certain corollaries become evident.

8.1. The Eucharist is Simultaneously an Absolute and Relative Sacrifice

Michael Schmaus, speaking about the Eucharist as a memorial (*i.e., anamnesis*), says that bringing back or recalling Jesus' death "… does not involve the presence of the historical death itself."[254] He says that asserting the presence of that historical event in the eucharistic sacrifice, besides straining "the concept of the memorial celebration … also risks making the eucharistic sacrifice absolute, over against the sacrifice of the cross, by according it an independence which, though based on the sacrifice of the cross, yet belongs to the eucharistic sacrifice itself."[255]

Schmaus' objection is without any foundation. First of all, the fact that the Eucharist ontologically contains what it signifies does not strain the concept of a memorial celebration. To the contrary, the Eucharist is, rather, a *perfect* memorial of Calvary and certainly one that only divine power could bring about. Moreover, the ontological identity of the historical sacrifice of Calvary and the Eucharistic Sacrifice absolutely precludes the possibility of the Eucharist being independent from Calvary because the Eucharistic Sacrifice **IS** Calvary! If the Eucharist and Calvary are ontologically the *identical sacrifice* —"*one single sacrifice*" according to The Catechism of the Catholic Church[256]—they cannot differ in what they substantially and existentially are. A thing cannot be independent of itself.

Every Eucharist *makes ontologically present* that unique historical death that it sacramentally signifies. This is to say that the Eucharist is simultaneously an absolute and a relative sacrifice.[257]

---

254   Schmaus, Michael, *Dogma, The Church as Sacrament* (Vol. 5; London: Sheed and Ward, 1990), p. 110.

255   *Ibid.*, pp. 110, 111.

256   CCC, n. 1367.

257   Ferland, Augustus. p.s.s, *Commentarius in Summam D. Thomae, De Sacramentis in Speciali, De Novissimis*, Montréal, Canada, Grand Séminaire, Faculté de Théologie, 1955, pp. 358, 359.

An **absolute sacrifice** is one that is sufficient unto itself because it contains all the elements of sacrifice: oblation and immolation. The Eucharist is an absolute sacrifice by reason of its ontological identity with the historical Sacrifice of Calvary. If the Eucharist did not have this identity it would be no sacrifice at all, because Calvary is the *unique* sacrifice of the Christian Dispensation. The Eucharistic Sacrifice does not multiply the historically unique *death* of Jesus; instead, it wondrously multiplies its *ontological presence in time and space* for the Church on earth.

However, the Eucharist is necessarily also a **relative sacrifice** by its very nature. It is such because of the sacramental manner in which it is offered. The Eucharist is a sacramental sacrifice and this means that it was instituted by the Lord to signify, commemorate and memorialize what happened on the cross of Calvary. This is so true that the Eucharistic Action would be totally incomprehensible without Calvary since its very sacramental signs refer to Calvary. To be relative to something is to be ordered to it, and since the Eucharist is the sign, commemoration and memorialization of Calvary, the Eucharist is obviously related to Calvary and is, for this reason, a *relative sacrifice*. The Eucharistic Sacrifice is *essentially* the same as and identical to Calvary, and, as such, is an absolute sacrifice. But the Eucharistic Sacrifice is **accidentally** different from Calvary in its sacramental mode of offering, and, as such, is also a relative sacrifice.

8.2. The Church Is Born Through the Eucharist of the Last Supper

The Constitution on the Sacred Liturgy speaks of the birth of the Church like the birth of Eve, the first "mother of all the living."[258] The Constitution declares: "For it was from the side of Christ as he slept the sleep of death upon the cross that there came forth 'the wondrous sacrament of the whole Church.'"[259] The CCC states: "As Eve was formed from the rib of the sleeping Adam, so the Church was born from the pierced heart of Christ, dead on the cross."[260]

If this teaching about the origin of the Church is placed within the perspective of what this study proposes concerning the Johannine teaching about the sacrificial nature of the Eucharist of the Last Supper, it implies an important added distinction from the way the nature of the Church and the salvific role of the Eucharistic Mystery are presently seen.

In St. Luke's Gospel Jesus says just before instituting the Eucharist: "I have earnestly desired to eat this Passover with you before I suffer"

---

258   Gn 3:20.
259   SC, n. 5.
260   CCC, n. 766.

(Lk 22:15). This phrase translated as "I have earnestly desired" is much more forceful in the Greek, which is translated as "with desire I have desired…" The point here is, why the Lord's consuming desire to institute the Eucharist *"before I suffer"*? The answer is found in the JLSA.

Should the Lord have instituted the Eucharist *after* his suffering and death, the Eucharist would simply have been the means to perpetuate the presence of his death for his Church and give to her his body and blood as her nourishment. However, in this case the Eucharist would not have been instrumental in the very origin of the Church. But the institution of the Eucharist **before the Lord suffered and died means that** *he intended the Eucharist to be the instrumental means for the origin of his Church before the event of Good Friday*. The Church was in fact born from the Calvary event—from the side of Christ as he slept on the cross— but precisely as this death was made ontologically present *at the Last Supper*. In this way the Church is completely dependent upon the cross for her very origin *through the Eucharistic Sacrifice*.

The Church's origin from the Eucharist on Holy Thursday indicates that she is *essentially* **eucharistic** because her very origin is essentially bound to the Eucharist and can never be separated from it.[261] The JLSA teaching

---

261 Because the Church owes not only her continued existence but also her very origin to the instrumentality of the Eucharist, she can never be separated from it. This important point sheds light upon the mysterious meaning of the eucharistic and ecclesial apparition that took place at Knock, Ireland, on Thursday evening, August 21, 1879. That apparition took place at the wall of the church dedicated to St. John the Baptist, who was Precursor of the Lamb of God and of the New Covenant. The Knock apparition is commonly considered Marian. However, that attribution does not do it justice. It has much wider dimensions. In the first place, Mary is not the center of the apparition. Instead it is the Sacrifice of the Altar wherein the Lamb of God who, by his death made present by the Eucharist, drives out the ruler of this world, establishes the Church (i.e. God's People of the New Israel) and is invested as its Messiah King. On the gospel side (left) and closest to the altar is St. John, dressed as a bishop, miter on his head and with the book of his gospel in his hand. He moves as if preaching. Here John, Apostle and Evangelist, teaches about what he wrote in his Last Supper account regarding the sacrificial nature of the Eucharist and the New Covenant it established. As on Calvary, Mary stands next to John. She is crowned and holds her hands in the *orans* position by which she indicates that she represents the Church. In the context of the apparition the Immaculate Virgin Mother of God is clearly the Church's **"example** as virgin and mother in an eminent and unique way…. She summons the faithful to her Son, to his sacrifice and to the Father's love. In seeking to further the glory of Christ, the Church becomes more and more like Mary, its **'exalted type'** in the order of faith, love and perfect union with Christ" (LG, nn. 63, 65). Mary as Co-Redemptrix, together with her Son, offers his Sacrifice to the heavenly Father for the salvation of mankind. Next to Mary is St. Joseph, Patron of the Universal Church, with his head reverently bowed in prayer. The apparition of Knock is concerned precisely with the doctrine of St. John found in the JLSA about the Eucharistic Sacrifice and the Church it established, of which Mary is the model and type. Without a doubt this apparition was granted to Ireland for the most admirable fidelity of its people to the Holy Sacrifice of the Mass and the Church which it established.

about the presence of the historical death of Jesus Christ at the Last Supper through the Eucharist reveals the fundamental role of the Eucharist of the Last Supper in the establishment of the New Covenant and the Church.[262] This Johannine teaching demonstrates how true it is that the Eucharist is the very source of all Christian life.[263]

There seems to be an additional reason for the Lord to have established his Church through the Eucharist. After instituting the Eucharist in the Cenacle, the Lord said: "... the ruler of this world is coming. He has no power over me; but I do as the Father has commanded me, so that the world may know that I love the Father. Rise, let us go from here."[264] By these words the Lord indicated that his final earthly work accomplished by means of the Eucharist on Holy Thursday has a different purpose from what he did on Good Friday. Holy Thursday's purpose was to complete his final earthly mission through the Eucharist, whereas Good Friday had the particular purpose of testifying to the unbelieving world Jesus' obedience to and love for his Father. Holy Thursday's work pertained to the realm of faith, and the Church belongs to this realm. By instituting the Church on Holy Thursday through the Eucharist, Jesus separated her from the Good Friday externals, the wiles and machinations of the devil, and associated the Church's origins only with himself and his sacrifice.

8.3. The Eucharist is the Mystery of Faith

As mentioned above, just after instituting the Eucharist the Lord indicated in Jn 14:30 the different purposes for Holy Thursday and Good Friday with regard to his greatest act of love for mankind. The Eucharist was instituted for the faithful who believe, who are not subjects of the ruler of this world, so that they may be present at Jesus' greatest act of love for them. That was the purpose of the institution of the Eucharist on Holy Thursday. The Eucharist belongs to the realm of faith; it can only be accepted by faith. On the other hand, the events of Good Friday confront the world with the external physical appearances of Jesus' death, appearances that are necessary for those who do not yet have faith.

---

262   This is contrary to what N. Ghir holds: "This covenant was formed mainly at the Last Supper and at the same time was sealed with Christ's Eucharistic blood in the chalice; it then obtained by the shedding of the blood of Christ its valid and complete confirmation." Ghir cites Suarez, whose text he has translated: *Sine dubio in ultima coena praecipue condidit (Christus) testamentum quod suo etiam sanguine tunc incruente immolato sancivit; postea vero in sacrificio cruento omnino stabilivit ac confirmavit* (Suarez, in III S. Thom., disp. XXXVII, sect. 4, n. 15). Cf. Ghir, Nicholas, *The Holy Sacrifice of the Mass, Dogmatically, Liturgically, and Ascetically Explained* (St. Louis: B. Herder Book Co., 1953), p. 99.
263   Cf. LG, n. 11.
264   Jn 14:30, 31.

From John's teaching about the Eucharist of the Last Supper, one is able to see that Jesus did not intend the faithful merely to look back through ages past to the hill of Calvary in order to unite themselves to his salvific sacrificial death. For Christ's faithful people, Calvary is not an "old rugged cross on a hill far away."[265] Instead, the Lord devised the Eucharistic Sacrifice so that those who have the knowledge of faith may celebrate the origin of his Church and be in real and constant contact with his all-saving death, the consummation of his love. The Eucharist is truly the mystery of faith, the awesome, astounding and unfathomable invention of the love of Jesus the High Priest.[266] He intended that his sacrifice of Calvary—the act of his greatest love—be present to his Church at all times through the Eucharistic Sacrifice. In the Eucharist, together with the Lord, the Church offers to the Father in the Holy Spirit, the perfect prayer of adoration, thanksgiving, petition and reparation.

8.4. The Eucharistic Covenant is the Formal Basis of the Christian Relationship

The Lord Jesus devised the Eucharist of the Last Supper as the means to establish his Covenant/Church *before* Good Friday. Consequently, the Eucharistic Sacrifice is the formal basis of the covenantal relationship between God and Christians and among Christians themselves.

In the JLSA teaching about the completeness of the sacrificial nature of the Eucharist of the Last Supper is found the strongest scriptural justification for one of the most profound statements of the Second Vatican Council: "The Eucharistic Sacrifice (is) the source and summit of the whole Christian life…." The Johannine teaching shows the full meaning of this statement by indicating that the Church is essentially a eucharistically-covenanted community because it receives from the Eucharistic Sacrifice not only its sustenance, but its very origin as well.

---

265   From the hymn *The Old Rugged Cross* by George Bennard.
266   Cf. Lk 22:15.

ABBA

The Last Supper

© 2000, Msgr. Anthony La Femina

Part II

The Eucharistic Covenant

CHAPTER 9

Introduction to Part II: The JLSA as a "Covenant Report"

Part II demonstrates that the JLSA reports on the nature of the Eucharistic Covenant established at the Last Supper. It will point out how the JLSA was greatly influenced by what was done in Deuteronomy in the second discourse of Moses which reports on the Mosaic Covenant.[1] The term "covenant report" as employed here signifies a document that recounts the makeup and terms of a covenant within a defined format.

Various components from OT covenant traditions are used in the JLSA. Part II will identify the presence of the elements, language and phraseology of those OT covenant traditions and explain their meaning with regard to the Eucharistic Covenant. By individuating the various OT covenantal components employed in the composition of the JLSA, this study will determine the specific nature of the Eucharistic Covenant and what this covenant both encompasses and requires. The very presence of the OT covenantal components will both confirm the JLSA's covenantal context and reveal the specific nature of the Eucharistic Covenant that Jesus instituted.

Aelred Lacomara, C.P., wrote an article about Jn 13:31-16:33 which he calls the Farewell Discourse (henceforth referred to as FD). In his article Lacomara noted the presence of certain treaty elements of the Hittite formulary employed in Deuteronomy.[2] He wrote: "… the fourth gospel, whenever it presents the person and mission of Jesus in a context of Moses-and-exodus typology is influenced, at least in part, by the OT forms and theology that are implicit in the presentation of Moses and his mission."

Lacomara explains both the external and internal resemblances of Jn 13-16 with the book of Deuteronomy. Regarding their external resemblances, he points out a similarity of circumstances inasmuch as both texts are concerned with the final discourses of their respective leaders in a covenant setting arising from the need of departing leaders to console, encourage, instruct and warn their respective communities. The internal resemblance of the texts derives from their use of the basic elements of that classical form used in

---

1   Dt 4:44-26:19; 28:1-46.
2   Lacomara, A. "Deuteronomy and the Farewell Discourse (Jn 13:31-16:33)," *CBQ*, 36 (January 1974), pp. 65-84.

ancient times for reporting on covenants between suzerains and vassals.[3] Lacomara points out, however, that in the FD one finds only the covenant's constitutive elements, but not its formal structure since "the elements ... are scattered all through the FD in the associative, conversational style that Jn uses in these chapters."[4]

Lacomara remarked that John follows the synoptic tradition by locating the New Covenant in the setting of the Last Supper. As such he sees the FD as "an extended commentary on the words 'of the new covenant'"[5] from the words of the institution of the Eucharist.[6]

The present study agrees with Lacomara's conclusions regarding the matter and manner of the FD's presentation of the various elements from treaty tradition. However, the present study is concerned with more of the Johannine Gospel than Lacomara's study, which is only concerned with Jn 13-16. The objective of our study differs from Lacomara's. He affirms the presence of certain covenantal elements, but he does not investigate the specific type of covenant established at the Last Supper.

There were many types of covenants by reason of their purposes: covenants between private individuals to confirm long-standing relationships; marriage covenants for uniting men and women and even strengthening the bonds between respective families or, in the case of royalty, between nations; covenants between rulers of different countries; royal investiture covenants, etc. The present study reveals the presence of certain OT covenant traditions not mentioned by Lacomara. These traditions make it possible to establish the particular purpose and specific nature of the Eucharistic Covenant of the Last Supper.

The purpose of the Eucharistic Covenant derives from the program for the Son of man's final earthly mission in Jn 12:23, 28, 31-33. The purpose

---

3   The elements of the covenant formulary will be enumerated and described further on.

4   Lacomara, A., "Deuteronomy and the Farewell Discourse (Jn 13:31-16:33)," *CBQ*, 36, p. 83.

5   *Ibid.,* p. 84.

6   Lacomara points out that the Last Supper opens with a purification ceremony (the Footwashing) which was one of the events accompanying the ratification of the covenant at Sinai in Ex 19:10-15. He notes that this ceremony, as an OT element that characterized covenant-making, is but another indication of John's intention to present the New Covenant in his Farewell Discourse. Lacomara finds the Footwashing to have a secondary symbolism for baptism whereby one enters the New Covenant. The conclusion of the present study treats the Footwashing in Part I. In contrast to Lacomara, this study finds the Footwashing to be the key to understanding the JLSA's teaching about the Eucharist. However, as Lacomara suggests, and for his same reason, the Footwashing as a purification ceremony may also well be another indication of the covenantal character of the JLSA and have a secondary symbolism for baptism.

is a twofold glorification, that of the Son of man and of God his Father. This glorification entailed Jesus' casting out Satan from the kingdom he usurped and the establishment of a universal new covenant.

The introduction to the Footwashing in Jn 13:1-3 indicates that its theological setting was the definitive battle between two opposing sovereigns: the devil, "the ruler of this world," and Jesus Messiah, to whom the Father "had given all things into his hands." From this specific purpose of Jesus' final mission, therefore, one is able to identify the specific nature of the Eucharistic Covenant. By this covenant Jesus would himself be glorified by his royal accession as Messiah of the new Israel and glorify his Father with other children.

Schnackenburg states that "the messianic question plays a significant, indeed amazing part, in John's gospel."[7] In fact, the messianic or royal mission of Jesus is the Johannine Gospel's preoccupation from its very inception. The Prologue's burden is the presentation of the Person of the Word-made-flesh and his earthly messianic mission. The Prologue's very first words, "in the beginning," indicate the parallelism of John's Gospel with the book of Genesis. As Genesis begins with the story of the creation, John's Gospel is the story of the perfecting of that creation by the establishment of the covenant through the Eucharist of the Last Supper. The Prologue begins by introducing Jesus.[8] He is the Word of God through whom all things were made,[9] and the light of men.[10] The Word became flesh and his glory was that of an only Son coming from the Father.[11] He will form the community of the New Covenant by sharing his divine Sonship with those who believe in him so that they might become children of God.[12] The Prologue concludes by explicitly giving the human name and title of the Word Incarnate: his name is "Jesus" and his title is "Christ,"[13] which is to say "Messiah." In this conclusion the Prologue explains that the earthly mission of Jesus, the Word-made-flesh, is to assume his sovereignty as Messiah of God's People for the revelation of God's name of Father, i.e. God's fatherhood.[14]

Immediately following the Prologue John develops his presentation of Jesus as Messiah under his use of the title "the Son of man." John indicates, through the prophetic testimony of the Baptist, that Jesus is the bearer of

---

7   Schnackenburg, Rudolf, *The Gospel According to St. John* (3 vols., New York: Crossroad, 1982), III, p. 339.
8   Cf. Jn 1:1, 2.
9   Cf. Jn 1:3, 4, 10.
10   Cf. Jn 1:4, 5.
11   Cf. Jn 1:14.
12   Cf. Jn 1:12.
13   Cf. Jn 1:17.
14   Cf. Jn 1:18.

the Spirit.[15] The Spirit descended and remained upon him[16] in fulfillment of the messianic prophecies of Isaiah.[17] This permanency of the Spirit in Jesus also alludes to King David who is the only king in Israel about whom this affirmation was made.[18] Jesus Messiah must communicate the Spirit for the establishment of God's people, the New Israel. John saw Jesus as the new David in accordance with the prophecy of Ezekiel: "I will appoint one shepherd over them to pasture them, my servant David; he shall pasture them and be their shepherd. I, the Lord, will be their God, and my servant David shall be prince among them. I the Lord have spoken."[19]

Then John exceptionally presents Jesus explicitly as "the Messiah" (Gr, *ton Messian*) to Simon Peter who represents the faithful people of Israel. Here, for the first time, John uses the transliterated Aramaic form for Messiah which he translates for his readers into the Greek title of "Christ."[20] Jesus is then explicitly recognized by Nathanael as John presented Jesus in the Prologue:[21] Nathanael exclaimed: "You are the Son of God; you are the king of Israel."[22] In this verse the Johannine Gospel makes it clear, by substituting "king of Israel" for the title "Messiah," that Jesus' authority is regal like David's.

John then presents Jesus as Messiah to the Gentiles, represented by the Samaritan woman.[23] John follows the same exceptional and identical procedure here as when he presents Jesus to Peter, by explicitly calling Jesus the Messiah, giving first the transliterated form of the Aramaic title "Messiah" which is then followed by the translated Greek form, "Christ."[24]

Apart from the fact that only John uses the Aramaic title for Jesus, it is interesting to note that John himself uses this title only twice in his gospel: firstly, when introducing Jesus to the faithful people of the old Israel in the person of Peter in Jn 1:41, and secondly in Jn 4:25, when introducing Jesus to the Gentiles in the person of the Samaritan woman. In this way John indicates that Jesus is to hold his kingly office over the New Israel to which all mankind is called, which is to say both Jew and Gentile.[25] This universal kingship over God's new People is precisely what the Johannine Jesus him-

---

15   Cf. Jn 1:32, 33.
16   Cf. Jn 1:33.
17   Cf. Is 11:2; 41:1; 61:1.
18   Cf. 1 Sam 16:143.
19   Ek 34:23, 24.
20   Cf. Jn 1:41.
21   Cf. Jn 1:17, 18.
22   Jn 1:49.
23   Cf. Jn 4:4-42.
24   Cf. Jn 4:25, 26.
25   Cf. Jn 12:34.

self affirms in his discourse at the Last Supper in Jn 17:2, 3, by uniting his royal title with his proper name: "Jesus Christ." This is the second and last instance of John's use of Jesus' proper name together with his royal title. John first did this at the close of the Prologue in Jn 1:17, and then, lastly, at the Last Supper.

Concluding his gospel, John says that accepting Jesus specifically as the divine Messiah is the faith required by his gospel: "… these (signs) are written that you may believe that Jesus is the Christ, the Son of God, and that believing you may have life in his name."[26]

Another important element in discerning the specific nature of the Eucharistic Covenant is John's teaching about the subordinate relationship of Jesus Messiah with God his Father. Jesus exercises a royal but inferior role as Messiah-King under the sovereignty of God his Father because, as Jesus himself said, "the Father is greater than I."[27] This relationship is analogous to that of suzerain and vassal in the vassal treaty genre.

If there is opposition between "the ruler of this world" and the Son of man, and if the Son of man's covenantal work is to bring judgment upon this world by driving out its ruler and taking back his usurped kingdom and subjects, these facts indicate that the JLSA Covenant is one of royal investiture. By the Eucharistic Covenant Jesus is enthroned as Messiah over the new Israel. In fact, among the OT covenant traditions found in the JLSA, there are elements adapted from the OT royal investiture traditions. The presence of these particular traditions in the JLSA lead to the conclusion that the covenant established at the Last Supper by the Eucharist is specifically presented by John as the Royal Investiture Covenant of Jesus as Messiah of the new Israel.

It should be no surprise that the Eucharistic Covenant is one of royal investiture since John states that the glorifications of the Son of man and his Father would only take place when Jesus will have been "lifted up" on the cross to draw all men to himself. While "lifted up" means Jesus' death, it also signifies his glorification by royal investiture as Messiah of the new Israel. In this way Jesus takes back for God the sovereignty over creation usurped by the devil.[28] This is stated very succinctly in the Liturgy: "The power of the cross reveals your judgment on this world and the kingship of Christ crucified."[29]

What has been said in this introduction to Part II does not intend to anticipate the conclusions of this study. These conclusions remain to be

---

26   Jn 20:31.
27   Jn 14:28.
28   Cf. Jn 12:31-33.
29   *Roman Missal*, Preface 17, Passion of the Lord, I.

proven. However, what has been said by way of introduction should be kept clearly in mind as the JLSA text is studied. This introduction serves to aid the reader in the process of identifying the various components of OT covenant tradition and seeing how they fit into the framework of a covenant of royal investiture.

Lacomara found that the FD included the basic elements of the traditional covenant form (i.e. of the ancient vassal treaty), though it does not follow the strict covenant formulary.[30] He means that the elements of the same type are not placed in close enough conjunction, nor are the different elements adequately correlated with one another into a sufficiently well-knit structure to be called a covenant formulary in the strict sense. The covenant elements are scattered throughout the FD in the associative conversational style that the Johannine Gospel uses in these chapters. Unlike Deuteronomy, John's treatment was parenetic rather than legalistic in form. It has been noted, however, that this study examines a more extensive text of the Johannine Last Supper Account than Lacomara's FD, and has a different objective than Lacomara's study. This study signals additional OT covenant elements that are intertwined with the treaty elements. It was precisely the combination of all these elements that enabled this study to specify the nature of the covenant established at the Last Supper.

---

30   Cf. Lacomara, A., "Deuteronomy and the Farewell Discourse (Jn 13:31-16:33)," *CBQ*, 36 (1947), pp. 83, 84.

CHAPTER 10

OT Covenant Traditions in the JLSA

Before analyzing the text of the JLSA itself, the OT covenant traditions employed in the composition of the JLSA must be examined.

10.1. Two Introductory Elements

The *"Mise-en-scene"* and the "Proclamation of Covenant" were two OT elements used to introduce discourses related to covenant traditions.[31]

The *Mise-en-scene* was the normal opening for covenants-turned-speeches. It contained historical material that positioned the speech in time and place and created a platform for its delivery.[32] An important example is found in Dt 1-3. These chapters constitute the physical, temporal and theological setting for the second Mosaic discourse of Deuteronomy. Other examples of a *Mise-en-scene* are found in Dt 4:44-49; 28:69; Jos 23:1, 2; 24: 1, 2; 1 Sam 12:6-7.

The purpose of the **Proclamation of Covenant** was to mark the beginning of a new era and the opening of a covenant situation.[33] A new era and the opening of a covenant situation were common whenever a change in leaders or government took place. Covenant and death became closely associated because of the passing of the leader. In this case the covenant formulary took on the character of a last will and testament. Such was the situation at the passing of Moses, Joshua and Jesus. Speaking about the use of the vassal treaty analogy in the second discourse of Moses in Deuteronomy, McCarthy observes: "It is thus that a covenantal formulation becomes a speech, a farewell address or, better, a testamentary discourse, for in it the ideal leader is represented as leaving the people its heritage, a defined and committed relation to its God."[34]

10.2. Vassal Treaty Analogy in Deuteronomy

In his book, *Treaty and Covenant*, Dennis J. McCarthy, S.J., notes the theological development in the understanding of "covenant" in Israel. He

---

31 Cf. McCarthy, *Treaty and Covenant,* pp. 159, 186, 188ff, 199, 202, 217.
32 Cf. McCarthy, *Treaty and Covenant,* pp. 159, 186, 189, 190, 199.
33 Examples of such a proclamation may be found in Dt 5:1; 29:1; Jos 23:2; 24:2; 1 Sam 12:13.
34 McCarthy, Dennis J., *Treaty and Covenant,* p. 187.

states: "The ancient religious covenant was originally cultic, and it developed over a long period toward expression in a structure analogous to the treaty without losing the manifold, rich meaning of its cultic expressions."[35] McCarthy notes that the articulation of the relationship between Israel and Yahweh according to the treaty genre was first made sometime after 700 BC. It was employed in the central portion of Deuteronomy (4:44-26:19; 28:1-46).[36]

The expression "treaty genre" refers to the particular way of reporting a covenant that was generally composed of six elements.[37] This genre of covenant reporting was used in forming the empires of the Ancient Near East. The expression "treaty genre" has a specifically different meaning from the expressions "covenant formulary" or "covenant formulation." The latter simply designate any report about covenant-making, but without any special connection with the treaty genre.

The vassal treaty genre was utilized in the Ancient Near East from as early as 2,500 BC for making and reporting treaties between suzerains and lesser sovereigns.[38] A significant number of these treaties was discovered in the 1920s.[39] Their importance for religion, however, began to be realized only about thirty years later when a similarity was thought to exist between the ancient treaty texts and certain OT biblical covenant texts. The OT practice of employing the elements of the treaty was a religious adaptation of the vassal treaty formulary.

The treaty formulary was similar to a royal decree or grant in that the treaty was conceived as the proclamation of the royal and powerful word of the suzerain, who was called the "Great King."[40] However, the treaty did not proclaim the royal word arbitrarily as in a decree or edict. The vassal king's acceptance of the treaty under oath was necessary and his acceptance was

---

35   McCarthy, *Treaty and Covenant*, p. 14.
36   McCarthy, *Treaty and Covenant*, p. 15.
37   These elements will be treated in the following chapter.
38   Baltzer notes that under certain circumstances even a collective entity such as a group of important men or an entire nation might be parties to a vassal treaty. Cf. *The Covenant Formulary*, p. 17.
39   Cf. McCarthy, Dennis J., *Treaty and Covenant,* pp. 2, 4; Clifford, Richard, *Deuteronomy with an Excursus on Covenant and Law*, edd. Carroll Stuhlmueller and Martin McNamara ("Old Testament Message, A Biblical-Theological Commentary," Vol. 4; Wilmington, Delaware: Michael Glazier, Inc., 1982), p. 188; Craigie, Peter C., *The Book of Deuteronomy* ("The New International Commentary on the Old Testament;" Grand Rapids, Mich.: William B. Eerdmans Publ. Co., 1981), p. 22.
40   Cf. McCarthy, Dennis J., *Treaty and Covenant,* p. 39, 292. McCarthy states on p. 78: "The treaty, then, is the word of the king." It is interesting to note that the title "Great King" is used in various parts of the OT to indicate one of the rank of suzerain: 2 Kgs 18:19, 28; Tb 13:15; Jdt 2:5, 3:2; Pss 47:3, 48:3, 95:3, 136:17; Is 36:4, 13; Hos 5:13, 10:6.

not taken for granted. The inferior king's sovereignty was respected; it was subordinated but not eliminated. By making the treaty the inferior king was not only protected against any arbitrary action of the suzerain in his regard, but also assured of the suzerain's love and protection from his enemies. The vassal treaty was the foundation of the Ancient Near Eastern empires since it protected their political structure and extended their sovereignty.

With regard to the nature of the vassal treaty, McCarthy states: "… it is the relationship created by oath which is at the heart of the vassal (treaty)."[41] The vassal treaty was the vassal's sworn response to the powerful and royal word of the Great King. The suzerain himself made no oath. The vassal's oath was not simply an external mark of the treaty; it was, rather, the treaty's very essence.[42] The treaty genre so emphasized the acceptance of its solemn obligation by oath that the word for "treaty" was taken from the word for "oath" in Akkadian, Hittite and Aramaic.[43]

From ancient times the OT Scriptures based the relationship between Yahweh and his people on the concept of covenant. This covenant tradition gradually matured through efforts to probe the meaning of the covenant that was originally expressed in symbolic ritual.[44] These efforts finally blossomed into the vassal treaty analogy found in the second Mosaic discourse of Deuteronomy.[45]

---

41 McCarthy, Dennis J., *Treaty and Covenant*, p. 41.

42 In this regard McCarthy states: "The treaty is in its very nature a bond established by an oath, and this appears in the essential of its expression, its literary form, namely the promulgation of terms and some adumbration of an oath in the list of gods invoked as witnesses or in the curse or blessing which is conditioned on fidelity to the word given." Cf. *Treaty and Covenant*, p. 77.

43 Cf. McCarthy, Dennis J., *Treaty and Covenant*, p. 31.

44 The developing traditions of the Sinai Covenant strongly emphasized symbolic ritual. Only the final presentation of the Sinai Covenant in Ex 19:3b-8 resorts more to explanation by word. However, even though it plays down liturgical action, it still remains attached to cult. Cf. McCarthy, Dennis J., *Treaty and Covenant*, pp. 275-279.

45 Regarding this point Clifford writes: "As attractive as the impulse is to find evidence of the covenant formulary in the Mosaic period (usually understood as the thirteenth century BC), the wiser course is to follow such cautious specialists as Dennis McCarthy who sees the Deuteronomic central discourse of 4:44-28:68 as the first self-conscious and full-scale adaptation by Israel of the covenant formulary. The Mosaic, and even the patriarchal covenants were of course true covenants. In a 'society of gentlemen' such important transactions could not but be covenants. But the adaptation of the specialized covenant formulary is the contribution of the Deuteronomist. One can also admit that the mature formulation of Deuteronomy had forerunners, 'pre-Deuteronomic' speeches such as 1 Samuel 12 and Joshua 24." Clifford then goes on to explain how, when, and from where, Israel came to use the covenant formulary. Cf. *Deuteronomy with an Excursus on Covenant and Law*, eds. Carroll Stuhlmueller and Martin McNamara, ("Old Testament Message, A Biblical-Theological Commentary," Vol. 4; Wilmington, Delaware: Michael Glazier, Inc., 1982), p. 189, 190. One may also consult the opinions of Craigie, Peter C., *The Book of Deuteronomy*, ("The New International Commen-

According to a plausible theory, the treaty formulary was adapted in the central portion of Deuteronomy during the second half of the eighth century BC to express the covenant relationship between Yahweh and his people. At that time Judah was politically threatened and had to rediscover the meaning of the Mosaic Covenant.[46] Thus, the author of the central portion of Deuteronomy likened the situation of Judah to that of the people of Israel waiting for God to let them into the Promised Land. Once again in Deuteronomy Moses explained the meaning of his covenant and how to live it. This time, however, the Mosaic Covenant was explained through the vassal treaty analogy.

McCarthy pointed out the advantages of using the treaty analogy for expressing the people's relationship to Yahweh.[47] Since the Mosaic Covenant in Deuteronomy was based upon word and was articulated in words instead of being expressed by symbolic cult, its meaning was more evident. The treaty analogy was most suitable for encouraging personal commitment to Yahweh and clarifying precisely what Yahweh's religion involved. The treaty's stress on personal relationship made the vassal treaty genre a fruitful source of exhortations to fidelity. It even gave reasons to hope for a return to Yahweh when infidelity was repented.

"Word" is at the heart of the treaty genre. In this particular literary form for expressing covenant, word simultaneously explained and established the treaty. The treaty genre insisted upon the verbalization of the agreement to avoid those misunderstandings that were common in treaties expressed by symbolic cultic action. The vassal treaty left little to the imagination because it spelled out in words, with the help of its constitutive elements, the nature of the relationship it was defining. The treaty analogy thus enabled the sacred authors to accomplish what they had been seeking for so long: the explicit verbal explanation of what was only symbolically expressed in their covenant ritual.[48] The use of the treaty analogy made it possible for the people to understand what they normally only experienced in symbolic liturgical rites. By making use of the treaty genre, the deuteronomic authors were able to indicate clearly the nature of the relationships involved in the Mosaic Covenant between Yahweh and Israel. At the same time, the genre provided the sacred authors with a fruitful source of exhortation to encourage personal commit-

---

tary on the Old Testament;" Grand Rapids, Mich.: William B. Eerdmans Publ. Co., 1981), pp. 22-29; Gerhard von Rad, *Deuteronomy, A Commentary*, trans. Dorothea Barton ("Old Testament Library;" London: SCM Press Ltd, 1979), pp. 21, 22.

46   See Clifford, Richard, *Deuteronomy with an Excursus on Covenant and Law*, edd. Carroll Stuhlmueller and Martin McNamara ("Old Testament Message, A Biblical-Theological Commentary," Vol. 4; Wilmington, Delaware: Michael Glazier, Inc., 1982), p. 190.

47   Cf. McCarthy, *Treaty and Covenant*, p. 15.

48   *Ibid.*, pp. 15, 16.

ment to the covenant. The genre especially emphasized the command to love and the exclusive service owed to the suzerain by the vassal.

The treaty genre had its own particular structure, phraseology and vocabulary, along with many other details.[49] The treaty formulary consisted of three essential elements: the stipulations or obligations, the invocation of the gods, and the curse formula. However, a typical treaty was composed of six elements:[50] (1) the Titulary Clause or Preamble, (2) the Historical Prologue, (3) the Statement of Relationship, (4) the Stipulations, (5) the Divine Witness Clause, and (6) the Curse-Blessing Formula.

The **Titulary Clause** was the introductory section of the vassal treaty. Since the treaty was the suzerain's message to the lesser king, the Great King opened the treaty by identifying himself as author of the sovereign word being proclaimed. It commenced with: "These are the words of ...." The Titulary Clause, however, was more than a simple introduction. It served as a justification of the suzerain's authority; it exalted the suzerain's might and magnified his word as royal and powerful by giving the Great King's name, genealogy, awesome appellatives and titles.[51]

In the **Historical Prologue** the Great King narrated a selective history of the relationship that existed between himself and the inferior king. It reported the suzerain's gracious benefits in order to justify the commands that would be part of the treaty agreement. The Historical Prologue narrated facts that constituted the foundation for the treaty relationship and served to dispose the inferior sovereign to consent to the treaty. By his acceptance, the inferior king acknowledged the suzerain as his rightful lord. The Historical Prologue often concluded with the bestowal of authority and the feudal benefice or estate upon the vassal.

---

49   The covenant formulary was a type of literary form. Cf. McCarthy, Dennis J., *Treaty and Covenant*, p. 11.

50   Cf. McCarthy, *Treaty and Covenant*, pp. 1, 2; Clifford, Richard, *Deuteronomy with an Excursus on Covenant and Law*, eds. Carroll Stuhlmueller and Martin McNamara, ("Old Testament Message, A Biblical-Theological Commentary," Vol. 4; Wilmington, Delaware: Michael Glazier, Inc., 1982), p. 4; Baltzer, Klaus, *The Covenant Formulary in Old Testament, Jewish, and Early Christian Writings*, trans. D.E. Green (Philadelphia: Fortress Press, 1971), pp. 9-18.

McCarthy notes (*Treaty and Covenant*, p. 63-66) that certain scholars speak of a Document Clause as one of the elements of the treaty genre. This clause gave directions regarding the placement of the treaty document and its public reading. However, the clause is lacking in most treaties. Two authors who speak of the Document Clause as a treaty element are: Hillers, Delbert R., *Covenant: The History of a Biblical Idea*. Eds. George E. Owen *et al.*, "Seminars in the History of Ideas." Baltimore: The Johns Hopkins Press, 1969, pp. 25-45; Mendenhall, G., "Covenant," *IDB*, I, pp. 714, 715.

51   Cf. Baltzer, Klaus, *The Covenant Formulary in Old Testament, Jewish, and Early Christian Writings*, trans. D.E. Green (Philadelphia: Fortress Press, 1971), p. 11.

The **Statement of Relationship** made clear, brief statements about the juridical fact of a basic relationship between the covenanting parties. These statements, however, had no set place in the treaty. Instead, they were dispersed throughout the treaty.

The basic relationship between the covenanting parties was precisely the reason for the particular commands given the vassal in the Stipulation Clause. The Statement of Relationship clarified the juridical aspect of the covenant relationship and made clear that the vassal's loyalty was a consequence of his relationship with the overlord. Thus, for example, the Statement could declare that the Great King made a treaty or friendship or that he made so-and-so a king. The suzerain was called "lord" and "father," which were terms signifying that he was the recognized lord.[52] The vassal was called "son," "servant," or even "slave," indicating that the vassal held an honorable and privileged position of subordination and fidelity.[53]

The treaty created not only a juridical bond but also an affective one.[54] Through general statements and imagery, the suzerain delineated the basic relationship that was to exist between himself and his vassal. He also summarized the purpose of the commands that entailed loyalty and love. The general imperatives of loyalty and friendship were thus an important part of this Statement.[55]

The Statement of Relationship defined the relationship between the covenanting parties in general terms, whereas the Stipulation Clause defined it in specific terms.

The purpose of the **Stipulation Clause** in the treaty was to define how the covenanted parties were to live out their already-existing personal relationship. The covenant perpetuated a pre-existing relationship and perpetuated it as sacred, personal, and family-like. Therefore, since the relationship preceded the covenant, the relationship was not a reward for the observance of the stipulations. The Stipulation Clause of the treaty genre should be regarded as a mode of commitment to the sovereign; a way by which the vassal lives out his extant relationship with the sovereign from day to day.

The vassal made an irrevocable choice by his oath and the stipulations had the calculated purpose of leaving no doubt in the vassal's mind about

---

52   McCarthy, *Treaty and Covenant,,* pp. 98, 107, 226.
53   McCarthy, *Treaty and Covenant,* pp. 35, 79, 107, 266. McCarthy notes that the general concept of covenant or treaty was connected with the idea of kinship and that even in a purely political treaty with Assyria, King Ahaz in 2 Kgs 16:7, called himself the son of his tyrannical overlord. Cf. "Notes on the Love of God in Deuteronomy and the Father-Son Relationship between Yahweh and Israel," *CBQ,* 27 (1965), p. 147.
54   McCarthy, Dennis J., *Treaty and Covenant,* pp. 43,161.
55   Cf. McCarthy, *Treaty and Covenant,* pp. 55, 56.

his choice. The stipulations commanded perfect service. However, since the treaty also created an affective relationship, the stipulations commanded love above all. The vassal was to love the suzerain as himself and his own family, and the suzerain was to take the vassal to his heart as his friend.[56] The vassal must be ready to die for his overlord; and no one has greater love than this.[57] The stipulations were laced with passionate rhetoric that exhorted the vassal to complete confidence in his overlord, even when circumstances would indicate otherwise. The stipulations even warned the vassal against murmuring. The vassal was forbidden relationships with other independent sovereigns; the vassal's friends and enemies were to be those of his overlord. Moreover, the vassal was to assist the suzerain in any military campaign when so commanded. These and other mandates minutely defined what the vassal was to do in order to live out the covenant union in everyday life.

In the **Divine Witness Clause** or **List of Gods**, certain deities were invoked and constituted as protectors, guarantors and avengers of the treaty provisions. The gods invoked were generally those of both the suzerain and vassal. The invocation of the gods derived from the sacred oath of the treaty. The Divine Witness Clause provided ample assurance that the gods would intervene against any violation by the vassal of the relationship that they were pledged to protect. At times natural phenomena such as heaven and earth were divinized and invoked in the treaty as qualified witnesses. Moreover, the treaty document itself, because witnessed by the deity, was frequently considered to be an active divine witness-agent that proclaimed the treaty by its own power.

Last but not least is the **Curse-Blessing Formula**. It was made up of a list of sanctions intended to enforce observance of the stipulations. The curses and blessings were explicit and efficacious motives for the vassal's fidelity to his oath. While the blessings were not always in the treaty, the curses were always present because the family-like relationship of covenant could only end by the death of one of the parties; there was no other way to be rid of an unfaithful party.

Regarding the curses Baltzer states: "In the curses, death and destruction in every possible form are threatened.... The curse is inexorable."[58] The treaty clearly linked the Stipulations to the Curse-Blessing Formula so that the vassal had no doubt that his future happiness or complete destruction— even by the suzerain as an agent of the gods—depended upon how well he observed the treaty.

---

56 McCarthy, *Treaty and Covenant*, p. 81, n. 88.
57 McCarthy, *Treaty and Covenant*, pp. 160, 161, n. 6.
58 Baltzer, Klaus, *The Covenant Formulary*, p. 15.

10.3. Royal Investiture Traditions

The royal investiture traditions in the OT have their origin in 1 Sam 12. McCarthy notes that this chapter contains fragments that are the oldest evidence of the covenant formulation in the OT. This is most significant since covenant is connected with kingship.[59] McCarthy says that 1 Sam 12 "... deals with ... integrating kingship into the basic covenant concept."[60]

The OT's explicit connection of king and covenant, together with its statements about the king's anointing and other features of royal ceremony and ideology, indicate that the Messiah was Yahweh's covenanted subject with many characteristics of the vassal king of treaty tradition. There is an especially striking similarity of the relationships between the Messiah and Yahweh and the vassal king and the Great King as well as between the royal investiture in ancient Israel and in treaty tradition.[61]

10.3.1. The Royal Protocol

Both 2 Kgs 11 and 2 Chr 23 report on the coronation ceremony of King Joash or Jehoash, who was the only surviving son of Ahaziah (837-800 BC). He was invested king of Judah by the priest, Jehoiada. According to 2 Kgs 11:12 and 2 Chr 23:11, the one to be enthroned, the "son of the king" (Hb *ben-hammelek*), was given a "protocol" (Hb *edut*) during the coronation rites. This protocol was a document justifying the royal title of the one being invested for assuming office and rule. Its transmission followed the custom of Egyptian royal tradition.[62] In Egypt the protocol was allegedly written by the deity itself and gave the name, genealogy, titles and appellatives of the Pharaoh who was presented as the deity's natural son. Von Rad notes, however, that since the royal protocol in Judah obviously made no such mythological claims, this "protocol," for the Hebrew mind, could only be a document inscribed with a covenant between Yahweh and the king.[63] In the protocol, the king in Judah was presented as Yahweh's son *per adoptionem*.[64] This sonship would probably be expressed in accordance with the protocol given by Yahweh in Ps 2:7-9 or the covenant established by Yahweh with David in 2 Sam 7:8-16; Ps 89:20-30; 132:11, 12. Allusion to such a testimony/covenant document is found in the "Last Words of David" (2 Sam

---

59   Cf. McCarthy, Dennis J., *Treaty and Covenant,* p. 284.

60   McCarthy, Dennis J., *Treaty and Covenant,* p. 284.

61   Cf. McCarthy, Dennis J., *Treaty and Covenant,* pp. 70, 215: n. 11.

62   Cf. von Rad, Gerhard, *Old Testament Theology,* trans. D.M.G. Stalker (2 vols; London: SCM Press Ltd, 1982-1985), I, p. 40; de Vaux, Roland, *Ancient Israel, Its Life and Institutions,* trans. John McHugh (London: Darton, Longman & Todd, 1980), p. 103.

63   Cf. von Rad, Gerhard, *Old Testament Theology,* trans. D.M.G. Stalker (2 vols; London: SCM Press Ltd, 1982-1985), I, p. 41.

64   Von Rad, Gerhard, *Old Testament Theology,* p. 103.

23:5) and in Ps 132:12. There also seems to be a reference to this covenant protocol in Ps 89:40. It is likely that the "decree" of Yahweh mentioned in Ps 2:6-9, which speaks of the coronation of the king, could very well be the Royal Protocol since the Hebrew word used for "decree" (*hoq*) is a synonym for *edut*.[65]

10.3.2. The Twofold Covenant

In the OT royal investiture tradition, a twofold covenant was reported during the investiture of the Messiah in Judah. One covenant, found in 1 Sam 12:16ff, 2 Kgs 11:17a and 2 Chr 23:16, is between the Nation (*i.e.* Messiah-with-people) and Yahweh. The other covenant, found in 1 Sam 12:1-15, 2 Kgs 11:17b and 2 Chr 23:3, is between the Messiah king and his subjects.

Baltzer, describing the investiture of the vassal, notes that "a double oath ceremony is clearly recognizable as the actual nucleus: an oath to the Great King taken by the vassal, and an oath taken by the people of the 'land' to the vassal. In this double ceremony, the investiture agrees completely with what we have ascertained concerning the nature of the two 'covenants' in Israel."[66]

10.3.3. The Royal Provision Clause

The Royal Provision Clause was a type of proclamation/presentation used for setting up kings both in Israel and Judah. An example of this clause is found in 1 Sam 12:13: "Now you have the king you want, a king the LORD has given you." Other Royal Provision Clauses are found in 2 Kgs 9:3: "Thus says the LORD: 'I anoint you king over Israel'"; in 2 Kgs 9:6: "Thus says the LORD, the God of Israel: 'I anoint you king over the people of the LORD, over Israel'"; and in 2 Chr 23:3: "Here is the king's son who must reign, as the LORD promised concerning the sons of David."

The Royal Provision Clause had a juridical cast; it affirmed the kingship of the one being invested and presented him to the people as Yahweh's own choice.[67] In the Royal Provision Clause Yahweh is like the treaty suzerain while the Messiah-king is like the vassal king. [68]

The "acclamation" by the people in the royal investiture ceremony was an affirmation of the Royal Provision Clause. Concerning this acclamation de Vaux writes: "… this acclamation does not mean that the people chose

---

65   Cf. de Vaux, Roland, *Ancient Israel, Its Life and Institutions*, trans. John McHugh (London: Darton, Longman & Todd, 1980), p. 103.

66   Baltzer, Klaus, *The Covenant Formulary*, p. 80. Cf. also McCarthy, *Treaty and Covenant*, p. 215, n. 11.

67   Cf. McCarthy, *Treaty and Covenant*, p. 214, n. 7.

68   Cf. McCarthy, *Treaty and Covenant*, pp. 214, 217.

the king, but that the people accepted the choice made by Yahweh .... Men recognize the king's authority and submit to it."[69]

10.4. Statement of Covenant-making

The Statement of Covenant-making was a regular element of Israelite genre structure for reporting covenants.[70] It consisted of emphatic affirmations that a covenant had indeed been made or sworn. An example of such a statement may be found in Dt 26:17-19.[71]

McCarthy notes that while the rites establishing the covenants were not commonly mentioned in treaty documents, the treaty genre did not necessarily exclude every mention that the treaty was based upon a pledged word.[72] And thus we have seen in Chapter 2 that the JLSA does mention Peter's covenantal oath in allowing Jesus to wash his feet.

69   De Vaux, Roland, *Ancient Israel, Its Life and Institutions*, trans. John McHugh (London: Darton, Longman & Todd, 1980), p. 106.
70   Cf. McCarthy, *Treaty and Covenant*, pp.19, n. 36; 20; 182, n. 53, 183.
71   For other examples see Gn 21:22-34; 26:23-33; Jos 9:15-20.
72   Cf. McCarthy, *Treaty and Covenant*, pp. 19, 182.

CHAPTER 11

Two Introductory Elements of the JLSA

The JLSA report on its covenant is composed of certain elements like other covenants-turned-speeches in the OT. The report begins with the two introductory elements: the *mise-en-scene* and the Proclamation of Covenant. However, while the *mise-en-scene* normally precedes the Proclamation of Covenant, this order has been reversed in the JLSA. These two introduction elements will be treated here as they appear in the JLSA.

11.1. Proclamation of Covenant

In the human undertaking of dividing the Fourth Gospel into chapter and verse, the discourse of Jn 12:44-50 was understood as the conclusion of Chapter 12. This study proposes, however, that the JLSA is introduced by Jn 12:44-50 because these verses serve as its Proclamation of Covenant.

The passage opens with the Greek verb *krazein (krazo)* which signifies "to cry out." It is most interesting to note that this verb is used to introduce two previous public proclamations of Jesus about his messianic mission.[73] The first of these proclamations is Jn 7:28, 29. Here Jesus proclaims his divine origin and mission as Messiah and his personal knowledge of the One who sent him. In the second proclamation of Jn 7:37, 39, Jesus makes explicit the connection between his messianic mission and the Spirit of which he is the bearer and source. The present passage of Jn 12:44-50 is proposed as the Proclamation of the JLSA Covenant because it is a timeless universal proclamation which summarizes Jesus' messianic mission and contains all the important themes previously treated in the Fourth Gospel.

Jn 12:44-50 is fittingly regarded as both "timeless"[74] and without context.[75] It is a universal proclamation since it is concerned with God's word/commandment that is directed to any and every person.[76] This proclamation is an appeal directed to stimulate a positive response.[77]

---

73   Mateos & Barreto, *Il Vangelo di Giovanni*, pp. 541, 542.

74   *JBC*, p. 450, n. 63:135.

75   Cf. Sanders, J.N. and Mastin, B.A., *A Commentary on the Gospel According to St. John* ("Black's New Testament Commentaries;" London: Adam & Charles Black, 1977), p. 301. R.H. Lightfoot says that this passage is "assigned to no especial place or season." See: *St. John's Gospel, A Commentary*, ed. C.F. Evans (Oxford: Clarendon Press, 1983), p. 245.

76   Cf. Jn 12:44, 45, 48.

77   Cf. Morris, Leon, *The Gospel According to John, the English Text with Introduction,*

It is most important to note that Jn 12:44-50 is a summary of all the previous themes treated in John's gospel because it connects the previous activity of Jesus with that which follows and completes it, *i.e.*, the royal investiture covenant of Jesus Messiah. C.H. Dodd observes: "The passage however does not only serve to summarize the purport of the preceding discourses. It forms an apt transition to the second main part of the gospel ...."[78] John 12:44-50 has striking similarities with the discourse of Moses in Dt 5:1. It presents Jesus as the Prophet-like-Moses in Dt 18:18,19.[79] As Moses mediated on behalf of Yahweh,[80] so Jesus mediates on behalf of God his Father. It should be noted that as word played a central role in the treaty and in Deuteronomy,[81] the centrality of word is also verified in this proclamation of Jesus who is personally God's Word and proclaims God's word.

Jesus explicitly stated that the word he proclaims is the Father's "commandment,"[82] the substance of which is "eternal life."[83] This commandment somewhat resembles those given by Yahweh through Moses. They are the principle of life for God's People.[84] Since sonship deals with family, the "eternal life" which Jesus received from his Father and promises to bestow upon his disciples, denotes the covenantal character of this proclamation. Covenant is a family-like union, a sharing in a common family-like life. It is precisely by receiving the eternal life of Jesus that one enters into the family-like union of covenant with the Father, which is to say becomes a child of God as in Jn 1:12.

When Jesus spoke of "the Father who sent me"[85] and stated that he spoke at his Father's command,[86] Jesus made allusion to his role as mediator of the New Covenant. McCarthy notes that the special role of Moses as mediator in Deuteronomy is a variation of the traditional treaty genre. The mediator of the vassal treaty was outside the treaty and had no special importance. He merely read the words of the Great King. Instead, the position of Moses is most prominent. As Lacomara notes: "Moses is not a mere spokesman for

Exposition and Notes ("The International Commentary on the New Testament;" Grand Rapids, Michigan: Wm. B. Eerdmans Publ. Co., 1979), pp. 571, 607; Mateo, J., Barreto J. et al., *Il Vangelo di Giovanni, analisi linguistica e commento esegetico* ("Lettura del Nuovo Testatmento;" Assisi: Cittadella Editrice, 1982), p. 541.
78   Dodd, C.H., *The Interpretation of the Fourth Gospel*, p. 383.
79   Cf. Brown, *The Gospel According to John*, I, pp. 491, 492.
80   Cf. Dt 5:5, 22-33.
81   The treaty was presented as the proclamation of the royal and powerful word of the suzerain or great king.
82   Jn 12:50.
83   *Ibid.*
84   Cf. Dt 8:3; 32:46, 47.
85   Cf. Jn 12:49; also Jn 12:44, 45.
86   Cf. Jn 12:49, 50.

Yahweh in Dt; he is a lawgiver for Yahweh."[87] This was due to the specifically religious nature of the Sinai Covenant. Yahweh is a transcendent God who reveals himself in human history. A person in some official position such as prophet, king or priest normally performed the mediation for this type of covenant.[88] Thus, what the Proclamation of Covenant in Dt 5:1 did for Moses, Jn 12:44-50 does for Jesus: it fulfills the theological function of making explicit the role of Jesus as mediator.

Though the JLSA presents Jesus as the "prophet-like-Moses,"[89] it is clear that Jesus, in his covenant, has a very different position than Moses in the Sinai Covenant.[90] The basis for the unique status of Moses as Yahweh's mediator and lawgiver in his covenant was that Moses was the confidante of Yahweh according to Dt 34:10 and Num 12:6-8.[91] However, Moses, despite his singular status, was on the same level as the people to whom he proclaimed God's word. Moses never made the claims made by Jesus. Jesus requires the same faith in his Person as that due to God his Father, who is in the position of suzerain of the Mosaic Covenant.[92] Jesus says that to see him is to see the Father.[93] Jesus is the light of the world to keep men from remaining in the darkness.[94]

It is most significant that at the very beginning of the JLSA, John alludes to the special dignity of Jesus. Though raised above the rest of mankind and equal in nature to the Father, he is presented, nonetheless, in a subordinate role to the Father. John will further develop this subordinate role of Jesus as a royal figure in the vassal position with regard to God his Father as was the Messiah with regard to Yahweh. As Messiah, Jesus rules over the kingdom that belongs to God his Father. It is precisely because of his role as Messiah-King that Jesus declared: "… the Father is greater than I."[95]

Jn 12:44-50 introduces Jesus' final messianic proclamation that is concerned with covenant in the classical OT covenant traditions of Dt 5:1; 29:1; Jos 23:2; 24:2; and 1 Sam 12:1-6. As a Proclamation of Covenant, this discourse summarizes all of Jesus' previous activity and is directed to all

---

87   Lacomara, A., "Deuteronomy and the Farewell Discourse (Jn 13:31-16:33)," *CBQ*, 36 (1974), p. 67.
88   Cf. McCarthy, *Treaty and Covenant*, p. 249.
89   Cf. Dt. 18:18, 19.
90   Cf. Dt 5:1, 22-33.
91   Cf. Lacomara, A., "Deuteronomy and the Farewell Discourse (Jn 13:31-16:33)," *CBQ*, 36 (1974), p. 67.
92   Cf. Jn 12:44.
93   Cf. Jn 12:45.
94   Cf. Jn 12:44-46. This Johannine light/darkness theme flashes back to the Prologue where the Word is the light of men shining on in the darkness that cannot overpower it (Jn 1:4, 5).
95   Jn 14:28.

mankind as the Son of man is about to terminate his earthly activity. "The hour" of the Son of man—his time to pass from this world to the Father—is about to begin. Thus, the proclamation of Jn 12:44-50 concludes an era and clearly marks the opening of a new one within a covenantal and testamentary situation. It presents Jesus' life and messianic activity as a continuum that is directed to its completion and realization through the establishment of the Eucharistic Covenant at the Last Supper. Jn 12:44-50 is a testamentary discourse wherein Jesus, a royal figure who is equal to his Father in nature but inferior because of his service as Messiah-King, leaves his people a defined and committed covenantal relationship to God his Father. All considered, Jn 12:44-50 perfectly fulfills all the requirements for a Proclamation of Covenant in accordance with OT covenant traditions. Therefore, this study proposes Jn 12:44-50 as the Proclamation of the Eucharistic Covenant in the JLSA.

11.2. *Mise-en-scene*

A *mise-en-scene* basically means to set a stage, to create the context of a drama. The *mise-en-scene* identifies the components of the stage, explains their significance and connects them to the ensuing drama. It defines implicitly in a single shot everything vis-à-vis the personages or actions within the drama.

When treating the introduction to the Footwashing (Jn 13:1-3) in Chapter 5, the specific function of these verses as the *mise-en-scene* was not addressed. However, it was noted how these verses specified the chronological and theological time of the Footwashing as well as the physical or material and theological setting of the Footwashing. But Jn 13:1-3 also presents the characters of the drama: Jesus, the Father, the disciples, the devil and Judas the betrayer, and it makes special mention of the special power exceeding the powers of nature bestowed upon Jesus. It presents these important elements in the decisive moment when Jesus will accomplish his earthly messianic mission. The stage is set for a deadly combat between Jesus and the devil. Both are presented in the JLSA as two opposing and warring sovereigns.

What is most important to note in this *mise-en-scene* is the mention in Jn 13:3b of the special power conferred upon Jesus by the Father. It gives him the power to accomplish his mission outside the boundaries of the laws of our nature governing time and space and also assures Jesus of final victory. This statement has a juridical ring, which, in this context of the definitive battle between combatant sovereigns, assures Jesus of final victory and betokens his covenant of royal investiture as Messiah of God the Father.

In accord with the requirements of OT covenant tradition for the *mise-en-scene*, Jn 13:1-3 masterfully sets the stage for the establishment of Jesus' royal investiture at the Last Supper.

CHAPTER 12

Royal Investiture Traditions and Vassal Treaty Analogy in the JLSA

It was previously noted that according to Jn 12:23, 28, the purpose of Jesus' final work in "the hour" was a twofold glorification: that of the Son of man and of God's name of Father. This purpose would be perfectly accomplished by the Son of man's Covenant of Royal Investiture. That the specific nature of the Eucharistic Covenant as one of royal investiture is brought to light by John's use of OT royal investiture traditions together with the vassal treaty analogy in the composition of his report on the covenant established at the Last Supper through the Eucharist.

The JLSA's use of the royal investiture traditions and the vassal treaty analogy will be treated together in this chapter since they are so closely intertwined in the JLSA text.

12.1. The Royal Protocol

The vassal treaty normally opens with the Titulary Clause or Preamble to identify the Great King and his powerful word. Instead the JLSA replaces the Titulary by giving the Royal Protocol of Jesus Christ. According to the JLSA Proclamation of Covenant, God proclaims his word/covenant through Jesus Christ. his mediator, who is personally his Father's Royal Word. Thus by giving Jesus' Royal Protocol the JLSA identifies not only Jesus Christ but also God the Father who occupies the position analogous to the "Great King" of vassal treaty tradition.

The JLSA's Royal Protocol gives Jesus' *name* and *genealogy*:

13:3	*Jesus – knowing ... that he **had come from God...***
16:27	***... I came from the Father***
28	***I came from the Father and have come into the world...***
17:1	***... Father ... glorify your Son ...***

In the above texts, Jesus affirms both his human and divine origins. The human name of the incarnate Son of God is "Jesus." In the JLSA, Jesus calls

God "Father" six times,[96] refers to him eleven times as "my Father,"[97] and, in addressing God, calls himself twice "your Son."[98] Jesus came from God who is his Father (term *"a quo"*) and came into the world (term *"ad quem"*) as the Son of man.

The JLSA meticulously gives the genealogy of Jesus. It identifies the Father of Jesus as "God."[99] The Father of Jesus is called "God" ten times. By this title he is presented in the JLSA as the One who revealed his covenant name of Yahweh to Moses.[100] He is the God of Israel whose original purpose is salvation for mankind[101] through Israel.[102] The God of Israel is the God of Abraham, Isaac and Jacob.[103] He is *Yahweh,* who is the true God as opposed to false ones because he is the living and eternal God.[104] However, he who is "exalted over the changes and chances of time"[105] is without beginning or end and therefore has no genealogy.

The name of God is *"Father."*[106] John already gave God the name of "Father" in the Prologue (Jn 1:14,18). In treaty language the suzerain was also called "Father." This name designated him as the vassal's "recognized" overlord.[107] Deuteronomy understood Israel's relationship to Yahweh as that of a son.[108] In Deuteronomy the analogy of Yahweh as Father of Israel was thought to be the most perfect expression for Yahweh's covenant love. In the JLSA, however, the term signifies reality rather than figure. The JLSA Covenant reveals the reality of God's name of Father by revealing his Fatherhood through and in his natural and only-begotten Son.[109] The JLSA designates God as "Father" fifty-two times.[110]

---

96   Jn 17:1, 5, 11, 21, 24, 25.

97   Jn 14:2, 7, 20, 21, 3; 15:1, 8, 10, 15, 23, 24.

98   Jn 17:1.

99   Cf. Jn 13:3, 31, 32; 14:1; 16:2, 27, 30; 17:3.

100   Cf. B.W. Anderson, "God, names of," *IDB,* II, 409-411.

101   Cf. Gn 3:15; Is 19:19-25; Mal 1:11.

102   Cf. Jn 4:22.

103   God is called the "God of Abraham" in Gn 31:42, 53 (cf. Ex 3:6), the "Awesome One of Isaac" in Gn 31:42, and the "Mighty One of Jacob" in Gn 49:24.

104   Cf. Gn 21:33; Jer 10:10.

105   Cf. Walther Eichrodt, *Theology of the Old Testament,* trans. John Baker (2 vols.; London: SCM Press Ltd, 1983) I, 182.

106   Jn 12:49; 13:1, 3; 14:2, 5, 7, 13, 16, 20, 21, 23, 24, 26, 28, 31;15:1, 8, 10, 15, 16, 23, 24, 26; 16:3, 10, 15, 17, 23, 25, 26, 27, 28, 32; 17:1, 5, 11, 21, 24, 25.

107   *E.g.* 2 Kgs 16:7. Cf. McCarthy, *Treaty and Covenant,* pp. 98, 104, 128; M. Weinfeld, "Covenant, Davidic," *IDB,* Suppl., 190, 191.

108   Dt 8:5; 14:1; 32:5, 6. Cf. also von Rad, *Deuteronomy,* p. 64.

109   Cf. Jn 17:6, 26.

110   Jn 12:49; 13:1, 3; 14:2, 5, 7-13, 16, 20, 21, 23, 24, 26, 28, 31; 15:1, 8-10, 15, 16, 23, 24, 26; 16:3, 10, 15, 17, 23, 25-28, 32; 17:1, 5, 11, 21, 24, 25.

The appellatives of God the Father are: *"the **only true** God,"*[111] *"**Holy Father**,"*[112] and *"**righteous** Father."*[113] These identifications of Jesus' Father are rich in meaning and intimately connected with the OT covenants.

The appellative *"only"* indicates Yahweh's unity and uniqueness. The covenants of Israel are built upon the fundamental dogma of monotheism that is prominently and clearly professed in one of Israel's most beloved prayers, the *Shemà* of Deuteronomy.[114]

The appellative *"true"* characterizes Yahweh with regard to his covenant relationship with Israel.[115] For the Greek mind, truth is known as the proper object of the intellect. For the Hebrew mind, however, the root of the word for truth (*'emet*) has the notion of what is "firm" and "reliable." Therefore, the Hebrew mind understood the "true" thing or person as the objective foundation for one's faith or trust. What or who is "true" is the reality to which one can give credence because it is solid, steadfast, unchangeable, faithful, genuine, dependable, reliable, and incapable of betrayal. Yahweh is true because he is all of these *par excellence*. God is true because he is the only One on whom Israel can rely or lean upon for support.

The Hebrew word for *"holy"* comes from the root, *qds*, which basically seems to imply separation.[116] God is holy because he is perfect and, as such, he is apart from everything and everyone created. He is "the Holy One," and to speak of his holiness is to touch God's "innermost reality."[117] God's holiness can be described, not so much as an attribute of his perfection, but as God's very substance, to which all his specific perfections are attributed. Sin is diametrically opposed to God's holiness. However, while God demonstrates his holiness by his hatred for sin and his judgment of those who commit it,[118] he especially demonstrates his holiness by being the savior and redeemer of Israel. For this reason God is called "the Holy One of Israel."[119] Israel, because of its covenant, was called to be holy as Yahweh is holy.[120] This appellative "holy," therefore, has a most prominent place in the covenant terminology of Israel. By calling the Father of Jesus "holy," the JLSA identifies him as the "holy God"[121] who is "the Holy One of Israel."

---

111   Jn 17:3.
112   Jn 17:11.
113   Jn 17:25.
114   Dt 6:4; cf. also Dt 32:39; Craigie, *The Book of Deuteronomy*, p. 169.
115   Dt 7:9; 32:4; Ex 34:6.
116   Cf. John L. McKenzie, "holy," *DOB*, p. 365; J. Muilenburg, "holiness," *IDB*, II, 617.
117   Cf. J. Muilenburg, "holiness," *IDB*, II, 616.
118   Nm 20:13; Ezk 38:16.
119   Is 43:3, 14-15.
120   Ex 19:6; Lv 20:8, 26; Dt 7:6; 14:2, 21; 26:19; Jer 2:3; Ezk 37:28.
121   Jos 24:19.

By the appellative *"righteous,"* the JLSA presents the Father as respecting his covenant relationship with Israel.[122] God is righteous because he is true, and he is true because he is the Savior of Israel.[123] The connection between God's truth and righteousness is pointed out in Dt 32:4: "The Rock, his work is perfect; for all his ways are justice. A God of faithfulness (true) and without iniquity, just and right is he." In this way Deuteronomy indicates the unchanging nature of the God of the covenant.[124] The JLSA has also used these two appellatives, "true" and "righteous," to show God's unchangeableness in this Eucharistic Covenant by establishing the New Israel.

John's presentation of God the Father of Jesus in the JLSA is of capital importance. Through John's deliberate and choice use of covenant language and terminology, he attests to the continuity of the previous OT covenants with this final one of the God of Israel in his Son at the Last Supper.

The JLSA Royal Protocol thus recalls the Word's incarnation spoken of in the Prologue[125] and, at the same time, reports the genealogy of Jesus as Messiah of the New Israel. Jesus is clearly not Yahweh's son *per adoptionem*. He, instead, is unique as the natural Son of God. In establishing the natural divine Sonship of Jesus, the JLSA makes it clear that, because of his natural filial relationship to God, there is between Jesus and his Father a perfect unity in nature[126] and operation[127] as well as a perfect community of possessions.[128]

---

122   Cf. E.R. Achtemeir, "Righteousness in the OT," *IDB*, IV, 81-83.
123   Is 45:21.
124   Cf. Craigie, *The Book of Deuteronomy*, p. 378.
125   Cf. Jn 1:14, 18.
126   The JLSA indicates the **perfect unity in nature** of Jesus and the Father by stating that they are: (a) **one** (Jn 17:11, 21, 22): the Father lives in Jesus (Jn 14:10; 17:23); Jesus is in the Father (Jn 14:10, 11, 20; 17:21) and the Father is in Jesus (Jn 14:10, 11; 17:21). Jesus can never be alone because the Father is with Him (Jn 16:32). (b) **equal**: they are both the object of faith (Jn 14:1); to know Jesus is to know the Father (Jn 14:7); to see Jesus is to see the Father (Jn 14:9); not to know Jesus is not to know the Father (Jn 16:3); to hate Jesus is to hate the Father (Jn 15:23, 24); eternal life is to know God and Jesus Messiah (Jn 17:3); Jesus is co-existent with the Father (Jn 17:5, 24); Jesus consecrates himself (Jn 17:19); Jesus alone has proper knowledge of the Father (Jn 16:25; 17:6, 8, 25, 26).
127   The **unity** of the Father and the Son **in operation** is indicated by the following. The Spirit of truth comes from both the Father and Jesus (Jn 14:16, 26; 15:26; 16:13-15). They both send the Spirit (Jn 14:16, 26; 15:26); both come together to dwell in God's people (Jn 14:18, 21, 23); both made the covenant election of God's people (Jn 13:18; 15:16, 19; 17:6, 9, 24); both answer prayers (Jn 14:13, 14; 15:16; 16:23, 24, 26); the Father lives in Jesus accomplishing his works (Jn 14:10, 11).
128   The JLSA affirms the **perfect community of possessions** between Jesus and his Father by stating that Jesus received all he possesses from the Father (Jn 17:7), but that he possesses with the Father all that the Father possesses (Jn 16:15; 17:10). In particular, Jesus possesses the divine name (Jn 13:19; 14:13, 14; 15:16, 21; 16:23, 24, 26; 17:6, 11, 12) and the Father's word (Jn 14:24; 17:14).

The JLSA also gives the *titles* of Jesus:

13:31   **"... the Son of man ...."**
17:3   **"...** *Jesus* **Christ** *whom you have sent"*

The title "the Son of man"[129] is Jesus' title before his royal accession as Messiah. This title is used only once in the JLSA: precisely when Jesus declares accomplished what was spoken of in Jn 12:23, 28, 31-33 about the glorification of the Son of man. It is most significant, as was previously mentioned in Part I, that after that announcement of his glorification by his messianic investiture in Jn 13:31, the Fourth Gospel no longer uses this title to designate Jesus. Instead, from that point on it uses exclusively his title of *Messiah,* i.e. "the anointed one" (Gr *christos*). John states that faith in Jesus as Messiah, the Son of God, is necessary to obtain eternal life.[130]

The JLSA gives the *appellatives* of Jesus:

14:6   *"I am the way, and the truth and the life...."*

"The way" is often used in the OT to refer to the stipulations of Israel's covenant, which is the Law (Hb *Torah*).[131] The Torah was the practical guide of life for the chosen people of the Mosaic Covenant to respond faithfully to Yahweh's covenant love and to obtain the blessings of faithfulness. The Law was "the way of truth"[132] because the one who followed it faithfully lived his covenant relationship with Yahweh. Thus Ps 86:11 says: "Teach me your way, O Yahweh; I will walk in your truth ...." Those who were faithful to their covenant relationship with Yahweh were promised life.[133]

Thus, the three appellatives—*"the way," "the truth," "the life"*—are rich in OT covenant meaning. They are connected to each other through the Law that was given by Yahweh on Mt. Sinai through Moses to the Israelites.

The Law was the way, the truth and the life for God's chosen people of the OT, and obedience to the Law was Israel's response to God's love of election. Election and covenant are correlative terms; it is because of Yahweh's election of Israel that he proceeded to define their relationship by covenant. Election, in fact, is realized by, and perpetuated in, covenant.[134] The Law epitomized the Mosaic Covenant as the revelation of Yahweh's saving will. The people depended upon the Law for their existence. The

---

129   This title was carefully examined in Part I, Chapter 2 of this study.
130   Cf. Jn 20:31.
131   Dt 9:12; 31:39; 1 Sam 12:23; Is 30:21; Mal 2:8.
132   Ps 119:30.
133   Cf. Dt 4:1; 5:16, 33; 6:2, 24; 16:20; 30:6, 15, 19, 20; 32:45-47.
134   Cf. B.D. Napier, "Prophet," *IDB*, III, p. 913. Cf. G.E. Mendenhall, "Election," *IDB*, II, pp. 76, 77, 79.

Law constituted the stipulations of the Sinai Covenant and was the "practical guide" for Israel to live out its election as the covenanted family of Yahweh and to enjoy his blessings.

By understanding the position of the Torah in the OT, one is able to fathom in what manner Jesus' appellatives in Jn 14:6 connect him with the Mosaic Covenant. Jesus himself, God's only Son, replaces the Torah and its Covenant as their fulfillment. He accomplishes this precisely in his office as Messiah-king of the New Covenant.[135]

What Jesus affirms through his appellatives in Jn 14:6, John already stated in Jn 1:17: "For the law was given through Moses; grace and truth came through Jesus Christ." Speaking of the Incarnate Word in Jn 1:14, John states that Jesus is full of "grace and truth." The pairing of these two words recalls the Hebrew usage of pairing their equivalents (*hesed we'emet*) to signify Yahweh's faithful covenantal love for his People. Thus, the Word Incarnate is full of this love of Yahweh for his People. The epitome of Yahweh's covenantal love in the OT was the revelation of the Law. It meant the way, the truth and the life for his chosen people. Jn 1:17 affirms the continuity of and difference between the Mosaic and the Christian Covenants. It says that Yahweh's enduring love is now that of a Father because he has sent to us his only Son who is the fulfillment of his faithful covenant love.[136] It is this love that makes those bound together in covenant exist in a family-like relationship. If the Law given to Moses meant the way, the truth and the life for the chosen people of the Mosaic Covenant, then Jesus Messiah is its complete fulfillment. Jesus brings to those of the Christian Covenant the divine paternal love revealing God's Fatherhood. Jesus, therefore, is the only way to the Father because he is the very truth of the Father and possesses, as natural Son, the love and eternal life of the Father.

By identifying Jesus as "*the way*," the JLSA speaks of Jesus as the Revealer of God and the only access to him. By calling Jesus "*the truth*" and

---

135   Cf. Jn 1:17, 18.

136   Could it be said that because God was considered Father of his People Israel in the OT, the New Covenant merely elucidated upon the theme of God's Fatherhood? The OT knew God as Father only in a very analogical sense: as the Creator who takes pleasure in the work that he has made, a work that has "come forth"—likened to generation—from him (Is 63:15,16). Moreover, the word "father" was a covenantal term which recognized the suzerain as legitimate lord. Thus was the term used in Deuteronomy for Yahweh. However, the People of the New Covenant know, experience and possess God as a true Father who generates a Son. This very Fatherhood is shared in by the people of the NT through a true rebirth (Jn 1:12, 13) by water and the Spirit (Jn 3:5). It is a Fatherhood that is conferred by sharing through grace the very glory (*i.e.* divine filial life) that the Father gave to Jesus, his incarnate Son, upon taking human nature. The divine Fatherhood that Jesus came to reveal by the New Covenant is *essentially* different from that Fatherhood of God that the OT Israel knew and experienced.

"*the life*," the JLSA affirms that Jesus is the manifest and visible presence of the Reality he reveals and to which he is the only way: Jesus and the Father are one.[137]

Because Jesus is one with the Father he is the very presence of the Father's innermost reality, his faithful holiness. He is, therefore, "*the truth*." God shows himself to men in his Son Jesus as the One who is unchangeable. He is always faithful to his original purpose of salvation for all men through Israel and to his covenant for the salvation of Israel.

All things considered, the appellatives for Jesus Messiah clearly express and confirm the change of covenants, though with continuity, in the divine economy of salvation.

Having carefully examined the above texts proposed as the JLSA Royal Protocol, it seems that they amply fulfill their purpose as a Royal Protocol of Jesus Messiah. By clearly indicating his divine natural Sonship, the JLSA Royal Protocol fully justifies his singular right to be invested with the office and governance of Messiah King of God's New Israel. The JLSA Royal Protocol also clearly indicates God, in the suzerain's position, for whom Jesus mediates his own Covenant of Royal Investiture. The Royal Protocol analogically places the Father and Jesus respectively in the positions of su-zerain and vassal of the vassal treaty.

12.2. The Statement of Relationship for the Twofold Covenant of Investiture

The Statement of Relationship belongs to treaty tradition. This statement defined in general terms the juridical fact of the basic relationship between the covenanting parties. Craigie calls this element the "General Stipulations" and says that it served to summarize the purpose of the detailed commands of the Stipulation Clause.[138] This is to say that the Statement of Relationship gave the general dimensions of the covenant, whereas the Stipulation Clause defined its specific dimensions. Deuteronomy itself is interspersed with statements of relationship.

As already indicated, the royal investiture covenant is a twofold cov-enant, one between Yahweh and the nation (Messiah-with-people), and the other between the Messiah King and his subjects. The Statement of Relationship states in a precise way the relationships between the covenant-ing parties, and the JLSA Statement of Relationship reflects the nature of the relationships established by the JLSA royal investiture covenant. Like the OT Royal Investiture Covenant of King Joash of Judah recorded in 2 Kgs 11

---

137   Cf. Jn 17:11, 22; see also Jn 10:30.
138   Craigie, *The Book of Deuteronomy*, p. 23.

and 2 Chr 23, the texts proposed as the JLSA Statement of Relationship describe a union, on the one hand, between the Father and the New Israel (Messiah-with-people), and, on the other hand, between Jesus Messiah and his people.

12.2.1. Relationship Between the Father and the Nation

> 15:1   *"I am the **true vine**, and my **Father** is the **vinedresser**."*
> 2   *"**Every branch of mine** that bears no fruit, he takes away,*
>   *and every branch that does bear fruit he prunes,*
>   *that it may bear more fruit."*

Jesus speaks in Jn 15:1, 2 about the "true vine" which belongs to his Father as vinedresser. In so doing he refers to a union between God his Father and the New Israel, which is parallel to the union between Yahweh and Messiah-with-People (i.e. the nation) by the OT Royal Investiture Covenants spoken of in 1 Sam 12:24, 25 as well as in 2 Kgs 11:17a and 2 Chr 23:16.

The vine and the vineyard are OT figures signifying Israel, Yahweh's chosen people.[139] This nation was described as a luxuriant vine, planted and tended by Yahweh himself. But notwithstanding his loving care, it was without fruit. One of the best passages summing up the OT teaching regarding the infidelity of Israel as Yahweh's vine or vineyard is found in Jer 2:21.[140] Here Israel, Yahweh's "choice vine, wholly of pure seed," proves itself to be a "degenerate" and "wild" vine. This OT background clarifies Jesus' statement about his being "the *true* vine," one that always bears fruit pleasing to the Father.

The words of Jesus in Jn 15:1, 2 are of enormous import because they indicate the unique place that Jesus occupies in the Christian Covenant and what this means for his disciples. ***The true Israel, God's faithful nation, is Jesus himself.*** By calling himself "the true vine," Jesus defines God's nation in terms of himself. A sovereign's name is often used, in a moral sense, interchangeably with his nation because of his position in that nation. However, Jesus is personally the nation of the New Israel in much more than a moral sense because there is much more than a mere moral union between Jesus Messiah and his disciples.

According to Jn 15:8, the true vine glorifies the Father by bringing forth much fruit. By calling himself the "true" vine, Jesus refers to his unique fidelity to his Father. The word "true" renders the Hebrew *émet*, expressing the idea of "trustworthiness." Jesus is saying that he is the vine that can be

---

139   *E.g.* Ps 80:9-16; Is 5:1-7; Jer 2:21; 6:9; Ezk 15; 17:5-10; 19:10-12; Hos 10:1.
140   Cf. also Ps 80:9-14; Ezk 15; Hos 10:1.

trusted to produce fruit after its kind.[141] In fact, *Jesus **alone** is capable of bringing forth fruit pleasing to God, the vinedresser.* Therefore, true fidelity from the New Israel is possible only because this Nation is God's Son himself, and his disciples are members as parts of him: branches of the vine, members of his body.

While Jesus uses the pronoun "I" in the first verse of this statement regarding the true vine—i.e. the nation (Messiah-with-People) of the New Israel—it is clear from the remainder of the statement that this nation is to be understood as Jesus-*with-disciples*. Immediately after speaking of himself as the vine, Jesus speaks of the branches, part of that vine. Jesus specifies that the branches are his disciples and that they can produce fruit only in union with him, that is to say, only if they live "in him." Thus, the nation of the New Israel is Jesus Messiah also in a corporate sense: Jesus together with his disciples (Messiah-with-People).

In the statement about "the true vine," the familiar OT figures of Israel as the vine/vineyard and of Yahweh as its vinedresser have been used by John to indicate continuity between Yahweh's covenant with Ancient Israel and the Christian Covenant. By his use of this OT imagery, John makes a basic statement about the relationship of the parties of the JLSA Royal Investiture Covenant. In the place of Yahweh is God, the Father of Jesus. As vinedresser, the Father is in a sovereign position because the vine depends upon him, it exists to bear fruit for him and to glorify him. In the vassal position is the New Israel: Jesus, together with his people, i.e. Jesus Messiah-with-People (Jn 15:1,2).

As Messiah, Jesus is placed over God's people but is in an inferior position with regard to the Father. For this reason Jesus says that "the Father is greater than I."[142] As Son of man, Jesus' earthly task was to glorify God by the fulfillment of his mission of revealing God's Fatherhood. He was sent by the Father and comes into the world to execute the Father's commandment for the eternal life of mankind. As God's Incarnate Son, Jesus is in a royal position regarding mankind. However, because the Father sent him on a mission in a position equivalent to a vassal king, Jesus is in a subordinate, even though royal position, with regard to his Father. The Father is, therefore, likened to the "Great King" of the suzerainty treaties, while Jesus is likened to a vassal king.

---

141   Cf. also the texts which affirm this: Mt 7:17-18: "So every sound tree bears good fruit, but the bad tree bears evil fruit. A sound tree cannot bear evil fruit, nor can a bad tree bear good fruit;" Lk 6:43: "For no good tree bears bad fruit, nor again does a bad tree bear good fruit; for each tree is known by its own fruit."

142   Jn 14:28.

12.2.2. Relationship Between Jesus Messiah and His People

15:4   *"**Abide in me, and I in you**. As the **branch** cannot
         bear fruit by itself, unless it abides in the **vine**,
         neither can you, unless you abide in me."*

5   *"**I am the vine, you are the branches. He who
         abides in me**, and I in him, he it is that **bears much fruit**,
         for **apart from me you do can nothing**."*

The JLSA also speaks about the relationship between Jesus Messiah and his people in Jn 15:4, 5. Jesus likens this relationship to a vine and its branches. He defines the bond between God's people and himself in line with his office as Messiah-King. This relationship is parallel to that relationship between Messiah-with-People spoken of in the OT Royal Investiture Covenants of 1 Sam 12:1, 2, 2 Kgs 11:17b, and 2 Chr 23:3.

While a king might personify himself as the whole nation, no ruler would ever presume to use the allegory of the vine and the branches to define his relationship with his subjects. The imagery employed by Jesus indicates the **special character** of the union existing between himself and his disciples. It is not the ordinary moral bond between king and subjects. Here, Jesus speaks of his people as "abiding in" himself, and he abiding "in" them.

Because Jesus is absolutely essential to the "true" Israel, his disciples' union with him is necessarily more intimate than the moral tie between a usual sovereign and his subjects. This special union between Jesus and his disciples derives from their incorporation into him though a participation in his gift of his own divine filial life. They are so incorporated into Jesus that they live by his very own life: the eternal life of the only-begotten Son coming from the Father.

12.3. The Royal Provision Clause

17:2   *"... you have given him power over all flesh,
         to give eternal life to all whom you have given him."*

3   *"And **this is eternal life, that they know you the only true
         God and Jesus Christ whom you have sent**."*

As a report about a royal investiture covenant, the JLSA employs a Royal Provision Clause in OT tradition to present Jesus to mankind as the choice of God the Father (who is also called "Yahweh"[143]) to be Messiah-King of the New Israel. This clause speaks about the authority given to Jesus by the Father *"over all flesh"* for the purpose of bestowing eternal life, i.e. a share in the filial life of Jesus, a life he received from God his Father. The royal

---

143   Cf. Jn 8:54.

investiture of Jesus, his office and authority are, therefore, essentially linked to his bestowal of eternal life upon mankind.

However, the question arises as to why the JLSA Royal Provision Clause defines eternal life itself as *"**knowing**"* the only true God and him whom he sent, Jesus Christ. This verb, "to know," is used in the same manner in Hos 8:2, where the Israelites claim to *"know"* God within a covenantal context.[144] About this Riemann writes: "The people's claim to 'know' God (vs. 2) is almost certainly to be understood as a claim that they acknowledge his legitimate authority as overlord."[145] Riemann goes on to explain that the verb "to know" is occasionally used in this legal sense "… to refer to mutual recognition on the part of suzerain and vassal, and has its equivalent in the treaties...."[146] Hillers also points out that oftentimes when treating the relationship between Yahweh and Israel, the usage of the word "to know" in biblical Hebrew is borrowed from international relations. In Hittite and Akkadian texts, Near Eastern kings use "to know" in two technical legal senses: (1) to recognize as legitimate suzerain or vassal, and (2) to recognize treaty stipulations as binding.[147] Speaking about traces of the treaty genre in the OT, McCarthy notes the equation of the Hebrew word "know" (Hb *yd'*) with the Akkadian (*idu*). This Akkadian word signified in the treaty "to recognize" (in the political sense) and "to serve faithfully." McCarthy writes: "Perhaps Israel was called on to recognize Yahweh's lordship in an analogous sense and so to serve him. But *yd'* is a technical word in the liturgy and in wisdom circles with a very similar semantic field … each case must be studied carefully in its own right to find its true setting and exact import."[148]

Considering what Riemann, Hillers and McCarthy report about the use of the word "to know" within a covenantal context, there could be no more appropriate use of this verb than here in the Royal Provision Clause of the JLSA. Because of the covenantal context of the JLSA and the nature of Jn 17:3 as a Royal Provision Clause, **the verb "to know" in Jn 17:3 surely means to recognize and faithfully serve as true Lord the Father, who is "the only true God," and his incarnate Son, "Jesus Messiah."**[149]

By defining eternal life as recognizing and faithfully serving God and his Messiah as rightful Lord, the JLSA Royal Provision Clause thus clearly

---

144   Cf. Hos 8:1-3.

145   P.A. Riemann, "Mosaic Covenant," *IDB* , Suppl., p. 195.

146   *Ibid.*, pp. 195, 196.

147   Hillers, *Covenant, The History of a Biblical Idea*, pp.121-123.

148   McCarthy, *Old Testament Covenant*, p. 78.

149   For other such examples see Hos 2:22; 8:2; 13:4; Dt 4:39. Cf. McCarthy, *Treaty and Covenant*, pp. 168, 186, 288, 349; Brown, *The Gospel According to John*, II, 631; McKenzie, *DB*, p. 486.

proclaims and presents Jesus as God's choice for Messiah King. This Royal Provision Clause warns the people that, without the recognition of and faithful service to "the only true God" and "Jesus Messiah," it is impossible to attain eternal life.[150] The technical usage of the verb "to know" here in the JLSA seems further confirmed by the fact that, in connection with Jesus, John uses the royal title of the Messiah King of Israel: "Jesus *christos*" (Gr for "Messiah"). It is most extraordinary for Jesus to call himself by his own name together with this title.[151] However, considering the text's royal investiture context and its nature as a Royal Provision Clause, the title's use in Jn 17:3 is most logically and fittingly employed.

Both the use of *christos* and the statement that Jesus is sent by the Father serve to indicate the Son of man's subordination to the Father like the king of Ancient Israel was subordinate to Yahweh or like the vassal king to the Great King. Thus, Jn 17:3 well illustrates what Jesus said in Jn 14:28, that the Father is greater than he. It also affirms Jesus' sovereign place over all mankind because of his mission to bestow eternal life upon all persons.

The function of the OT Royal Provision Clause was to proclaim the kingship of the one being invested and to present him to the people as the choice of Yahweh himself. The text proposed in Jn 17:2, 3 as the JLSA Royal Provision Clause perfectly fulfills this function. It makes clear that God the Father is the suzerain who is setting up his Incarnate Son as Messiah over the kingdom of the New Israel. If people wish to obtain eternal life, they must recognize and faithfully serve as rightful Lord "the only true God" and "Jesus Messiah."

12.4. Historical Prologue

In treaty tradition, the Historical Prologue recalls the benefits bestowed by the suzerain upon his vassal *previous* to making covenant. The narration of these benefits served as an objective basis and a subjective incentive for

---

150   Cf. also Jn 20:31.

151   The name of Jesus with this title appears like this in only one other text, Jn 1:17, where it is used, like here, in relation to God's faithfulness to his covenant and promises. In Jn 17:3, however, Jesus *calls himself* by this title. This seems so strange that Brown says "it is anomalous that Jesus should call himself 'Jesus Christ'" (Brown, *The Gospel According to John*, II, 741). About Jn 17:3, Schnackenburg writes: "The name 'Jesus Christ' is unsuitable and contrary to the style of the prayer as a whole, as spoken by Jesus. There is only one other text in which this occurs. This is in 1:17, which is a commentary following the Logos hymn, but the name of 'Jesus Christ' is meaningful in this verse, in contrast with the name 'Moses'" (Schnackenburg, *The Gospel According to St. John*, III, 172). These comments are made because the commentators do not know that the JLSA is dealing with Jesus' royal investiture covenant. Jesus is the one to proclaim his Royal Provision Clause because he himself is the mediator of the JLSA Covenant.

the acceptance of the Great King's stipulations by the inferior king with his people. The Historical Prologue, along with the selective history, contained a great deal of parenesis or persuasive exhortation.

In accordance with the twofold covenant about which it reports, the JLSA Historical Prologue provides grounds for the parties' acceptance of the stipulations of the Royal Investiture Covenant. It lists, on the one hand, the benefits of the Father to Jesus Messiah, and, on the other hand, the benefits of both the Father and Jesus Messiah to the chosen people of the New Israel.

12.4.1. Benefits of the Father to Jesus Messiah

The texts indicated below make clear what Jesus Messiah owes to God his Father: his covenant election which brought him the gift of glory of the divine Sonship, his mission, his universal dominion and extraordinary authority, as well as his disciples. These benefits indicate the subordinate position of Jesus Messiah to his Father. In keeping with the treaty analogy, the enumerated benefits are both objectively and subjectively solid grounds for the acceptance by Jesus of the stipulations of his Royal Investiture Covenant. These benefits will now be examined individually.

12.4.1.1. Gift of Glory/Divine Name

Jesus speaks of two gifts he received from his Father: (1) the gift of glory in Jn 17:24 and (2) the gift of God's name in Jn 17:11,12.

- Gift of Glory:

17:22   *"The glory <u>which you have given me</u>...."*

24   *" ... my glory <u>which you have given me</u> in your love for me before the foundation of the world."*

- Gift of the <u>Divine Name</u>:

17:11   *"**Holy Father**, keep them in **your name, <u>which you have given me</u>** ...*

12   *... your name, <u>which you have given me</u>."*

In Jn 17:24, Jesus speaks about a gift of glory that he received from his Father as his personal heritage: *"...my glory which you have given me in your love for me before the foundation of the world."*

The Johannine Prologue speaks of "the glory of an only Son coming from the Father."[152] Could this be the glory/heritage of which Jesus speaks? Prat points out that Jesus receives "the glory of an only Son coming from the Father" by reason of his eternal generation as the Word of God.[153] This

---

152   Jn 1:14.
153   Prat, *Jesus Christ*, II, p. 306.

particular glory is in no way communicable to any other person. It belongs solely to God's only Son by reason of his eternal generation from the Father and, therefore, *before his incarnation.* Consequently, this cannot be the glory/heritage that Jesus shares with his disciples (see Jn 13:8; 17:22).

The glory of which Jesus speaks in Jn 17:24 is a **glory that he received from his Father as the God-Man**; it is a glory that belongs to him as God's *incarnate* Son. By this gift the Father united the human nature that the Son would assume to his divine nature in the Person of his Son. Because of this gift Jesus the man is truly God the Son: Jesus is both the Son of God and the Son of man.

According to Jn 17:24, the Father bestowed Jesus' gift of glory *by the operation of the divine paternal love*. Jesus is not speaking here of the glory that he had as the Son from his eternal generation because, *in the order of nature*, the paternal love of the Father follows the generation of the Son. (God must first have a Son before he can love him.) Instead, the gift of glory that Jesus speaks of in Jn 17:24 is the glory that the Father bestowed at the moment of his incarnation. Jesus received this gift by the operation of the divine paternal love (who is the Spirit[154]) that the Father had for him from his eternal generation. This operation of the divine paternal love in Jn 17:24 took place in time in the womb of the Blessed Virgin Mary.[155]

In theological language Jesus' gift of glory is called the "hypostatic union." By reason of this gift of glory, the man Jesus is the natural and only-begotten Son of God. It is precisely this glory that allowed Jesus to have exclusively God as his natural Father.[156] Jesus, the God-Man, shares this glory with his disciples by giving them to be reborn by the operation of the Spirit as God's children in himself.[157] In sharing his heritage, his divine Sonship, with his disciples, Jesus gives them, in the words of Peter, "to share in the divine nature."[158]

John also presents the above gift of glory as the gift of God's name of Father. Speaking to his Father in prayer, Jesus referred to this gift: "… *your name, which you have given me.*"[159] By reason of his gift of glory the man Jesus, as the natural Son of God, has the personal and exclusive right to God as Father. It was through the signal and unique grace of the hypostatic union that Jesus was able to call God by his name of "Father" in the univocal sense of the word.

---

154   See below in Chapter 14.
155   Cf. Lk 1:34: "The Holy Spirit will come upon you, and the power of the Most High will overshadow you; therefore the child to be born will be called holy, the Son of God."
156   Cf. Jn 17:11, 12.
157   Cf. Jn 1:12, 13; 3:3, 5, 6. This is the gift of adoptive sonship.
158   2 Pt 1:4.
159   Jn 17:11, 12.

The gifts of glory/divine name constitute God's revelation of his Fatherhood to Jesus. These two gifts are two ways of expressing the one benefit/heritage that Jesus received from his Father. The gift of glory/divine name made Jesus capable of accomplishing his mission of revealing God's Fatherhood to mankind: "No one has ever seen God; the only Son, who is in the bosom of the Father, he has made him known."[160] Since the Christian Covenant is ordered to the revelation of God's name of Father, Jesus' gift of glory/divine name constitutes Jesus' *covenant election*. This election is the special love of God whereby he chose Jesus to be his Incarnate Son and Messiah of the New Israel, "the first-born among many brothers."[161] It is this elective love for Jesus that God the Father perpetuates by the JLSA Covenant of Royal Investiture.[162]

12.4.1.2. Universal and Everlasting Authority

> 17:2   " *...you have given him power over all flesh, to give eternal life to all whom you have given him.*"

Since the JLSA reports about Jesus' royal investiture covenant, it speaks of the authority bestowed upon him by his Father. Because of his royal office as Messiah, Jesus' task is to bring all men to salvation, which means consequently to bestow eternal life upon men. This authority is, therefore, universal, extending to *every* human person without exception.

12.4.1.3. Disciples

> 17:6   " *... the men whom you gave me out of the world; they were yours, and you gave them to me ....*"
>
> 9   " *... those whom you have given me...*"
>
> 10   "*...all mine are yours, and yours are mine...*"
>
> 24   "*... they, also, whom you have given me ....*"

The above verses speak of those subject to Jesus' authority in a more limited and special sense. These are the ones whom the Father gave Jesus as "his own," those Jesus himself had chosen from the world. These disciples are a gift to Jesus from his Father. Included among these subjects are all those, until the end of time, who will believe in Jesus: "those who will believe in me through their word."[163]

---

160   Jn 1:18.
161   Rom 8:29.
162   Cf. Napier, B.D., "Prophet," *IDB*, III, p. 913. Napaier states that election is realized and perpetuated in covenant.
163   Jn 17:20.

12.4.2. Benefits of the Father and Jesus Messiah to People

The following texts indicate the benefits received by the people of the New Israel from God the Father and from Jesus Messiah. These benefits serve to elicit their gratitude and motivate them to accept the commandments in the Stipulation Clause.

12.4.2.1. Covenant Election

Bestowed by Jesus:

13:1   *"Having loved his own who were in the world."*

18   *" ... for I know **whom I have chosen.**"*

15:16   *"You did not choose me, but **I chose you.**"*

19   *"... I chose you out of the world."*

The JLSA speaks three times of Jesus choosing his people. They are his peculiar possession: *"his own."*[164] This term is similar to those used in the vassal treaty and in Deuteronomy.[165] The verb "to choose"—with God as subject and Israel as object—was only first used in Deuteronomy, even though Israel's concept and conviction of being "elected" was of ancient origin.[166] Speaking of this choice, Mendenhall states that "the religious meaning of God's 'choosing' must be looked for within the framework of the religious bond which held early Israel together. This can only be the covenant tradition."[167] Covenant is thus seen as maintaining and perpetuating the relationship initiated by election. In fact, as previously mentioned, covenant and election are correlative terms. The classical phrase denoting Yahweh's covenant election of his people in Deuteronomy is that they are a people *"peculiarly his own"* in the sense of his *peculiar property* or *treasure.*[168] This term describes a subject in connection with his duties as a vassal. It signifies that the person or persons so designated are favored, not by a natural, but by an *elected* relationship. It is a term used by the Great King for a favored vassal and is a motive for the vassal's obedience.[169] The people of the JLSA Covenant, just as the people of Yahweh in Deuteronomy, are objects of covenant election. Since it is Jesus who chose them, they are the objects of his personal covenant election; they are his people as vassal king.

Bestowed by the Father:

17:6   *"...the men whom you gave me out of the world;*
         they were yours, and you gave them to me..."

---

164   Cf. Jn 1:11; 13:1.
165   Cf. Dt 7:6; 14:2; 26:18.
166   Cf. G.E. Mendenhall, "Election," *IDB,* II, pp. 76, 77, 79.
167   Cf. G.E. Mendenhall, "Election," *IDB,* II, p. 79.
168   Dt 7:6; 14:2; 26:18.
169   Cf. McCarthy, *Treaty and Covenant,* pp. 162, 171, 270, 288.

> 9 *"...those whom you have given me, for they are yours."*
> 10 *"...all mine are yours, and yours are mine..."*

Yet, God the Father is also the one who bestows this covenant election since these people were and really are his own. He gave them to Jesus but they still belong to him. This is to say that Jesus elected or chose those persons whom the Father had predestined. Thus, the disciples of Jesus owe their covenant election to God the Father as well as to Jesus. They belong to both the Father and Jesus as their own special possession.

12.4.2.2. Protection

> 17:12 *"... I kept them in your name, which you have given me; I have guarded them, and none of them is lost but the son of perdition...."* [170]

The JLSA presents Jesus as battling with the ruler of this world. But Jesus kept careful watch over "his own" so that they were not harmed by the enemy. He protected them by revealing God to them as Father, i.e., by making them his Father's children. Thus, this protection of Jesus' subjects is a benefit they received both from Jesus and from the Father. Jesus preserved his people by reason of his own gift of covenant election whereby he received the gift of divine Sonship, a gift he calls his glory. Jesus kept those he had chosen from harm because the Father, to whom they also belong, chose them for Jesus.

12.5. Stipulation Clause

McCarthy calls the Stipulation Clause the "particular terms" of the treaty. The one general aim of the stipulations was to render "effective the object of the treaty-making by assuring the vassal's submission to and support of the ... kingdom." [171] The Stipulation Clause gave the detailed dimensions of covenant life; it defined the meaning of covenant fidelity by commanding what covenant

---

170   This verse continues with reference to Judas: "... but the son of perdition, that the scripture might be fulfilled." In Jn 13:18, again with reference to the role of Judas, Jesus would seem to indicate that the choice of Judas was no mistake. There was a purpose for Jesus' choice of Judas, and Jesus made his choice with full knowledge of what would happen. However, Jesus' purpose was not that Judas betray him but that the Scripture be fulfilled. Jesus' choice, therefore, involved permission, not approval. This seems to be indicated in Jn 13:27 where Jesus tells Judas: "What you are going to do, do quickly." Jesus freely accepted his death and how it was to take place; this was the command of his Father (Jn 10:7-18). It was by this death that Jesus would glorify the Father and show the world that he loves the Father (cf. Jn 14:30, 31). Jesus' death was the defeat of Satan, and the Fourth Gospel is very clear that Judas, by his own free choice, was an instrument of that illegitimate ruler. Jesus only sent Judas on his way once Judas allowed Satan to enter into his heart (Jn 13:27).

171   McCarthy, *Treaty and Covenant*, p. 57.

life involved.[172] It is very important to note, however, that the stipulations were not envisioned as conditions necessary for the treaty's continued existence. This is to say that the non-observance of the stipulations did not cancel the covenant and its obligations; this could only happen with the death of one of the parties. But it is true that whoever did not follow the stipulations rendered the family-like union *de facto* no longer extant, but only as far as they were concerned.[173] They were subject to the covenant curses for infidelity.

The function of the Stipulation Clause was to articulate in detail precisely how the vassal and his people were to live so as to preserve the family-like union in their daily life.[174] The JLSA stipulations are in accordance with the treaty tradition as it is reflected in Deuteronomy.

It is significant that each of the JLSA stipulations, in accordance with the treaty genre, is linked to the past history of benefits received. This history was intended to ground and motivate the vassal's total obedience, fidelity, and dedication.

12.5.1. Commandment of Love

The introduction to the JLSA Commandment of Love is found in Jn 13:14-17. In these verses Jesus instructs his disciples about the Footwashing's significance. This instruction is theologically grounded in the covenant union of the disciples with the Son of man. By incorporation into Jesus, the disciples share in his very mission and are commissioned to continue his mission: "As you (*i.e.* the Father) sent me into the world, so I have sent them into the world."[175] This is to say that the disciples are to accomplish their mission in union with Jesus. Through the fulfillment of their apostolic mandate, the world will come to believe in Jesus and in the mission that he received from the Father for mankind.[176]

The position of the introduction to the Commandment of Love indicates *the commandment's special relationship to the Eucharist* because it follows the Footwashing and immediately precedes the association of the betrayal by Judas in 13:21-31a[177] with the declaration of the glorification of the Son of man and of God in him in Jn 13:31b.

---

172   *Ibid.*, p. 185.
173   It is important to note the distinction here between *de facto* and *de jure*. *De facto* the union does not exist, but it does exist *de jure*.
174   McCarthy, *Treaty and Covenant*, p. 295.
175   Jn 17:18.
176   Cf. Jn 17: 20, 21.
177   Jn 13:31a is concerned with the betrayal of Judas. The mention of the betrayal was made by John just after the Footwashing and immediately before the statement of the double glorification to connect the Footwashing with the Eucharist in the Johannine analogy. It has been pointed out in Part I of this study how the betrayal is connected to the Eucharist in the Synoptic and Pauline Accounts of its institution and is part of Eucharistic tradition.

It is important to note that the Commandment of Love is in **two parts**: (1) for the nation of the New Israel as a whole, and (2) for the individual members of that nation.

12.5.1.1. For the New Israel

13:34   *"A new commandment I give you, that you love*
          one another; even as I have loved you, that
          you also love one another."

35   *"By this all men will know that you are my disciples,*
          if you have love for one another."

To whom is this command directed? Verses 34 and 35 follow upon the declaration that the glorifications of the Son of man and of God had just been accomplished. This declaration, through the Johannine analogy of the Footwashing/Eucharist, indicates that the New Israel had just been formed by the Eucharistic Covenant celebration. Jesus first commands his nation about how it is to exercise its *communal responsibility* in living out its covenant relationship together with him. The New Israel, one with its Messiah-king, must continue his mission in the world.

In this stipulation directed to the New Israel, its members are commanded to love one another just as Jesus loved them. However, the exact nature of Jesus' love is defined only in the second part of the Commandment of Love that is directed to each individual disciple.

12.5.1.2. For Individual Disciples

15: 9   *"As the Father has loved me, so I have loved you.*
          Abide in my love.

10   *If you keep my commandments, you will abide in my love,*
          just as I have kept my Father's commandments and
          abide in his love."

12   "This is **my commandment, that you love one another**
          as I have loved you.

13   *Greater love has no man than this, that a man lay down*
          his life for his friends.

14   *You are my friends if you do what I command you.*

15   *No longer do I call you servants, for the servant does not*
          know what his master is doing; but I have called you friends,
          for all that I have heard from my Father I have made known
          to you.

16   *You did not choose me, but I chose you and appointed you*
          *that **you should go and bear fruit and that your fruit***
          ***should abide;** so that whatever you ask the Father*

in my name, he may give it to you.
17   **This I command you, to love one another."**

This stipulation is based upon Jesus' statement in Jn 15:5 about his relationship with his disciples, which he likened to a vine and its branches. This stipulation, therefore, instructs each disciple how to live out **individually** in everyday life his or her covenant relationship with Jesus, the vine, and the Father, the vinedresser.

The content of this stipulation—love—is consistent with the previous stipulation for the nation of the New Israel. However, the communal Commandment of Love is only fully explained within the context of this stipulation directed to the individuals who make up the new Nation. This stipulation distinguishes personal responsibility from the communal responsibility of the whole nation to highlight the importance of the individual's commitment and fidelity since the whole is no greater than all its parts.

The first verse of this stipulation indicates the **nature of Jesus' love for his disciples**. Jesus says that he loved his disciples *in the same way that the Father loved him*. This verse is of *capital importance* because it reveals the *specific nature* of the love stipulated both for the New Israel[178] and for its individual members.[179]

The Historical Prologue indicated precisely how the Father loved Jesus: by giving him, at the time of his incarnation, a gift of glory/divine name that was the gift of divine Sonship. This gift is the revelation made to Jesus of God's name of Father. By reason of this gift, Jesus is the Incarnate Son of God, the God-Man. God the Father loved his Son by revealing his Fatherhood to Jesus. Jesus, in turn, loved his People when, "lifted up from earth" by means of the Eucharist of the Last Supper, he created the covenant union whereby men and women, being united to himself, share by grace in the revelation God made to him of his Fatherhood.

Therefore, when Jesus stated in Jn 15:9 that he loved his disciples just as the Father loved him, *he meant precisely that he loved his disciples by revealing God's Fatherhood to them, just as the Father loved him by revealing his Fatherhood to him.* The revelation of God's Fatherhood was accomplished through the bestowal and operation of the divine paternal love which is the Spirit. The divine paternal love belongs by exclusive right to Jesus as "the only Son coming from the Father."[180] His disciples possess God's paternal love only by reason of their union with Jesus through grace.

---

178   See Jn 13:34, 35.
179   See Jn 15:9, 12, 17.
180   Jn 1:14.

God can be Father of Jesus' disciples only if they are incorporated into him as branches of the true vine. Jesus is the unique access to God the Father: "No one comes to the Father but through me."[181]

The command of Jn 15:9 to remain in Jesus' love goes to the very heart of the relationship of Jesus Messiah and his disciples. Here Jesus speaks of the divine paternal love that belongs to him by unique right of his eternal generation. By the bestowal of, and through the operation of, this paternal love, Jesus incorporated the disciples into himself. He made them children of God in the only-begotten Son. Therefore, the command to remain in Jesus' love is but another indication of the disciples' utter dependence upon Jesus to fulfill the Commandment of Love. The commandment of Jn 15:9, therefore, prepares for the substance of what is stipulated in the "new commandment" of Jn 15:12,17.

Jn 15:12 states what Jesus' disciples must do to remain in his love, to remain part of him as branches of the vine. If Jesus' love for his disciples consisted in revealing to them the Fatherhood of God, Jesus' disciples must continue Jesus' own revelatory mission of God's Fatherhood. *The New Commandment ordains that the disciples must, together with Jesus Messiah, reveal God's Fatherhood to mankind.* In this way will every human be offered the choice of accepting the Christian Covenant of eternal life and effectively remaining part of that Covenant.

The New Commandment is essentially apostolic. It is a rephrasing of the apostolic commission in Mt 28:18-20: "*And Jesus came and said to them, 'All authority in heaven and on earth has been given to me. Go therefore and make disciples of all nations, baptizing them in the name of the Father and of the Son and of the Holy Spirit, teaching them to observe all that I have commanded you; and behold, I am with you always to the close of the age.'*"

The New Commandment governs not only the internal life of the New Israel but also that of the whole world.[182] In fact, the New Commandment is called "the fundamental law of human perfection and consequently of the transformation of the world."[183] The New Commandment entails both corporate and individual cooperation with Jesus for the revelation of God's Fatherhood. Only in the fulfillment of the New Commandment can the universal brotherhood of mankind be realized. This brotherhood is accomplished through the Fatherhood of God in his Son.[184]

---

181   Jn 14:6.
182   The Royal Provision Clause of Jn 17:2 indicates that the authority of Jesus extends over "all mankind" for the purpose of bestowing eternal life.
183   GS, n. 38.
184   Jn 17:18.

The command to reveal God's fatherhood in union with Jesus is the duty of the New Israel (Jn 13:34, 35) and of the individual members of the New Israel as branches of the vine (Jn 15:9,12,17). This commandment has all mankind as its object since all persons are called to be part of the Christian Covenant.[185]

The New Commandment may be better understood by comparing it to the two great commandments of the Mosaic Covenant.[186] The first requires the love of God with one's whole being; the second, love of one's neighbor as oneself. The New Commandment, however, does not speak about the love of God because it presupposes a far greater union of man with God than could ever be contemplated in the Mosaic Covenant. The New Commandment presupposes a covenant union with God through incorporation into his incarnate Son like branches on a vine. Moreover, the action commanded, both for God's nation and its individual members, is essentially supernatural. By his human nature alone man is absolutely incapable of fulfilling it. It can be performed uniquely by reason of incorporation into God's only Son: "… no one has ever seen God. It is God the only Son, ever at the Father's side, who has revealed him."[187]

Besides being apostolic, the **New Commandment is also essentially eucharistic**. While this commandment supposes the Christian Covenant relationship with the Father in the life and activity of his Son, it also supposes that union with Jesus' life and activity be specifically within the Eucharistic Sacrifice. The action whereby Jesus reveals God's Fatherhood is that very sacrifice which is enveloped and made present in the celebration of the Eucharist. The Eucharistic Sacrifice, in establishing the Christian Covenant, glorified the Son of man as Messiah-King and glorified God in the Son of man. It accomplished both these glorifications through the revelation of God's Fatherhood. Therefore, fulfilling the Commandment of Love is grounded upon a living participation in Jesus' love and activity that are made present in the Eucharistic Sacrifice. For this reason the document, *Eucharisticum mysterium*, states that one who participates in Holy Mass "… will seek to fill the world with the Spirit of Christ and 'in all things, in the very midst of human affairs, to become a witness of Christ.'"[188] This activity of filling the world with the Spirit of Christ is the work of evangelization which has as its goal "to serve man by revealing to him the love of God made manifest in Jesus Christ."[189] This love of God that is to be revealed is

---

185   Cf. Jn 12:44-50; 17:2.
186   Dt 6:5; Lv 19:18; cf. also Mt 22:34-40; Mk 12:29-31.
187   Jn 1:18.
188   EM, n. 14; cf. also PO, n. 4.
189   RM, n. 2.

precisely God's paternal love. It became manifest through the revelation of his Fatherhood by his only Son.

The work of evangelization is, therefore, clearly connected with the Eucharistic Sacrifice. While this revelation was made upon the cross, it was *first*—before Good Friday—made present to mankind by the Eucharist of the Last Supper. It continues to be made present in the Sacrifice of the Mass. Thus, to fulfill the New Commandment is to evangelize in union with Jesus Messiah through the Eucharistic Mystery.

The work of evangelization incumbent upon the disciples of Jesus Christ has Christian conversion as its aim: "a complete and sincere adherence to Christ and his Gospel through faith."[190] This conversion consists in "accepting, by a personal decision, the saving sovereignty of Christ and becoming his disciple."[191] However, to be an evangelizer one must be evangelized in order to perfect what was begun at baptism by the revelation of God's Fatherhood. To be an evangelizer one must be God the Father's faithful little child[192] who shares "in the image of his Son, that the Son might be the first-born of many brothers."[193] This is evangelical holiness. Pope John Paul II pointed out: "What truth of the Gospel message is, in fact, more fundamental and more universal than this one: God is our Father and we are His children?"[194] Spiritual childhood is the spirituality of the Gospel and it is genuine eucharistic spirituality; it is the spirituality of authentic worshipers of God the Father, those who adore him "in spirit and in truth."[195] It is the spirituality commanded by Jesus Christ as necessary for entrance into the kingdom of heaven.

Speaking about the treaty's peculiar genre of commanding love, McCarthy notes that some Hittite stipulation clauses stated that "one must even be ready to die for his lord and no man has greater love than this."[196] In Jn 15:13, however, the command is indirect because Jesus makes a statement about his own love. But since the disciples' intensity of love is to imitate that of Jesus, Jn 15:3 means that the physical element of suffering or even death is not discounted when carrying out the Commandment of Love. Actually, the way this command is articulated is much more powerful than a direct command. It is founded upon the behavior of Jesus who, though "lord

---

190   *Ibid.*, n. 46.
191   *Ibid.*
192   Cf. Mt 19:14; Mk 10:15; Lk 18:16, 17.
193   Rom 8:29.
194   Homily at Lisieux, n. 2, June 2, 1980.
195   Cf. Jn 4:23, 24.
196   McCarthy, *Treaty and Covenant*, p. 161. It should be noted how this command bears an uncanny resemblance to Jn 15:13: "There is no greater love than this: to lay down one's life for one's friends."

and master," gave his life for his slaves whom he has chosen and made his friends. As mentioned before, this talk of "lord," "master," "slaves," "chosen ones," and "friends" is typical treaty vocabulary and was used to obtain the total dedication required by the sovereign.

12.5.2. Prohibition of Relationship with World

> 15:18   *"If the world hates you, know it has hated me*
> *before it hated you.*
>
> 19   **If you were of the world**, *the world would love its own;*
> *but because you are not of the world, but* **I chose you**
> **out of the world;** *therefore the world hates you. "*

This stipulation prohibiting relationship with the world regards the exclusivity of the relationship of the people of the New Israel with God the Father and Jesus, his Messiah. This exclusivity derives from the fact that these people were chosen precisely out of the world to belong to the Father. The present stipulation recalls the exclusivity of Israel in Dt 7:6-8: "For you are a people sacred to the LORD, your God; he has chosen you from all the nations on the face of the earth to be a people peculiarly his own ... because the LORD loved you ...." Exclusivity is also a typical treaty command. The vassal was to be a friend only to the overlord's friends and an enemy to all his enemies.[197]

The JLSA presents Jesus in opposition to the devil, "the ruler of this world,"[198] whose illegitimate kingdom is opposed to the kingdom of "Jesus Messiah" and of his Father, "the only true God."[199] The JLSA also indicates Satan's subjects: those to whom Jesus has come and spoken but who have not accepted his word.[200] Jesus has come into the world as its light to speak the Father's word, his commandment of eternal life for all men.[201] It is precisely by refusing to accept this mighty and powerful royal word proclaiming the Eucharistic Covenant that man incurs guilt.

Though the imperative forms are lacking in this stipulation, we have here an example of a most powerful and convincing way of commanding. This command is a perfect example of what a treaty stipulation should be. McCarthy notes that the precise purpose of every stipulation was to deny the vassal any other choice but to obey.[202] The vassal had already made an irrevocable choice by consenting to the covenant; there is no other choice left

---

197   Cf. McCarthy, *Treaty and Covenant*, pp. 32, 56, n. 27; Mendenhall, "Covenant," *IDB*, p. 714.
198   Jn 14:30; 16:11; cf. Jn 12:31.
199   Jn 17:3.
200   Cf. Jn 15:22 and the Proclamation of Covenant in 12:44-50.
201   Cf. Jn 12:50.
202   Cf. McCarthy, *Treaty and Covenant*, p. 235.

but to render perfect service to the overlord. This stipulation commands the unswerving loyalty required by treaty tradition.

This loyalty is ultimately based upon the vassal's covenant election by the sovereign. Jesus chose his people from the world.[203] This recalls what he said shortly before: "You did not choose me, but I chose you ...."[204] The concept of election goes back to the term, "his own," which was used to designate Jesus' disciples in Jn 13:1. Nonetheless, there is no doubt that at some time or other election demands the inferior's consent. In the JLSA Covenant, the disciples' consent was given at the Footwashing. However, since the overlord's election is antecedent to the consent of the inferior and is the basis for his making covenant with the inferior, the overlord's election is of far greater importance than the inferior's consent to accept the covenant. Thus, because of the honor which Jesus bestowed upon his disciples by choosing them, Jesus takes it for granted that his disciples could not possibly belong to or have anything to do with the kingdom of the world, which is diametrically opposed to his own.

This stipulation commanding exclusive relationship very much resembles Dt 14:2, where Yahweh's people are forbidden to imitate practices implying a tie to other lords because "the Lord has chosen you to be a people for his own possession, out of all the peoples that are on the face of the earth."[205]

12.5.3. Absolute Faith and Complete Confidence

12:44   ***"He who believes in me**, believes not in me but in him who sent me."*

14:1   ***"Let not your hearts be troubled; believe in God, believe also in me."***[206]

27   ***"Let not your hearts be troubled, neither let them be afraid."***[207]

16:33   ***"Be of good cheer, I have overcome the world."***

Often the treaty, along with prohibitions against murmuring or uttering unfriendly words about the sovereign, contained exhortations to trust the sovereign, to believe and have complete confidence in him, even when circumstances would seem to indicate otherwise.[208] This is because treaty tradi-

---

203   Cf. Jn 15:19.

204   Jn 15:16.

205   Cf. McCarthy, *Treaty and Covenant*, p. 171.

206   This translation was made directly from the Greek text. Brown notes that the word for "heart" is in the singular according to the Aramaic and Hebrew preference for a distributive singular (*The Gospel According to John*, II, 618).

207   See preceding footnote.

208   Cf. Mendenhall, "Covenant," *IDB*, I, p. 715; JBC, [77:79], p. 749; McCarthy, *Treaty and Covenant*, pp. 82, 83.

tion is concerned with *personal* relationship, not impersonal contractual relationship. Thus, this type of exhortation was natural to the treaty genre. The treaty aimed at obtaining that total commitment and dedication to the lord that had already been pledged by oath. There was no longer any choice.[209]

In the very opening words of the Proclamation of Covenant, Jesus requires faith in himself. He says that this faith is placed not so much in himself as in the One who sent him. These commands, calling for absolute faith, complete confidence and dedication, are based upon the blessings promised by Jesus. They are not, as in Deuteronomy, grounded by historical narrative or hortatory material about having seen and witnessed the power of God or of Jesus. The power and might of both Jesus and God are taken for granted here. The previous part of the Fourth Gospel as well as the JLSA Historical Prologue provide ample signs of the power of God and Jesus. The fact that this power is so obviously taken for granted demonstrates how much more intimate this Christian Covenant is than the Mosaic Covenant in Deuteronomy.

12.6. Divine Witness Clause

In the Ancient Near East the distinction between covenant and contract was clear. The contract was a human affair and consequently could be enforced before a court through the testimony of witnesses. However, the covenant's binding force derived from its oath invoking the deity as witness. Because of this oath of the vassal the deity became judge, guarantor, and avenger of the covenant. As witness, the deity would judge the conduct of the parties regarding their fidelity to the covenant stipulations. Then, as guarantor and avenger of the covenant, the deity would mete out accordingly the blessings or curses listed in the Curse-Blessing Formula.

The JLSA Divine Witness Clause names the Paraclete and the disciples of Jesus as the covenant witnesses. There is no difficulty regarding the Paraclete as a divine witness. However, the fact that Jesus also named his disciples as witnesses requires some examination.

12.6.1. The Paraclete

14:16   *"And I will ask the Father, and he will give you **another Paraclete**, to be with you forever, even **the Spirit of truth** ...."*

15:26   *"But when **the Paraclete** comes, whom I shall send to you from the Father, even the Spirit of truth, who proceeds form the Father, he **will bear witness to me** ...."*

---

209   Cf. McCarthy, *Treaty and Covenant*, p. 235.

> 16:8   *"And when he comes, **he will convince the world of sin and of righteousness and of judgment;***
>
> 9   *of sin, because they do not believe in me;*
>
> 10   *of righteousness, because I go to the Father, and you will see me no more;*
>
> 11   *of judgment, because the ruler of this world is judged."*

The Spirit appears at the very beginning of the Fourth Gospel.[210] He has a most prominent place in the life and career of Jesus Messiah and is the vital principle for the new birth of men.[211] The Spirit is also called the "holy Spirit"[212] and "the Spirit of truth."[213]

What does the designation "holy" signify when applied to the Spirit? The Spirit is "holy" by reason of his origin and mission from the Father and the Son. The Father is "holy"[214] because he is "the only true God,"[215] "the Holy One of Israel."[216] God's holiness is the most perfect designation of his nature because holiness is God's innermost reality, the sum total of all his attributes. God's holiness makes him different (separate) from everything else. God is all goodness and therefore righteous by his very nature. He demonstrates his holiness by his activity, especially by saving Israel because of his covenant relationship. The Spirit is a divine Person together with the Father and the Son, and his earthly mission is to cooperate with the Father and Jesus for the salvation of Israel.

The specification of the Spirit as "the Spirit of truth," apart from referring to his origin from the Father who is "the only true God," also points out the Spirit's particular relationship to Jesus, who is "the truth."[217] As "the truth," Jesus executes the Father's faithfulness to his covenantal relationship with Israel. And since Jesus is personally the truth of the Father, the designation "the Spirit of truth," associates the Spirit's role in the saving design of the Father to the mission of Jesus.

The JLSA uses the term "Paraclete" four times.[218] The JLSA speaks of the Spirit as "Paraclete" for the first time in Jn 14:16. The JLSA refers

---

210   Jn 1:32, 33.
211   Cf. Jn 3:3-8.
212   Cf. Jn 1:33; 14:26; 20:22.
213   Cf. Jn 14:17; 15:26; 16:13.
214   Jn 17:11.
215   Jn 17:3.
216   Cf. 2 Kgs 19:22; Ps 71:22; 78:41; 89:19; Sir 50:17; Is 1:4; 5:19, 24; 10:20; 12:6; 17:7; 29:19; 30:11,12,15; 31:1; 37:23; 41:14, 16, 20; 43:3, 14; 45:11; 47:4; 48:17; 49:7; 54:5; 55:5; 60:9, 14; Jer 50:29; 51:5.
217   Jn 14:6.
218   See Jn 14:16, 26; 15:26; 16:7.

three times to the Paraclete as "the Spirit of truth"[219] and once as "the holy Spirit."[220]

Jesus calls the Spirit "another Paraclete"[221] because he, Jesus, is the first Paraclete. However, because Jesus is to return to the Father, the Spirit takes his place with the disciples as *"another* Paraclete." Thus, in this role the Spirit's mission is a continuation of and dependent upon the mission of Jesus himself. As originator of these saving missions, the Father is "just"[222] because he upholds his covenant relationship with Israel.

"Paraclete" (Gr. *parakletos*) is a combination of two Greek words: *para* meaning "near to" or "by the side of," and *kaleo* meaning "to call to" or "to send for." This word is not used in the Septuagint and only five times in the NT.[223] Etymologically, "paraclete" indicates one who is called to assist and help. The active sense of the word indicates one who gives helpful service, who counsels, exhorts, strengthens and comforts another.[224] In its passive sense, "paraclete" has a forensic meaning as one who is called in the capacity of a prosecuting attorney.[225] Schnackenburg notes that in this sense "paraclete" is related to a Hebrew and Aramaic term that signifies a defending counsel.[226]

In the JLSA, the Paraclete is called to witness to the Royal Investiture Covenant by which God establishes the Son of man as Messiah of the New Israel. All mankind is commanded to be part of the New Israel. The JLSA Proclamation of Covenant states that man will be condemned for not accepting the word which Jesus spoke at the Father's command;[227] and that word is Jesus Christ himself. Thus, since the JLSA Covenant is precisely concerned with this Word's royal investiture, persons will be judged on their acceptance or rejection of Jesus as Messiah-king. This is clearly enunciated in the Royal Provision Clause: to obtain eternal life, every person must recognize and faithfully serve as rightful Lord "the only true God and Jesus Christ whom you have sent."[228]

"Paraclete" in its forensic sense is well suited to the function of the divine witness in vassal treaty tradition. In this tradition the deity is called to

---

219   See Jn 14:17; 15:26; 16:13.
220   See Jn 16:13.
221   Jn 14:16.
222   Jn 17:25.
223   Cf. Jn 14:16, 26; 15:26; 16:7; 1 Jn 2:1.
224   Cf. G.W.H. Lampe, "Paraclete," *IDB*, III, 654.
225   Cf. Brown, *The Gospel According to John,* II, p. 1136; Nolli, *Evangelo Secondo Giovanni*, 590.
226   Cf. Schnackenburg, *The Gospel According to St. John,* III, 139-150.
227   Cf. Jn 12:48, 49.
228   Jn 17:3.

witness as judge, protector, guarantor and avenger of the covenant. By proving the world wrong about its behavior regarding the person and mission of Jesus Christ, the Spirit's activity as Paraclete in its forensic sense is well suited to the function of the divine witness, whose task is to witness to the parties' fidelity or infidelity regarding the Great King's Covenant. The Spirit is sent as a divine witness to the conduct of humanity regarding the acceptance or rejection of Jesus and his covenant. With regard to the followers of the "ruler of this world," the Spirit, in his capacity of a prosecuting attorney, bears witness to the Father, the Great King, against the world for its refusal to accept the royal enthronement covenant by which the Father has set up his Son Jesus as Messiah of his kingdom.

The JLSA carefully explains how the Paraclete will execute his mission of Divine Witness. In continuing Jesus' saving mission from the Father, the Paraclete bears witness on behalf of Jesus by proving the world wrong in its refusal to *"know (i.e.* acknowledge and faithfully serve as rightful Lord) you, the only true God, and Jesus Christ whom you have sent."[229] Because of the world's refusal to accept Jesus' Royal Investiture Covenant, the Paraclete will convict the world for its understanding of sin, because sin ultimately consists in rejecting Jesus Christ whom God sent to reveal his Fatherhood. The Paraclete will show that the world was mistaken in its understanding of righteousness since it was Jesus who was found righteous before God and was resurrected from the dead. Furthermore, the Paraclete will prove the world wrong about judgment, for it is not Jesus but Satan, the ruler of this world, who is rightfully the object of a condemnatory sentence.

12.6.2. The Disciples

15:27   *"And **you also are witnesses, because you have been with me from the beginning.**"*

The introduction of human witnesses into the Divine Witness Clause is foreign to the vassal treaty genre. In the Ancient Near East, one of the clear differences between the contract and treaty consisted in their witnesses. Should it be necessary to terminate the contract or enforce its terms, human witnesses could be obliged to testify in court. The treaty, however, being a sacred agreement sworn by oath, was solely subject to the divine forum. The only witnesses to the treaty were the various gods of the suzerain and vassal. The treaty had no human witnesses. While it is true that at certain times human witnesses were included in a treaty document containing transcriptions of former treaties, these witnesses were named to certify the validity of the transcriptions rather than to sanction the treaty as the deity.[230]

---

229   Jn 17:3.
230   Cf. McCarthy, *Treaty and Covenant*, p. 71, n. 67.

Jos 24 has many details from treaty tradition. In Jos 24:22, Joshua calls the people to be witnesses "against yourselves" when they are about to renew their covenant with Yahweh. It might seem at first hand that this invocation of humans as witnesses at a covenant celebration might be a precedent for the JLSA's designation of human covenant witnesses. This, however, is not the case. What in Jos 24:22 seems like the summoning of the people as witnesses, is really a self-conditioned curse. The passage is, therefore, only a parallel to summoning the deity in treaty tradition since being witnesses "against themselves" means that the people are cursing themselves.[231]

In the JLSA, there are no ominous overtones evoked with regard to the disciples as there are for the people in Jos 24. The disciples are clearly called to be witnesses of the JLSA Royal Investiture Covenant. The disciples of Jn 15:27 are given the special honor of being chosen to be witnesses over all mankind, together with the Paraclete, the Spirit of truth, regarding the acceptance or rejection of Jesus as Messiah king.

The NT has a tradition that sheds light upon the problem of human witnesses in the JLSA Covenant. According to the tradition found in Luke and in the Acts of the Apostles, one of the special offices of Jesus' disciples is to be his witnesses.[232] Again, along the same lines, but expressed in a manner more like the concept of the divine witnesses in treaty tradition, the disciples in Matthew and Luke are to be seated upon twelve thrones judging the twelve tribes of Israel.[233] It is interesting that Jesus' affirmation in Luke was made precisely at the Last Supper when a discussion arose among the apostles about who should be regarded as the greatest. Thus, this NT tradition and the JLSA shed light upon each other.

In the JLSA the disciples, because of their association with the divine mission of the Paraclete in the work of judging mankind, should not be seen as if they were gods who apply sanctions by their proper power. Rather, they have been appointed to share in the witnessing of the Paraclete through the mission they received. They, like the Spirit of truth and together with him, have their mission from Jesus who is the truth.

However, who, precisely, are the disciples Jesus is naming as covenant witnesses? Are they only those to whom Jesus was speaking at the Last Supper, or does the "you" include all the disciples of Jesus until the end of time? The solution depends upon the meaning of the qualifying phrase: "... *for you have been with me from the beginning.*"

---

231   Cf. McCarthy, *Treaty and Covenant*, p. 230.
232   Lk 24:48; Acts 1:8, 22; 2:32; 3:15; 5:32; 10:39, 42; 13:31.
233   Mt 19:28; Lk 22:30.

If "from the beginning" (Gr. *ap'arches*) signifies the commencement of Jesus' public ministry, then the clause is restrictive and can mean that only the Twelve are designated as covenant witnesses. Brown is of this opinion, and it seems to be the correct interpretation:

> "In the setting of the Last Supper, *ap'arches* means from the beginning of Jesus' ministry when disciples began to follow him.... The theme that those who were with Jesus during his ministry were privileged witnesses is found also in the Lucan writings: Luke i 2 speaks of "those who from the beginning were eyewitnesses"; Acts i 21 specifies that the place of Judas had to be filled from "the men who accompanied us during all the time that the Lord Jesus went in and out among us."[234]

On the other hand it is possible to see the "you" in Jn 15:27 as referring to those designated by "his own" in Jn 13:1. Thus, Jesus would be speaking of all those who have a common origin in the eternal counsels of God and were represented by the disciples present at the Last Supper. Or again, the "you" of Jn 15:27 could refer to all the disciples who had been with Jesus "from the beginning" which, in this case, would mean "since their conversion."[235]

However, substantially the same phrase, "from the beginning," is used just three verses later in Jn 16:4b, where it clearly means "from the commencement of Jesus' public ministry."[236] Thus, with due consideration of the text and context—because the two phrases follow in such close succession, and because there is nothing to indicate any difference in usage—it would seem that the two phrases have the same meaning: at the beginning of Jesus' public ministry. If this is so, then the disciples designated as witnesses of the Christian Covenant are only those present at the Last Supper, those who were with Jesus from the commencement of his public ministry. This would, moreover, be most consonant with the traditions in Matthew and Luke which speak specifically about "twelve thrones."

12.7. Curse-Blessing Formula

Certain elements were never absent from the treaties because they were considered essential. These elements were the list of obligations to be assumed (Stipulation Clause) and the invocation of the deity as witness to the oath (Divine Witness Clause) together with the list of divine sanctions (Curse-Blessing Formula). The sanctions in the Curse-Blessing Formula had the purpose of enforcing the stipulations that indicated how the family-like union was to be lived. These sanctions were designated in view of the fidelity or infidelity of the covenanting parties. Thus, the abovementioned three es-

---

234   Cf. Brown, *The Gospel According to John*, II, 690.
235   Cf. Brown, *The Gospel According to John*, II, 690.
236   Cf. Brown, *The Gospel According to John*, II, 704.

sential elements of the treaty genre were closely connected: the observance of the stipulations was assured by the deity who, having been made witness to the covenant because of the oath, would surely bestow blessings upon the faithful party or execute curses upon the unfaithful one.

The treaty speaks of curses or blessings as specific harms or benefits invoked from the deity by the suzerain as punishment for an unfaithful vassal or as recompense for a faithful vassal. The Johannine texts that are proposed as curses and blessings resemble other OT passages that are more properly called threats, promises, or conditioned predictions.[237] A curse or blessing is a human being's imprecation or prayer directed to the deity for harm or benefit upon someone. The difficulty arises here when applying the definition of a human thing such as a blessing or curse to God himself. God does not pray for something to happen but merely states that it will happen, either certainly or under particular conditions. The terms of the JLSA Covenant depend entirely upon God who personally established it. Consequently, while the Johannine texts proposed here, like similar OT texts, are only analogously called curses and blessings, they are in the position of and perform the function of the curses and blessings invoked by the suzerain of treaty tradition.

The curses and blessings of the JLSA Covenant will now be individuated and examined. Where pertinent, their resemblance to the curses and blessings in Deuteronomy will be indicated.

In general, the principal blessing of Deuteronomy was life. This blessing was associated with the blessing of the Promised Land. The principal curse of Deuteronomy was death. Moses, having concluded the covenant, declared to Israel: "See, I have set before you this day life and good, death and evil. If you obey the commandments of the LORD your God which I command you this day ... you shall live and multiply, and the LORD your God will bless you in the land which you are entering to take possession of it" (Dt 30:15, 16); "I have set before you life and death, blessing and curse; therefore choose life, that you and your descendants may live.... for that means life to you and length of days, that you may dwell in the land which the LORD swore to your fathers, to Abraham, to Isaac, and to Jacob, to give them" (Dt 30:19).[238] While the JLSA's principal curse and blessing are similar to those of Deuteronomy, they are also vastly different.

The JLSA reports about the Royal Investiture Covenant of Jesus Messiah. This covenant concerns the action whereby "the only true God" invested his incarnate Son, Jesus the Son of man, as Messiah king of the New Israel. Jesus

---

237   Cf. McCarthy, *Treaty and Covenant*, p. 11.
238   Cf. also Dt 32:46, 47. In Deuteronomy, life and death are tied to the land as either a blessing or a curse (*e.g.* Dt 4:11, 40; 5:33, etc.). See also Clifford, *Deuteronomy*, pp. 147-150.

has been given authority over all mankind. Consequently, every human person owes him absolute obedience and submission. This is very clear in the JLSA Proclamation of Covenant (Jn 12:44-50). Those who reject the JLSA Royal Investiture Covenant—either by refusal to accept it or by infidelity to it—are subjects of the illegitimate ruler of this world and are consequently liable to the JLSA curses. Those who accept and are faithful to the JLSA Covenant are living branches of the true vine and benefit from the covenant blessings.

12.7.1. Curses

There are two curses in the JLSA Covenant, and they cover all possible cases. There is a curse for refusal to accept the Christian Covenant and another curse for those who, having accepted it, subsequently prove to be unfaithful.

12.7.1.1. Curse for Refusal to Accept the JLSA Covenant

13:8　　*"If I do not wash you, you have no part with me."*

The first curse is contained in Jesus' answer to Peter's refusal to allow Jesus to wash his feet. This washing, according to Jn 15:1-4, is a very special one. To accept the washing is to accept the Father's covenant command of eternal life that Jesus presents in the Proclamation of Covenant.[239] This acceptance, because of the specific nature of the JLSA Covenant, signifies the acceptance of the revelation of God as Father and the royal investiture of God's Messiah.[240] Peter's refusal to be washed was a refusal to accept Jesus' mission from the Father.[241] Peter's response, therefore, was tantamount to a refusal of the JLSA Covenant. It consisted in a refusal to "*know* (*i.e.* recognize and faithfully serve as true Lord) you the only true God, and Jesus Christ whom you have sent."[242] Jesus declares that a person who refuses this covenant can have no part with him, which is to say, no share in his heritage.[243] The heritage Jesus shares with his disciples is essentially his own divine filial life. Jesus received this life from the Father and it is called "eternal life" in Jn 12:50 and Jn 17:2, 3. Since those who do not accept the JLSA Covenant cannot share Jesus' heritage of eternal life with him, the curse of Jn 13:8 clearly signifies eternal death.

12.7.1.2. Curse for Infidelity to the Covenant

15:6　　*"If a man does not abide in me, he is cast forth* as a branch and withers, and the branches are gathered, thrown *into the fire and burned."*

239　　Cf. Jn 12:44-50.
240　　Cf. Jn 17:2,3.
241　　Cf. Jn 14:31.
242　　Cf. Jn 17:3.
243　　See the explanation of the word "heritage" in Chapter 1.

This second curse follows upon the statement of Jesus wherein he describes his relationship with those who accept the Christian Covenant but are unfaithful to it. Jesus is "the true vine" and his disciples are "the branches." Whoever remains in Jesus produces fruits that glorify the Father.[244] However, if a person does not produce these fruits, the reason is that such a person is not faithfully living the covenant union. Such a person is an unproductive branch. That unproductive branch, therefore, by its own will, does not remain in Jesus, because Jesus is the true vine which *only* and *always* produces fruit pleasing to the Father. The true vine *cannot* ever produce bad fruit. Consequently, the unfaithful person's fate is to wither, be rejected, and thrown into the fire and burned. This description resembles the image of the judgment upon Israel because of its deliberate rejection of Yahweh in Ez 15:4-6 and 19:12.

12.7.2. Blessings

The following are the blessings promised for acceptance of and fidelity to the Royal Investiture Covenant of Jesus as Messiah.

12.7.2.1. Eternal Life

12:50   *"And I know that **his commandment is eternal life**.*
         What I say, therefore, I say as the Father has bidden me."

17:2   *"since you have given him (Jesus) power over all flesh,*
         to give eternal life to all whom you have given him."

3   *"And this is eternal life, that they know you, the only true*
         God, and Jesus Christ whom you have sent."

The principal covenant blessing of Deuteronomy is life. That life was understood as a nearness to God in the Promised Land. The deuteronomic blessing, however, is vastly different from the covenant blessing of *"eternal life"* in the JLSA.

The JLSA Proclamation of Covenant explains that the Father's commandment is one of "eternal life."[245] This life is the substance of Jesus' message and the object of his mission. In order to receive it, one must put faith and trust in Jesus and in the Father who sent him.

The Royal Provision Clause itself states that the Father gave Jesus authority over all mankind precisely so that he might bestow eternal life. The blessing of eternal life, therefore, is immediately connected with Jesus' Royal Investiture Covenant. The Royal Provision Clause defines the mes-

---

244   Cf. Jn 15:8.
245   Jn 12:50.

sianic blessing of eternal life precisely as the acceptance of Jesus Messiah's Royal Investiture Covenant. It determines that eternal life is recognizing and faithfully serving as rightful Lord the only true God and him whom God has sent, Jesus Messiah. This is restating what was substantially said in the Proclamation of Covenant where the Father's commandment is, *i.e.* means, eternal life. To fulfill this commandment one must recognize and serve faithfully as true Lord, Jesus and the One who sent him.

But while the JLSA defines eternal life as the acceptance of the Christian Covenant, it also explains this life in other ways. Eternal life is a sharing in the personal heritage of Jesus, the Son of God incarnate;[246] it is the life that Jesus received from the Father,[247] the Father's gift of glory to his Son.[248] The disciples of Jesus Messiah share in his life by incorporation into him through grace. This life consists in the revelation of God's Fatherhood. It is the object of Jesus' messianic mission for all mankind.

Jesus is the source of eternal life for his faithful disciples. However, this would be evident to his disciples only at a time after the Last Supper. Jesus told them in Jn 14:19, 20: "Yet a little while, and the world will see me no more, but you will see me; because I live, you will live also. In that day you will know that I am in my Father, and you in me, and I in you." Jesus spoke these words with reference to the time when he would have received his heavenly glorification at the side of his Father and the Spirit of truth would have come as "another Paraclete."[249]

In Jn 14:20, Jesus explains more about the eternal life of which he is the source. Jesus indicates that the relationship of his disciples to himself brings them into a relationship with the Father, whose commandment is eternal life.[250] The relationship of Jesus to his Father is immediate and direct: "I am in my Father."[251] However, the faithful disciples of Jesus do not have an immediate and direct relationship to Jesus' Father. Jesus does not speak of "our" Father, but of "my" Father. The relationship of Jesus' disciples to his Father is founded upon their incorporation into Jesus.[252] Jesus is the unique way to the Father, according to his words in Jn 14:6: "... no one comes to the Father but through me." For this reason Jesus is the source of eternal life for his faithful disciples. By participation in the eternal life of the Son of God incarnate, human persons enter by grace into the very unity of the Godhead.

---

246   Cf. Jn 13:8.
247   Cf. Jn 5:26; 6:57; Brown, *The Gospel According to John*, I, 507.
248   Cf. Jn 17:22, 24.
249   Cf. Jn 17:5. This function of the Paraclete as a covenant blessing will be explained below.
250   Cf. Jn 12:50; 17:2, 3.
251   Cf. Jn 14:11, 20; cf. Jn 17:21-23.
252   Cf. Jn 14:11, 20; 17:21-23, 26.

Jesus also states the conditions for obtaining the blessing of eternal life. The first parts of Jn 14:21 and 23 contain conditions which link the various aspects of the blessing of eternal life to the Stipulation Clause: "He who has my commandments and keeps them, he it is who loves me. … If a man loves me, he will keep my word." The connection of the blessings to fidelity to covenant stipulations is normal treaty practice, a practice followed in the central portion of Deuteronomy. The blessing was another motivation for observing the stipulations. The blessing of eternal life is conditioned by the disciple's love for Jesus.[253] Obedience to his commandments[254] and loyalty to his word[255] demonstrate this love. The blessing of eternal life is conditioned upon love for Jesus because of his divine Personality and office. Thus, the conditions to obtain the blessing of eternal life are in line with both the Proclamation of Covenant and the Royal Provision Clause of the Royal Investiture Covenant.

The JLSA indicates the various aspects of the blessing of eternal life. They are the possession of the Father's love, the possession of the love of Jesus and his self-manifestation, and the state of peace.

The first aspect of the blessing of eternal life is to be loved by the Father. Jesus states this in Jn 14:21: "He who has my commandments and keeps them, he it is who loves me, and he who loves me will be loved by my Father." In fact, the faithful disciples who accept the covenant are made parties to it by the bestowal of the divine paternal love according to Jn 17:26. This love, which is the Spirit,[256] operates the incorporation of the disciples into Jesus as branches into the vine so that they share in his heritage of eternal life. By their incorporation, God becomes their Father and they become his children in his only-begotten Son. This aspect of the blessing of eternal life pertains to the very nature of the eternal life that is the blessing of the Christian Covenant.

Continuing in Jn 14:21, Jesus points out the second aspect of the blessing of eternal life. He says he will manifest himself to one who loves him: "…I will love him and manifest myself to him." In fact, the incorporation of the faithful disciples into Jesus and their sharing his divine filial life constitutes a continual manifestation of Jesus to them and the possession of the love of the Father, whose children they have become.

The blessing of eternal life also means the indwelling of Jesus and the Father according to Jn 14:23. Jesus said: "If a man loves me, he will keep

---

253   Just as in Deuteronomy (*e.g.* Dt 6:5) and the vassal treaty tradition, love is commanded above all.

254   Cf. Jn 14:21.

255   Cf. Jn 14:23.

256   For the treatment of the identity of the Spirit, see Chapter 14 of this study.

my word, and my Father will love him, and we will come to him and make our home with him." Jesus and the Father are one because of their unity of nature. Consequently, they dwell together in the faithful subject who is incorporated into Jesus. By this indwelling, human persons enter into the very unity of the Godhead. As eternal life is a nearness to the Lord, it recalls the OT idea expressed in Ps 27:4: "that I may dwell in the house of the LORD all the days of my life." Yet, eternal life far surpasses the OT concept of nearness to the Lord, since this nearness is a mere proximity to the Lord in his earthly dwelling.

Eternal life is also the promised gift of messianic peace. Jesus speaks of this gift in Jn 14:27: "Peace I leave with you; my peace I give to you; not as the world gives do I give to you." Writing about this peace, Kasper notes: "Shalom (peace) is ... the embodiment of that salvation which was promised in the Old Testament and which, according to the New Testament, has come through Christ."[257]

Peace in the OT may be generally described as "the state of wholeness possessed by persons or groups, which may be health, prosperity, security, or the spiritual completeness of covenant."[258] Peace is an important covenantal term in the OT.[259] Among the elements of peace enumerated in Lv 26 are Yahweh's covenant and his dwelling in the midst of his people.[260] Writing about peace, von Rad states that the word "peace"

> ... designates the unimpairedness, the wholeness of a relationship of communion, and a state of harmonious equilibrium, the balancing of all claims and needs between two parties. Thus, the making of covenant is intended to secure a state of intactness, orderliness, and rightness between two parties, in order to make possible, on the basis of this legal foundation, a relationship in matters affecting common life.[261]

The notion of peace in the OT also followed the ideas of peace in treaty tradition. Peace is important in the treaty.[262] It is a state that the treaty aimed to achieve for the empire.[263] In fact, the treaty made friends of the covenanting parties[264] so that they enjoyed peace. Jesus, by establishing his covenant, made known to his disciples "all that I heard from my Father" and, for this

---

257   Walter Kasper, *Jesus the Christ* (New York: Paulist Press, 1977), p. 219.
258   E.M. Good, "Peace," *IDB*, III, 704.
259   *E.g.*, Dt 23:7 [Hb. 8]; Jos 9:15; 2 Sam 3:12-21; 1 Kgs 5:26.
260   Cf. Lv 26:8, 11, 12.
261   von Rad, *Old Testament Theology*, I, 130.
262   Cf. P.A. Riemann, "Covenant, Mosaic," *IDB*, Suppl.194; *JBC*, p. 749; Mendenhall, "Covenant," *IDB*, I, pp. 715, 719; Craigie, *The Book of Deuteronomy*, p. 298.
263   McCarthy, *Treaty and Covenant*, pp. 35, 36, 295.
264   McCarthy, *Old Testament Covenant*, p. 44; see also *Treaty and Covenant*, p. 43.

reason, said: "I call you friends."[265] Thus, peace is a blessing coming from Jesus' covenant.

In Jn 14:27 Jesus states that the peace he gives is not the peace given by the world. In Jn 16:33 Jesus explains why: his peace is to be found "in me." This peace of Jesus, therefore, is an aspect of the gift of eternal life that is the immediate consequence of union with Jesus through incorporation into him[266] and of the indwelling of Jesus and his Father.[267]

Speaking of his peace, Jesus exhorts his disciples to trust in him because he has overcome the world: "I have said this to you that in me you may have peace. In the world you have tribulation; but be of good cheer, I have overcome the world."[268] This exhortation is similar to the exhortation in Dt 20:3 where the Israelites are commanded to have courage when waging war against their enemies because Yahweh will give them victory. Jesus' gift of peace in the JLSA is one that enables his disciples in this world to be confident of victory in their inevitable battle with the world.

12.7.2.2. Abode in the Father's House

> 14:1   *"Let not your hearts be troubled: believe in God, believe also in me.*
>
> 2   **In my Father's house are many rooms**; *if it were not so, would I have told you that I go to prepare a place for you?*
>
> 3   **And when I go and prepare a place for you, I will come again and will take you to myself, that where I am you may be also."**

The text of the blessing of an abode in the Father's house immediately follows an exhortation-stipulation not to be upset, but to have faith in Jesus and his Father. This is similar to what is commonly found in the vassal treaty and in Deuteronomy where a promised blessing is linked to trust respectively in the suzerain or Yahweh. The exhortation-stipulation of Jn 14:1 goes back to the opening sentence of the Proclamation of Covenant that invites mankind to put faith in Jesus and the One who sent him.[269] The acceptance of this Proclamation is, in fact, intimately connected with the terms of the Royal Provision Clause according to which Jesus and the Father are recognized by accepting and serving them as rightful Lord.[270] Thus the exhortation-stipulation of Jn 14:1 links the blessing of an abode in the Father's

---

265   Jn 15:15.
266   Cf. Jn 14:20; 15:4-7; 17:23, 26.
267   Cf. Jn 14:23.
268   Cf. Jn 16:33.
269   Cf Jn 12:44.
270   Cf. Jn 17:2, 3.

house to the Royal Provision Clause. In this manner the present blessing should be seen as dependent upon fidelity to the Royal Investiture Covenant of Jesus Messiah.

The context of this covenant blessing of a dwelling place in the Father's house is the glorification of the Son of man in Jn 13:31. Having glorified God on earth by accomplishing his final earthly mission, Jesus returns to God to be glorified "in your own presence."[271] Jesus speaks of this heavenly glorification as imminent.[272] He tells his disciples that they will follow him, not "now" but "afterward."[273] It is on this note that Jesus speaks about the JLSA Covenant blessing of an abode "in my Father's house." He is going there to prepare a place for his disciples since in his Father's house "there are many dwelling places." Jesus himself will be the one to usher his disciples into the place he has gone to prepare: "I will come again and will take you to myself, that where I am you may be also."

The blessing of a dwelling place in the Father's house is linked to the blessing of eternal life since the heavenly dwelling place is the abode of the One who lives eternally. It should be noted that these two blessings of the New Covenant are analogous to those blessings in Deuteronomy of "life in the Promised Land." In the introductory chapters of the second Mosaic discourse, many of the units finish with blessings and curses which have to do with life/death in the Promised Land, such as Dt 6:14-19; 7:12-16; 11:13-17; 11-22.[274] This joining of life/death to the land is also found in the Curse-Blessing Formula of the second discourse of Moses in Dt 28. There, the individual blessings and curses generally involve some aspect of living a good and long life in the land or being cut off in diverse ways from such a life in the land.[275] The bonding of eternal life with an abode in the Father's house is another significant point where the JLSA is similar to the central portion of Deuteronomy. Deuteronomy offers life in the Promised Land as a blessing for the Mosaic Covenant, while the JLSA offers eternal life in a dwelling place in the Father's house as a blessing of the Eucharistic Covenant. However, while the blessings of the JLSA are on a parallel with those of Deuteronomy, they far surpass the deuteronomic blessings in their supernatural substance and magnificence.

---

271   Jn 17:5.

272   Cf. Jn 13:32; 17:5.

273   Cf. Jn 13:36.

274   Cf. McCarthy, *Treaty and Covenant*, p. 167.

275   Speaking about Dt 28, Clifford observes: "Both blessing and curse in the chapter are tied to the land. The land will or will not yield life to Israel according to their obedience. Yahweh will or will not afflict them with various forms of infertility or loss of land in military defeat on the same principle" (Clifford, *Deuteronomy*, p. 147).

12.7.2.3. Assistance of the Paraclete

14:15   ***"If you love me, you will keep my commandments.***
16   ***And I will ask the Father, and he will give you another***
        Paraclete, to be with you for ever."
25   *"These things I have spoken to you, while I am still with you.*
26   But ***the Paraclete, the Holy Spirit,*** *whom the Father*
        will send in my name, ***he will teach you all things,***
        and bring to your remembrance all that I have said to you."

The JLSA introduces the blessing of the assistance of the Paraclete with Jn 14:15, where fidelity is clearly the condition for obtaining this blessing.

Jesus is the first Paraclete. But because he returns to the Father, the Spirit is to take his place with the disciples as "another Paraclete." The mission of the Paraclete, therefore, is a continuation of and dependent upon the mission of Jesus himself. As originator of these saving missions, the Father is "just"[276] because he upholds his covenant relationship with Israel. At the time of his death Jesus completes his final earthly mission and returns to the Father, but the Paraclete will come in his place to be with God's People always.

The basic meaning of the term "paraclete" has already been explained.[277] As the Divine Witness of the JLSA Covenant, the meaning of the term "paraclete" is taken in its passive and forensic sense. However, as a covenant blessing, the Paraclete's role should be understood in its active sense: as one who gives helpful service, who counsels, exhorts, strengthens and comforts another.[278]

Jn 14:16 states that the Father will give the Paraclete at the request of Jesus. It is fitting that Jesus request this covenant blessing since he himself is the New Israel, which is the Father's faithful vine. His disciples are part of this nation because they are incorporated into Jesus and remain faithful to him. The blessing of the assistance of the Paraclete for "the true vine" is absolutely certain because Jesus, always faithful, always produces only good fruit that is pleasing to the Father.

The first section describing the Paraclete's assistance as covenant blessing is found in Jn 14:26. Here Jesus tells his disciples that he has given them the Father's word, which is the commandment for eternal life. The blessing of the assistance of the Paraclete insures that the Father's word always remain with Jesus' people. Jesus carefully explains that the Paraclete will keep

---

276   Jn 17:25.
277   Cf. above, in the Divine Witness Clause.
278   Cf. G.W.H. Lampe, "Paraclete," *IDB,* III, 654.

the Father's word alive in God's people by: (1) instructing them in every-thing, and (2) reminding them of all things Jesus already told them.

First of all, the Paraclete is to instruct God's people in everything. Since teaching is a gradual process, it seems that the Paraclete's role here is to en-able the Church, living in time, to understand the divine revelation of which she is the depository and interpreter.

In Jn 14:26, Jesus states that the Father will send the Paraclete, whom he calls "the Holy Spirit." The appellation "holy," recalling the Spirit's origin from the Father who is the Holy One of Israel,[279] affirms the Paraclete's divine nature. In this way Jn 14:26 teaches the divinity of the Paraclete and his power to accomplish his mission. The Paraclete's role in Jn 14:26 is to teach or recall to God's people all those things that Jesus taught during his lifetime.

The Lord reveals the second role of the Paraclete as covenant blessing in the following words:

> 16:7   *"Nevertheless I tell you the truth: it is to your advantage that I go away, for **if I do not go away, the Paraclete will not come to you; but if I go, I will send him to you.**"*
>
> 12   *"I have yet many things to say to you, but you cannot bear them now.*
>
> 13   *When **the Spirit of truth** comes, he **will guide you into all the truth;** for he will not speak on his own authority, but whatever he hears he will speak, and **he will declare to you the things that are to come.***
>
> 14   *He will glorify me, for he will take what is mine and declare it to you.*
>
> 15   *All that the Father has is mine; therefore I said that **he will take what is mine and declare it to you.**"*

In this role of the Paraclete as covenant blessing, Jesus specifies that he will send the Paraclete *after his departure from the world.* Why? Because the object of this activity, by reason of this specific blessing, is that the Paraclete tell the disciples the things which they were unable to bear during the short time he was here on earth. Regarding these matters, the Paraclete will "guide" the disciples "to all truth" and "will announce" to them "the things to come."

Does Jn 16:12,13 imply that the Paraclete will make further revelations following Jesus' departure? In this regard Brown lists the various opinions held by the commentators.[280] He himself is opposed to the idea of new

---

279   Cf. Jn 17:11; Is 43:3, 14, 15.

280   Brown, *The Gospel According to John,* II, 714 ff.

revelation: "It is unlikely that in Johannine thought there was any concept of further revelation after the ministry of Jesus, for Jesus is *the* revelation of the Father, the Word of God."[281] Another reason Brown gives against any new revelation is Jn 15:15: "I have made known to you *all* that I heard from my Father." Brown suggests that, rather than a new revelation, the Paraclete will give a full and practical understanding (*i.e.* for use in daily life) of what had already been revealed during Jesus' ministry.

On the other hand, it is also possible that Jesus is talking here about *new* revelation.[282] Jn 15:15 poses no problem because Jn 16:12, 13 does not contradict it. The phrase that Jesus "made known to you all that I heard from my Father" could be interpreted in the sense that Jesus accomplished his earthly mission[283] by the establishment of the Christian Covenant of Royal Investiture through the incorporation of "all men"[284] into himself. This incorporation marked the establishment of the covenant by which Jesus revealed God's Fatherhood to mankind and was invested as Messiah of the New Israel. The completion of this earthly covenantal work of the Son of man, however, does not necessarily exclude the revelation of further truths for the New Israel. Nor does it contradict the fact that Jesus is the very Revelation of God in Person and the truth itself. The Paraclete is spoken of here as the immediate revealer of the things that the disciples could not bear to receive at the time of the Last Supper. However, it is actually Jesus who continues his work of revelation because Jesus made it very clear that the Spirit only repeats what he received from Jesus himself.[285] Thus, Jesus is no less the revealer of those things made known after his death than of those which he revealed before it. One presumes that the JLSA was written with the specific time frame of the Last Supper in mind and that Jesus spoke within the time frame of the Last Supper.[286] Therefore, what does not come into the time frame of the Last Supper would be precisely what the disciples could not bear at that time. It is difficult to see how Johannine thought could preclude the concept of further revelation or, at least, a deeper understanding of revelation *after* the Last Supper. It seems that Jn 16:12, 13 reflects the Church's constant teaching that public revelation ended only with the death of John, the last apostle.

---

281   *Ibid.*, 714.

282   This "new" revelation could be understood as a fuller understanding of those truths that Jesus previously made known to his disciples.

283   Cf. Jn 17:4.

284   Cf. Jn 12:33.

285   Cf. Jn 16:13-15.

286   The Last Supper is cardinal to the Church, which was established at that point in time. The time of the glorification of the Son of man and of God in Jn 13:31 is designated as *"now."* This was the decisive moment of the Last Supper. It was the time of the establishment of the JLSA Covenant of the Royal Enthronement, by which God was made Father of men. It is with reference to the *"now"* that Jesus says in Jn 14:7: *"From this point on* (Gr: *ap' arti*) you know him; you have seen him."

The Paraclete, when spoken of in Jn 16:13 as revealer of those things not yet made known by Jesus, is called "the Spirit of truth." In this capacity the Paraclete acts properly *in the person of Jesus who is the truth,* and whose unique office, as God's only Son, is to reveal God's name of Father to all mankind. Thus, by calling the Paraclete "the Spirit of truth," the JLSA accentuates his particular relationship to Jesus as "the truth." In revealing the things not yet told by Jesus, the Paraclete will make known *what he receives from Jesus.* In this way the revelation is made by Jesus, the truth, through the Paraclete who is Jesus' own Spirit, "the Spirit of truth." In doing this, the Paraclete glorifies Jesus, since what he reveals comes *from* Jesus and is *about* Jesus, for it regards his Covenant of Royal Investiture. Moreover, what the Paraclete makes known is always the word which Jesus has received in turn from his Father, who is in the position of the Great King or overlord and upon whom all depends.

12.7.2.4. Blessings for the Mission of the New Israel

14:11   *"Believe me that I am in the Father and the
       Father in me; or else, believe me for the sake of
       the works themselves.*

12   *Truly, truly, I say to you,* **he who believes in me will
       also do the woks that I do,** *because I go to the Father.*

13   **Whatever you ask in my name, I will do it,** *that the
       Father may be glorified in the Son;*

14   **if you ask anything in my name, I will do it."**

The context of this blessing is the glorification of the Son of man and of God, announced in Jn 13:31. To accomplish this twofold glorification Jesus revealed to his disciples God's Fatherhood by incorporating them into himself. At the same time Jesus assumed his office as God's Messiah and formed, together with his disciples, the kingdom of the New Israel. In Jn 13:34, following the twofold glorification, Jesus gave the New Commandment for the New Israel. In Jn 14:7, he affirmed to his disciples that he had just revealed to them God as their Father.

In the blessing for the mission of the New Israel, Jesus promises his faithful disciples that: (1) they will perform the same and even greater works than he, and (2) he will do whatever they ask of him in his name in order to glorify the Father in the Son.

These promised blessings are founded upon the unity of Jesus with the Father and the unity of Jesus' disciples with himself and his Father. In the introduction to this blessing in Jn 14:11, Jesus calls upon his disciples to believe that he and the Father are one. They should believe this either because of Jesus himself or because of his works. If Jesus were not one with the Father, he could never have accomplished his works. He accomplished them precisely because "the Father who dwells in me does his works."[287] On the other hand, Jesus commanded his disciples to continue his mission on earth because they are incorporated into him and, together with him, form the New Israel, the true vine. Jesus thus promises the present blessings to his disciples for their cooperation with him in their common mission. Given the context, these blessings sanction the apostolic New Commandment of Love in Jn 13:34, 35 and Jn 15:12, 17.

In the present blessing Jesus assures his loyal disciples, both individually and collectively, that in fulfilling the New Commandment they will perform the same and even greater works than those which he himself performed. Moreover, Jesus promises that he himself will do whatever his disciples ask him in his name. He will do this precisely because his faithful subjects, together with him as the true vine, continue his mission upon the earth. By granting his disciples' requests in his name, Jesus continues his very own mission. Naturally, it is understood that these favors be requested for the accomplishment of the mission of the New Israel and not for personal motives. This is clear because the context of these blessings is precisely the stipulation for the mission of the New Israel.

12.7.2.5. Blessings for the Branches of the Vine

15:1	*"I am the true vine, and my Father is the vinedresser.*
2	*Every branch of mine that bears no fruit, he takes* away, *and every branch that does bear fruit he prunes, that it may bear more fruit."*
5	*"I am the vine, you are the branches.* **He who abides in me, and I in him, he it is that bears much fruit, for apart from me you can do nothing."**
7	*"If you abide in me, and my words abide in you,* **ask whatever you will, and it shall be done for you.**
8	*By this my Father is glorified, that you bear much fruit, and so prove to be my disciples."*
10	*"If you keep my commandments, you will abide in my love,* just as I have kept my Father's commandments and *abide in his love.*
11	*These things I have spoken to you, that* **my joy may be in you, and that your joy may be complete."**
16:23	**"**.... **if you ask anything of the Father, he will give it to you in my name.**

---

287   Jn 14:10.

24 *Hitherto you have asked nothing in my name;* **ask and**
you shall receive, that your joy may be full.

26 *In that day you will ask in my name; and I do not say*
to you that I shall pray the Father for you;

27 *for the Father himself loves you, because you have loved me*
and have believed that I came from God."

The blessings for the branches of the vine follow upon the Statement of Relationship between the parties to the JLSA Covenant in Jn 15:1, 5. They are, consequently, related to the Statement of Relationship regarding the branches of the true vine.

As vinegrower, the Father is, according to treaty tradition, in the position of the Great King or suzerain over the New Israel which Jesus likened to a vine. This vine belongs to the Father; it is in his care and he tends its branches. Jesus himself is the vine, God's Nation, and his faithful disciples, incorporated into him, are branches of the vine. They, together with Jesus, are in the position of vassal king.

In caring for the vine, the Father's attention is specifically concerned with the branches which he prunes and trims. By tending the vine the Father enables the branches to remain living and fruitful parts of the vine. Jesus says in Jn 15:8 that the Father is glorified by the disciples' bearing much fruit and becoming his disciples.

The blessings of abundant produce (Jn 15:5, 7), requests granted (Jn 16:23-27) and divine filial joy (Jn 15:11; 16:24) follow upon and regard the Statement of Relationship pertaining to Jesus, his disciples, and God the Father as, respectively, the true vine, the branches, and the vinegrower. Since the Father is the vinegrower who tends the vine's branches, it is fitting that he be the one who bestows these blessings.

While the blessings of abundant produce and requests granted are similar to the blessings for the mission of the New Israel, these blessings differ: (a) in the motive for their bestowal, as well as (b) in the one who bestows the blessings. The previous blessings for the fulfillment of the mission of the New Israel were granted by Jesus so as to glorify the Father in the Son. The mission of Jesus that is continued by his disciples has the specific purpose of glorifying the Father in the Son.[288] These present blessings, however, are granted by the Father because of the glory that he receives from the disciples of Jesus who are faithful to his Son's mission and, together with Jesus Messiah, contribute to bearing fruit pleasing to him.

---

288   Cf. Jn 12:23-36; 13:31.

The blessings of abundant produce and requests granted are promised to those who are faithful to their covenant relationship with Jesus as branches of the true vine. These blessings require that the disciples remain in Jesus, as branches living in the vine, and that they make Jesus' words (*i.e.* commands) their own. By so doing the disciples will experience the joy of Jesus which comes from possessing the paternal love of God.

CHAPTER 13

The JSLA Statement of Covenant-making

In OT covenant tradition the Statement of Covenant-making was an emphatic affirmation that a covenant (i.e. family-like union) had been made or sworn.[289]

1. The most significant JLSA Statement of Covenant-making is **Peter's oath for himself and the other disciples** to accept the ministry of Jesus by the Footwashing.[290] By this acceptance the disciples obtained a share in the heritage/birthright of Jesus Messiah. In this way Jesus loved his disciples the way the Father loved him.

13:6-9 "He came to Simon Peter; and Peter said to him, 'Lord, do you wash my feet?' Jesus answered him, 'What I am doing you do not know now, but afterward you will understand.' Peter said to him, 'You shall never wash my feet.' Jesus answered him, **'If I do not wash you, you have no part in me.'** Simon Peter said to him, **'Lord, not my feet only but also my hands and my head.'"**

Apart from the above, which is the very act of the covenant-making of the disciples through Peter their head, the JLSA also implied the covenant-making by many other statements in accordance with the various aspects under which the program for "the hour" viewed the New Covenant. These various statements of covenant-making will now be examined.

2. **Jesus requests his heavenly glorification from the Father because he had completed his earthly covenantal work and glorified his Father in himself.** This request is also an avowal that the covenant-making was completed:

13:31   **"Now is the Son of man glorified, and in him God is glorified...."**

17:4   *"I glorified you on earth, having accomplished the work which you gave me to do ....*

5   *... now, Father, glorify me in your own presence with the glory which I had with you before the world was made."*

3. A most significant affirmation that the covenant had been made at the Last Supper is the statement in Jn 14:6, 7 that **Jesus' disciples know and have seen his Father.**

---

289   See above in Chapter 10.
290   Cf. Jn 13:8, 9.

14:6   *"I am the way, and the truth, and the life; no one*
         comes to the Father but by me.

7   *If you had known me, you would have known me, and*
         you would have known my Father also; **henceforth**
         you know him and have seen him."

The JLSA Royal Provision Clause in Jn 17:2, 3 states that it is necessary "to know you, the only true God, and him whom you have sent, Jesus
Christ."[291] Here, "to know" means to acknowledge and faithfully serve as one's
rightful lord in covenant terminology.[292] Jesus' statement in Jn 14:6, 7 indicates that the disciples had complied with the terms of the Royal Provision
Clause. If the disciples really "knew," *i.e.* "acknowledged" him—who is the
way, the truth and life, the only access to the Father—as Lord, then they would
also recognize the Father as Lord. He then tells them in Jn 14:7b that, in fact,
from that point in time—just before the immediate present—they already did
know the Father; they "have seen" him. The verb used here "to see" (Gr *orao*),
when referring to God, means precisely to be admitted into his more immediate presence as in Mt 5:8 and Heb 12:14.[293] Since the disciples know Jesus
according to his words in Jn 14:7a, they also do know the Father.

In Jn 14:7 Jesus tells his disciples that they "know" the Father precisely
because God's Fatherhood had just been revealed to them at the Last Supper
in the Footwashing/Eucharistic Action. Since Jesus had incorporated them
into himself, his Father is also their Father and loves them with the very love
with which he loves his only-begotten Son. It is precisely because this union
of covenant had been established that Jesus exclaimed in Jn 13:31: "Now is
the Son of man glorified and God is glorified in him."

4. By covenant-making the **disciples were incorporated into Jesus** and
thus given a relationship to God himself. Also, by the incorporation of "all
men" into himself, Jesus was himself glorified by this union in his royal investiture as their Messiah king.[294]

The establishment of this union is affirmed in the following verses:

14:20   **"I am in my Father, and you in me, and I in you."**
15:4   **"Abide in me, and I in you."**

5. Another aspect of the JLSA covenant-making was to **bring judgment upon this world by driving out its ruler.**[295] The making of the

---

291   Jn 17:3.
292   Cf. P.A. Riemann, "Mosaic Covenant," IDB, Suppl., pp. 195,196; see above Pt. II, II, B, 3.
293   Cf. *The Analytical Greek Lexicon Revised*, ed. Moulton, Harold K. (Grand Rapids,
Michigan: Zondervan Publishing House, 1978), p. 291.
294   Cf. Jn 12:23; 13:31.
295   Cf. Jn 12:31, 32.

Royal Investiture Covenant was the decisive moment of the great battle of God and his Messiah with the devil. The JLSA affirms the judgment of the world and the victory over the devil to have been accomplished at the Last Supper:

14:30 *"… the ruler of this world is coming.*
He has no power over me."

16:11 *"… the ruler of this world is judged."*

33 *"I have overcome the world."*

6. Another avowal of the covenant's establishment is the **affirmation of the union established by the Son of man by drawing "all men" to himself** for the glorification of his Father. This union between the Father and Jesus and between Jesus and his disciples is affirmed and described in the following manner:

15:1 *"I am the true vine, and my Father is the vinedresser."*

5 *"I am the vine, you are the branches."*

7. In accordance with the vassal treaty analogy found in Deuteronomy, the JLSA presents its covenant as the **proclamation of the suzerain's royal and powerful word**. This proclamation is one of the aspects of Jesus' covenantal work. In the JLSA, God's word is proclaimed for the establishment of the Royal Investiture Covenant of the Son of man as Messiah of the New Israel. Jesus proclaims his Father's word as covenant mediator. This word is accepted by the disciples through their acceptance of Jesus' ministry in the Footwashing. Therefore, Jesus, having completed his last earthly work through the Footwashing, stated that he had completed the proclamation of the Father's word. The following statements signify that the JLSA Covenant had been established through the proclamation of that word:

15:3 *"You are already made clean by **the word I have spoken to you.**"*

15 *"…all that I have heard from my Father I have made*
known to you."

17:8 *"I have given them the words which you (the Father) gave*
me, and they received them…."

14 *"I have given them your* (i.e. the Father's) *word …."*

8. In order to create this union, **Jesus had to love his disciples as the Father had loved him:** "As the Father has loved me, so have I loved you."[296] **In so doing, Jesus gave his disciples the gift of glory that the Father had given him, a sharing in Jesus' filial relationship with the Father.** In the following verses the JLSA states that this was accomplished:

---

296   Jn 15:9.

17:6   *"I have manifested your name* (i.e. of Father) *to the men whom you gave me out of the world."*

22   *"The glory which you have given me I have given to them that they may be one even as we are one.*

23   *…you … have loved them even as you have loved me."*

26   *"I made known to them your name … that the love with which you have loved me may be in them, and I in them."*

CHAPTER 14

Observations and Insights

14.1. John's Treatment of NT Revelation Within the Framework of Covenant

Mendenhall questioned whether the NT considers "covenant" to be a concept inherited from Judaism or whether covenant was seriously considered as the formal basis of the relationship of the early Christians to each other and to Christ. He finally concluded that while the early Christians did regard themselves as a covenant-bound community, they considered the covenant to be a very open and creative reinterpretation of the older traditions.[297] Mendenhall arrived at this conclusion because, beyond the reference to the "blood of the covenant" in the Last Supper accounts of the Synoptics, he was unable to connect the Last Supper with OT covenant traditions.[298] Consequently he stated that "... unfortunately the clearest description of the NT church as a covenant-bound community comes from Pliny the Younger (*ca.* 112)." [299]

The response to Mendenhall's observation regarding covenant in the NT is given in this study's identification of specific elements of OT covenant tradition employed in the composition of the JLSA. As a result, this study proposes that the JLSA, which makes up over one quarter of the Johannine Gospel, explains Christian Revelation strictly within the framework of covenant theology.

Mendenhall considered the treaty/covenant genre too legalistic a framework for Christianity: "The NT experience of Christ was one which could not be contained within the framework of a quasi-legal terminology or pattern of thought and action."[300] The objection to the treaty/covenant genre as too legalistic a framework to be used as a valid expression for union between God and Israel was already raised in regard to the central portion of Deuteronomy. McCarthy explained that this objection originates from confusing "covenant" and "contract." In the contract, relationship is based upon the fulfillment of the contractual stipulations. The contractual stipulations are actually *sine-qua-non* conditions for the contract's existence. In the contract, where all is on a *quid pro quo* and *do ut des* basis, the

---

297 Mendenhall, "Covenant," *IDB*, I, p. 723.
298 *Ibid.*, pp. 722, 723.
299 *Ibid.*, p. 722.
300 *Ibid.*, 723.

relationship and the degree of its intensity is the guaranteed reward for the observance of the contractual stipulations. All of this, however, is foreign to the concept of covenant. The covenant relationship is sacred, personal, and family-like; it is not a reward for the observance of the stipulations. The purpose of the stipulations in the covenant was, not to create a relationship, but to confirm it and define how the covenanted parties were to live out their already-existing personal relationship. Thus the Stipulation Clause of the treaty genre should be regarded as a mode of commitment to the sovereign, a way by which the vassal lives out his extant relationship with the sovereign from day to day.

Covenant cannot be considered too legalistic a framework for expressing the relationship between God and mankind because the contractual *quid-pro-quo* relationship has no place in covenant. Instead, the treaty genre presented a manner for living out the personal family-like union of covenant. McCarthy says that in the treaty/covenant concept, "one does not earn a contracted reward, one lives a covenanted relationship. As a faithful vassal one gives tribute, a mark of submission and willing service." [301]

While a covenanted relationship with God is a gratuitous gift, the observance of the stipulations is necessary to keep this relationship *de facto* alive. The stipulations confirm and define the family-like relationship. To be unfaithful to this relationship would be effectively to end it, since grave unfaithfulness means, in practice, to deny the covenant any real existence in one's life.[302] While the covenant and its relationship are gratuitous gifts of God, these gifts are of no avail without fidelity to living the covenant. The threat of the Curse-Blessing Formula is confirmation of this fact.

The covenant framework cannot be too legalistic for a valid expression of union between God and mankind in the New Covenant dispensation because covenant is concerned with family-like relationship, and the Christian Covenant is concerned with an adoptive filial relationship to God in his only-begotten Son. Therefore, covenant is the *perfect* framework to express this Christian relationship.[303] John employed elements from OT covenant tradition to explain the nature of this family-like union established by the Eucharistic Covenant of the Last Supper. He employed the genre from Deuteronomy that was based upon word so as to be able to express in words the nature of the Eucharistic Covenant which, as a sacramental action, is expressed in signs. However, this symbolic form of covenant-making is, unfortunately, in constant danger of being misinterpreted and misunderstood.

---

301   McCarthy, *Treaty and Covenant*, p. 207.
302   *Ibid.,* p. 297.
303   It should be noted that this adoption is not by fiction of law but, rather, by sanctifying grace that transforms the soul.

The level-headedness of the genre chosen by John—a genre that explains in words the meaning of the symbolism involved in covenant-making—offsets such dangers regarding the establishment of, and the nature of, a union that is expressed through a symbolic or sacramental action.

14.2. The JLSA: Compendium of the New Covenant

Craigie rightly states that the basic principle for interpreting the theology of Deuteronomy is that book's character as a covenant document, which is to say, a report about the making of a covenant.[304] He says that Deuteronomy's "covenant...provides the framework within which the details of (its) theology are to be expressed."[305]

The JLSA reports the Royal Investiture Covenant of Jesus as Messiah of the New Israel by employing various OT covenant traditions. Although, unlike Deuteronomy, the JLSA does not follow the strict order of a covenant formulary, the JLSA, like Deuteronomy, is a report about covenant. Therefore, the covenantal character of the JLSA should be, as it is for Deuteronomy, its basic principle of interpretation.

Like Deuteronomy, the JLSA is intended to be a compendium, digest, or survey of the Christian faith. Paraphrasing von Rad's statement about the covenantal theology of Deuteronomy, the JLSA is intended to be something in the nature of a complete course of instruction embracing the sum total of God's Revelation and all that this involves for mankind.[306] Thus, in the light of the JLSA's covenantal character, its theology should be seen to present the mysteries of Christian Revelation and show their interrelationship more coherently than ever before. There are many scriptural and theological points in the JLSA that are now indicated as having very specific meaning from the covenantal perspective.

---

304   Craigie, *The Book of Deuteronomy*, p. 36. Speaking about the central portion of Deuteronomy, McCarthy writes in *Treaty and Covenant*, p. 286: "It is built as a treaty and this means it has a structure determined in many matters by an immemorial legal tradition for specifying relationships between notables, persons of consequence, beyond any relation given in nature like kinship."

305   Craigie, *The Book of Deuteronomy*, p. 36.

306   Cf. von Rad, *Deuteronomy*, p. 29. Von Rad states: "It is unnecessary to emphasize that behind this attempt (it was the first in Israel), beside the well-known practical and hortatory concern, there was also at the same time a strong effort toward theoretical and theological comprehension. With this awakened interest in the entirety of Yahweh's revelation, Deuteronomy is unmistakably on the way towards working out a canon, towards delimiting those traditions which possess authoritative significance for Israel. Deuteronomy does indeed... think of itself as...above all an oral interpretation of Israel's early traditions, making them relevant for the present."

14.3. The Covenantal Roles of the Holy Spirit

The JLSA states many important particulars concerning the roles of the Spirit. However, in this study's reading of the JLSA, these roles are more clearly defined from the covenantal perspective.

Jesus Messiah is the bearer of the Spirit.[307] He accomplishes his messianic mission of revealing God's Fatherhood by the bestowal of the Spirit upon those of mankind who accept God's covenant.[308] God the Father is revealed by the operation of the Spirit who effects in persons a participation in the eternal life of the Son of God incarnate.[309] This bestowal of the Spirit for eternal life, therefore, is intimately connected with the Royal Provision Clause of the Royal Investiture Covenant of Jesus Messiah: "Eternal life is this: to know you, the only true God, and him whom you have sent, Jesus Christ."[310]

In order to establish his covenant, Jesus loved his disciples just as the Father loved him.[311] The Father loved Jesus precisely by giving him the "gift of glory" whereby he revealed his Fatherhood to Jesus. Speaking to the Father about this gift Jesus said: "… this glory of mine which is your gift to me, *because of* (Gr *hoti*) the love you bore me before the world began."[312] The word *hoti* is a conjunction expressing a causal relationship with what precedes it. Thus, Jesus is saying that the Father gave him the gift of glory through the causality of the divine paternal love. However, since the operative principle for the Father's gift of glory to Jesus is the same as the operative principle for the gift of glory that Jesus gives to his disciples, it would seem that in his Last Supper Account John contradicts himself. In the JLSA, the divine paternal love is the operative principle of the Christian Covenant. In the preceding part of the Johannine Gospel the Spirit is the operative principle for making the "man of flesh" into the "man of spirit." ***This is not contradiction but identification.*** Jn 17:24 expressly but implicitly identifies the Spirit with the divine paternal love as the operative principle of the New Covenant. The divine paternal love is not an entity apart from God; instead, it is the very Person of the Spirit,[313] the "Person-Gift" who is the "uncreated

---

307   Cf. Jn 1:32.
308   Cf. Jn 1:33.
309   Cf. Jn 3:3-16, cf. also Jn 1:32, 33.
310   Jn 17:3.
311   Cf. Jn 13:34; 15:9, 12.
312   Jn 17:24.
313   Brown has an interesting comment about the identification of the love of God within the Trinity and the Spirit in Jn 17:26: "The medieval scholar Rupert of Deutz (PL 169:724 …) identifies the indwelling love described in 26c ("the love you had for me") as the Holy Spirit—clearly a reflection of later Trinitarian theology where the Spirit is the love between the Father and the Son. Yet he may not be far wrong in seeing that only through the Spirit can

Love-Gift."[314] Thus, John completes his teaching in the JLSA about the operative principle of the Christian Covenant. The Spirit—who is personally the divine paternal love—is the operative principle of the New Covenant.

The JLSA text also reveals the Spirit as the Bond of the Christian Covenant. Having bestowed the paternal love upon his disciples, Jesus said to them, speaking of the Spirit of truth, "...you do recognize him since *he remains with you* and *is within you*."[315] In this role the Spirit is seen as the Bond of the Christian Covenant. It is by his power and presence in the disciples who, incorporated into Jesus Christ the only-begotten Son, are caught up into the very unity of the Trinity itself.

The Spirit is identified in his other two roles as "another Paraclete." As such, the Spirit is: (1) Divine Witness to the New Covenant, and (2) gives his assistance as a covenant blessing. These two covenantal roles were not heretofore specifically identified.

By reflecting upon the Johannine teaching in the JLSA, one is able to see more clearly the intimate connection of the Spirit with the Christian Covenant. By means of the Eucharistic Action of the Last Supper, Jesus bestowed upon men the divine paternal love, who is the Spirit. This bestowal of the Spirit brought about the birth of the Church, the New Israel, by incorporating men into Jesus. Through the continual celebration of the Eucharistic Action, the Spirit continues to bestow eternal life upon men, bear witness to their fidelity and bless them in the execution of their mission.

14.4. The Two Glorifications of Jesus

The JLSA speaks about two glorifications of Jesus. The first glorification, his earthly one—announced in Jn 12:23-33 as proximate—is declared to have been accomplished at the Last Supper in Jn 13:31. The second glorification of Jesus, his heavenly one, is spoken of as not yet fulfilled in the JLSA in Jn 13:32; 17:1, 5, 24.

Within the covenantal context of the JLSA, the matter of these glorifications is of extreme importance. Regarding the earthly glorification of the Son of man, Jn 7:39 states that Jesus would not bestow the Spirit until he was glorified by his death. Only by this death would the New Covenant be definitively established. Therefore, confusion regarding the earthly glorification of Jesus and the bestowal of the Spirit has had unfortunate repercussions

---

the promises of Jesus in 26 be fulfilled." See *The Gospel According to John*, II, p. 781; cf. also Schnackenburg, *The Gospel According to St. John*, III, p. 197.

314   Cf. Encyclical Letter *Dominum et Vivificantem*, John Paul II, May 18, 1986.

315   Jn 14:17; cf. also Jn 17:26, where Jesus states that he has revealed the Father's name to the disciples so that the divine paternal love may live in them.

on understanding the establishment, nature and circumstances of the New Covenant. It is imperative to dispel the existing confusion in order to understand properly the role of the Eucharistic Action of the Last Supper and the New Covenant that it established.

The first glorification of Jesus as the Son of man relates to his royal office of Messiah. His royalty, though deriving from his divinity, belongs to him basically as son and heir of King David. As Messiah, Jesus is inferior to, and at the service of, God his Father. As such, Jesus is in the analogous position of a vassal of the treaty genre while God the Father has the position of the Great King. Both the incarnate state and royal position of Jesus indicate a mission of humble service in which Jesus is subject to the will and command of his Father. For this reason Jesus stated in Jn 14:28: "… the Father is greater than I."

This study proposes that the royal accession of Jesus as Messiah-King of God's New Israel took place at the Last Supper by the establishment of the New Covenant through the celebration of the Eucharist. This is the meaning of Jesus' declaration in Jn 13:31: "Now is the Son of man glorified and God is glorified in him." Because of John's analogical presentation of the Footwashing for the Eucharist of the Last Supper, the declaration of Jesus indicates the ontological presence of the death of Jesus on the cross through the celebration of that Eucharist. In this manner John asserts the sacrificial nature of the Eucharist of the Last Supper to be complete and, consequently, that the glorification of Jesus by his death was truly effected *before* Good Friday. The role of the Eucharist of the Last Supper was to establish the Community of the New Covenant *before* Calvary. Thus, in accordance with Jn 7:39, the Spirit as the divine paternal love was bestowed at the Last Supper as the life-giving operative Principle and Bond of the New Covenant for the revelation of God's Fatherhood. This bestowal is confirmed in Jn 14:17 where Jesus, speaking of the Spirit, tells the disciples: "… you do recognize him since *he remains* with you and *is* in you."[316]

Immediately following the declaration about his earthly glorification, Jesus speaks in Jn 13:32 about another glorification. This glorification had not yet taken place: "If God is glorified in him, God will also glorify him in himself, and *will glorify him at once.*" Jesus again refers to this still-unrealized glorification in Jn 17:5: "And now, Father, glorify me in your own

---

316   The Church was born by this bestowal of the Spirit. Therefore, it owes its very origin to the celebration of the Eucharist of the Last Supper. Consequently, a distinction should be made between the bestowal of the Spirit for the establishment of the New Covenant and its Community at the Last Supper, and the bestowal of the Spirit as the Paraclete at Pentecost. At Pentecost the Spirit was not bestowed as the operative Principle and Bond of the New Covenant, but rather as the already-established Church's covenant blessing.

presence with the glory which I had with you before the world was made." Jesus speaks here of this glorification as his due because of his divinity as only-begotten Son of the Father. This heavenly glorification also regards the continuation of his royal messianic mission. Jesus indicates this in Jn 17:1 where he asks the Father for this glorification so that he may continue to give glory to the Father by continuing his faithful service of revealing God's Fatherhood to mankind. This is also indicated in the last verse of the JLSA: "I have made known to them your name, and I will make it known, that the love with which you have loved me may be in them, and I in them."

The Eucharistic Covenant Action is the celebration of the two glorifications of Jesus Messiah: his death and resurrection/ascension. However, the Eucharist does not celebrate these glorifications in the same way. By its efficacious signs, the Eucharist makes present the ontological reality of the death of Jesus, his royal accession as Messiah of the New Israel. However, this ontological presence is accomplished by and in the Personal Presence of the gloriously risen Messiah, Son of God, who is seated at the right hand of the Father as Eternal High Priest.

14.5. The New Commandment: Expression of Authentic Evangelization

Through the celebration of the Eucharist of the Last Supper, Jesus accomplished his final earthly messianic mission of revealing God's Fatherhood by establishing the New Covenant and taking his position as Messiah King. In fulfilling this mission, Jesus loved his disciples as the Father loved him. He gave them a share in his birthright by incorporating them into himself through the bestowal of the divine paternal love, thus making them children of his Father. By reason of their incorporation into Jesus, his disciples must participate in his own mission and, therefore, Jesus commanded them to love others as he himself loved them.

The purpose of the New Commandment is the revelation of God's Fatherhood to all mankind. It is a rephrasing of the apostolic mandate in Mt 28:18-20. Jesus must draw all men to himself, and he wishes to continue this work through those incorporated into himself as branches of the true vine. The New Commandment is essentially supernatural and therefore requires of the Christian what is above every human capacity unaided by grace.

The New Commandment is apostolic since its practical fulfillment is accomplished only through evangelization in its multi-faceted activities. In order to accomplish this evangelization the Christian is required to live in a union of life and activity with Jesus Messiah through the Eucharist. It was through this action at the Last Supper that Jesus accomplished his mission and it is by union with his action through the Eucharistic Action that his dis-ciples will fulfill their mission. In this way the disciples of Jesus glorify the Father as branches of the true vine "in … bearing much fruit."[317] By a union of life and activity with Jesus Messiah in the Eucharist, the Christian fulfills the command to remain in Jesus so as to produce abundantly and bear fruit that endures.[318]

The spirituality required by the New Commandment is that of spiri-tual childhood. This is why Jesus, God's Son and the first-born of many brethren,[319] likened those in the kingdom of God to children.[320] Since the New Commandment's purpose is to fulfill the mission of Jesus himself—the revelation of God's Fatherhood—it is necessary for the followers of Jesus to be the Father's loving, humble and obedient children in his Son.

14.6. Baptism and the Eucharist

The Footwashing cannot have baptism as its primary signification because the Footwashing is an analogical presentation of the Eucharist. Nonetheless, striking similarities between the Footwashing and baptism lead one to see an allusion to baptism in the Footwashing since both: (1) wash with water, (2) cleanse from sin, and (3) bestow a share in the heritage of Jesus Messiah. And precisely because baptism does these things, it is closely related to the Eucharistic Covenant.

In fact, baptism is the sacrament whereby one becomes part of the Eucharistic Covenant. By baptism persons become branches of the true vine and adopted children of God. Moreover, John's choice of the Footwashing, so similar in its externals to baptism, teaches that baptism—the sacrament for individual spiritual birth—should be seen as drawing its efficacy to fulfill its specific purpose from the Source of all saving grace that is the Eucharistic Covenant Action that gave birth to the Universal Church.

14.7. The Place of the JLSA in the Fourth Gospel

This study's concern is the JLSA which begins with Jn 12:44 and ends with Jn 17:26. It is beyond the scope of this present work to study the rest of the Fourth Gospel's relationship to the JLSA, and in particular, that of Chapter 6, which treats of Jesus' promise of the Eucharist. However, hope-fully this study demonstrates that the JLSA affirms that the prophetic prom-ise of Chapter 6 was fulfilled at the Last Supper.

---

317   Jn 15:9.
318   Cf. Jn 15:5, 16.
319   Rom 8:29.
320   Cf. Jn 1:12; Mt 18:3; 19:14; Mk 10:14.

From a material point of view, the JLSA enjoys the most prominent place in the Fourth Gospel. It is the single largest section, making up more than one quarter of that entire gospel. The Last Supper is given more attention than any other event and its place in the middle of the Fourth Gospel leads one to attribute cardinal importance to it. These reasons seem serious enough to suppose that John considered the JLSA the very heart of his gospel.

The JLSA also holds first place in the Fourth Gospel by reason of the matter it treats. The Fourth Gospel dwells so long on the Last Supper because at that time Jesus completed his final earthly messianic mission with his glorification and that of God his Father. Jesus did this by making his death ontologically present *before* Good Friday and providing that his saving death would be present to all God's People of all times by means of the Eucharist, the greatest of all sacraments and the one by which Jesus gave birth to his Church. The very prominent place of JLSA within the Fourth Gospel indicates that John sees the Eucharist as central to his gospel message of salvation and that the Church is essentially a Eucharistic People.

Royal Investiture Covenant of Jesus Messiah

**Places in the JLSA (*Jn 12:44 – 17:26*) Related to
OT Covenant Elements and Traditions, Royal Investiture and
Elements of the Vassal Treaty Analogy**

I. TWO INTRODUCTORY ELEMENTS
   A. **PROCLAMATION OF COVENANT** *Jn 12:44-50*
   B. *MISE-EN-SCENE* *Jn 13:1-3*

**II. ELEMENTS OF ROYAL INVESTITURE TRADITION AND
VASSAL TREATY ANALOGY**
   A. **ROYAL PROTOCOL OF MESSIAH**
      1. Name (*"Jesus"*) *Jn 12:44; 13:1, 3; 17:3*
      2. Genealogy (*"Son of God"*) *Jn 14:13; 17:1*
         FATHER of Jesus:
         a) Name (*"Father"*) *Jn 12:49; 13:1, 3; 14:2, 5, 7-13, 16, 20,
         21, 23, 24, 26, 28, 31; 15:1, 8-10, 15, 16, 23, 24, 26; 16:3, 10,
         15, 17, 23, 25, 26, 27, 28, 32; 17:1, 5, 11, 21, 24, 25*
         b) Title (*"God"*) *Jn 13:3, 31, 32; 14:1; 16:2, 27, 30; 17:3*
         c) Appellatives (*"only"* – *"true"* – *"just"*) *Jn 17:3, 11, 25*
      3. Titles (*"the Son of man"* – *"Messiah"* or *"Christ"*)
         Jn 13:31; 17:3
      4. Appellatives (*"the way"* – *"the truth"* – *"the life"*) *Jn 14:6*

   B. **STATEMENT OF RELATIONSHIP FOR TWOFOLD
   INVESTITURE COVENANT**
      1. Between the Father and the New Israel (king-with-people)
         Jn 15:1, 2
      2. Between King (Jesus Messiah) and People *Jn 15:4, 5*

   C. **ROYAL PROVISION CLAUSE** *Jn 17:2, 3*

   D. **HISTORICAL PROLOGUE**
      1. Benefits of the Father to Jesus Messiah
         a) Gift of glory/Divine Sonship *Jn 17:22, 24; 17:11, 12*
         b) Universal and Everlasting Authority
            Jn 13:3; 16:15; 17:2, 10
         c) Subjects *Jn 17:2, 6, 9, 24*

2. Benefits of Jesus Messiah and Father to People
    a) Covenant Election:
        (1) by Jesus *Jn 13:1,18; 15:16, 19*
        (2) by God the Father *Jn 17:6, 9*
    b) Protection *Jn 17:12*

E. STIPULATION CLAUSE
1. New Commandment
    a) For the New Israel *Jn 13:34, 35*
    b) For individual subjects *Jn 15:9, 10, 12-17*
2. Prohibition of Relationship with World *Jn 15:18-25; 16:1-4*
3. Absolute Faith and Complete Confidence *Jn 14:1, 27; 16:33*

F. DIVINE WITNESS CLAUSE
1. Paraclete *Jn 15:26*
2. Disciples *Jn 15:27*

G. CURSE-BLESSING FORMULA
1. Curses
    a) For Refusal to Accept Covenant *Jn 13:8*
    b) For Infidelity to Covenant *Jn 15:6*
2. Blessings
    a) Eternal Life *Jn 12:50; 17:2, 3; 14:21, 23, 27; 16:33*
    b) Abode in the Father's House *Jn 14:2, 3*
    c) Assistance of the Paraclete *Jn 14:16, 26; 16:7, 13-15*
    d) Blessings for the Mission of the New Israel *Jn 14:12-14*
    e) Blessings for the Branches of the Vine
        Jn 15:5, 7, 11; 16:23-27

III. STATEMENT OF COVENANT-MAKING
1. Peter's oath accepting the Footwashing *Jn 13:6-9*
2. Jesus completed his work and glorified his Father in himself
    Jn 13:31; 17:4, 5
3. The disciples knew and saw the Father *Jn 14:6, 7*
4. Disciples incorporated into Jesus *Jn 14:20; 15:1*
5. Judgment brought upon the world and its ruler driven out
    Jn 14:30; 16:11, 33
6. Covenant union established *Jn 15:1, 5*
7. Proclamation of the Father's word completed *Jn 15:3, 18; 17:8, 14*
8. Jesus loved his disciples as the Father loved him
    Jn 17:6, 22, 23, 26

The Mass Is the Passion and Death of Our Lord

(Written by Mrs. Dorothy O'Neill Weimar, O.P., in obedience to her spiritual director)

Our Divine Lord told me that He would give me "a love beyond the imagination and knowledge of men." On another day Jesus told me: "You will sing the Mass with your heart," and that my heart would live within Father's.[321] When I told Father this he said, "If it's God's will, it's all right with me." So, there it has remained, and especially during Father's Mass.

As Father is one with Jesus, so, when he is vesting for Mass, I begin to feel the warm, living Blood of Jesus flowing around the flesh of Father's heart. I feel, through Father, Jesus' steps as He walks the road to the Garden of Olives. I feel the slight tenseness of His body, caused by the knowledge of what is to happen. The night air is moist and cool. I kneel with Him in the Garden. It is the Agony of Jesus in the Garden all over again. Sometimes I put my hand down, almost as if I doubted, to take a handful of the warm sand and let it sift through my fingers. How I am within Jesus at times, and yet myself, is, of course, as everything, by the power of God.

From the Garden we see down on the world: most often, fields of leaping flames, which Our Lord tells me are *sins of pride sweeping the world*. He has told me that *the sins of this generation cause Him His most bitter suffering*.

I feel the burning flesh of Jesus, and with my hand brush back His matted hair, and kiss away His tears. I feel Father's hands clasp over Jesus'. Then our souls leave—in some manner—our bodies, and go down through darkness. Everything around is slimy, moving, snake-like, creepy. On occasion, Lucifer has approached and threatened me for taking souls away from him. I hear souls screaming, moaning. The black cloak of penance is heavy over Father's shoulders.[322] The walking becomes almost impossible. Over and over I call: "Mary! Mary!" Sometimes I feel a Rosary made of living drops of Our Lord's blood between his fingers.[323] Then I feel that burning,

---

321   The priest referred to here was Dorothy's spiritual director, the Rev. Michael L. Novacki, O.P.

322   The black cloak referred to here is part of the Dominican habit and signifies penance.

323   St. Dominic told Dorothy that the Rosary was formed by the drops of Our Lord's

passionate, intense love of Jesus: His Heart pounds with love as we see these souls. They are buried and suffering in this slime of sin. Some are indifferent; others are reaching out for help. I see Father go to one and then to another. I hear him making love to them, whispering words of love to them, coaxing them; sometimes he holds one close to his heart.

We find ourselves back with Our Lord, perhaps just when I feel the kiss of Judas against Jesus' cheek. "Oh Jesus, it is my sins that have betrayed you." I feel each step of Jesus back into town; the Apostles run away; the mob mocks Him: they shove and push Him, pull His hair and beard; the trial goes on before the Sanhedrin; Peter denies Him. I live through the *bitter hours of unbelievable loneliness* at His feet in prison. In the morning, I hear the drunken mob returning. Our Lord is brought before the Sanhedrin; then to Pilate; then to Herod; and again back to Pilate. I hear him ask: "Are you a king?" I feel Our Lord's back slightly straighten and I heard Him answer: "**I am a King.**" Since then He has told me so often when he appears as "Christ the King" that His kingdom is in the hearts of men. And as they take Him away, they push and shove Him; they pull His hair; and one of the blows knocks Him over. When Father moved to the gospel side of the altar, for a minute I saw him. Then at the scourging I feel each blow against the flesh of Father's back: the rope that ties and burns His wrists; the crowning with thorns. Within Jesus' sorrowful Heart I hear the mob cry, "Crucify Him!"

Then I feel the weight of the cross cutting into His shoulder. Sometimes He stops and lets me kiss that wound. One would think that the pain of touching it would be unbearable; but no; it seems to ease His suffering. We walk a little farther, and Veronica rushes out to wipe His face. This courageous act of love causes the pain of Jesus to cease for a few seconds. I feel the pressure of her veil against Father's face.

I feel Jesus' tongue so thick, so swollen; the cool metal cup of wine mixed with myrrh against His lips—usually given to numb the pain of the flesh—but which consolation Jesus refuses, because it was not prompted by love as was Veronica's act. He looks to see what choice I will make. But, "My Beloved White Dove (Canticle of Canticles), what can I do but refuse." I kiss away the tears of blood that come from His eyes. I feel it all through Father. And then comes that most cruel of all moments when the first blow of the hammer sends the nail crushing through Jesus' hand.

Then for three long, bitter hours, I feel the terrible pain of Jesus' blood leaving His body drop by drop until this pain, caused by sin, becomes so terrible that only the Infinite Love of Jesus, Who bears it for us in reparation, can

---

blood. Mary said that the story of her Rosary is "the story of the Mass—the Life, Death, and Resurrection of Jesus."

and does act as an anesthetic. The pain is gone. There is only love. Suffering has become a joy. I feel the beating of Jesus' Heart. Through Father, I feel His arms outstretched as on the cross: Jesus is a Burning White Cross of Love. Great golden clouds, filled with angels, suddenly roll gloriously like thunder-clouds over the mud, the filth of Calvary. There is the throne of Our Heavenly Father. I see His arms outstretched to embrace Jesus. I feel the most precious blood of Jesus, His Infinite Love, flowing through His wounds down upon the world. IT IS THE CONSECRATION OF THE MASS. One day our Blessed Mother told me that at the Consecration, "Heaven and earth are united as one." Then, looking down from the Sacred Heart of Jesus upon the world, I see souls coming from all over: some come very quickly; others just slowly; others are carried by angels. These, I think are the dying.

What follows the Consecration, I can never describe except that the air is fragrant with the odor of spices and roses. I become so hungry for Our Lord's flesh and blood at this time. Sometimes I see our Lord coming swiftly as on a soft breeze, with His arms outstretched. At other times He comes from the cross; and sometimes, invisibly. As He comes close, I taste His flesh and feel each pore on Father's tongue, then going slowly into his throat and into his heart. On First Friday I taste His burning flesh. On occasion, His flesh tastes as a rose petal, that is, His Infant flesh. From Jesus' hands held like a cup we drink His most precious blood. Our souls just leap with joy. I feel His kiss against Father's cheek. Sometimes He says, "With desire, I have desired to eat this Pasch with you." I feel the breath of the Holy Ghost filling Father's heart. I feel Jesus' flesh drawing us into Himself. I melt at His feet and our souls sing of love to Him. It is after this that Jesus talks to me. When the priest distributes Holy Communion, I often see Our Lord in soft white garments, barefooted, coming to the spiritually lame, halt, and blind. I do not see the priest, but only Christ. As Jesus raises His hand in absolution,[324] our souls sing this prayer to Him:

> O Thou Who of old didst love Thy hand to lay
> On the dull vacant eyes that craved for light,
> Behold! I come to Thee, and crying pray:
> "O Christ, O Son of David, give me sight!
> A faith scarce clouded by the mists of earth,
> A faith pierced Heaven, I ask of Thee;
> Faith to prize all things by their lasting worth;
> Thou canst, Thou wilt—O Lord, that I may see!"[325]

---

324   According to the Roman Missal (1948), the rubrics required the priest to impart absolution at Mass before distributing Holy Communion.

325   This prayer was composed by Mother Mary Loyola (1845-1930).

As Jesus goes to each soul I see His arms embrace that soul, and it disappears, for it becomes one with Him. The life of the priest in black may appear dull and boring to the world, and, at times, even to the priest himself because he is human. But if priests would only remember that they are the most adventurous, the most daring, the most thrilling of lovers when they bring Christ's love to a soul in sin, there could be no dullness to amount to anything. Their hearts contain the love of Christ: all of the passion of Magdalen, the fire of St. Paul, the recklessness of St. Peter, the gentleness of St. John. If they would only see the Light of the Holy Ghost Who causes souls of sinners to melt at their spoken words, as Magdalen did when her eyes met the eyes of Jesus for the first time! Priests are lovers who, one with Christ, at the Consecration unite Heaven and earth.

Just as I share in the sufferings of Our Lord through Father, so too, I receive His flesh and blood through Father.[326] Our Lord asked me to sacrifice the joy of receiving Him in the customary manner, because He desires to show how close the soul of every mortal is within the Heart of Jesus at the Mass. To those who assist at Mass, of course, more graces are given. But Jesus' Heart burns with love for each and every soul on earth and in purgatory, as well as for those in Heaven. His priests, who are one with Him, share in that all-embracing love of souls, and all souls are thus in the heart of every priest.

---

326   This extraordinary manner of receiving Our Lord in Holy Communion lasted only for a period of time. Our Lord subsequently allowed Dorothy to resume receiving Holy Communion in the accustomed manner.

Bibliography

Achtemeir, E.R. "Righteousness in the OT," *IDB*, IV, 81-83.

Anderson, B.W. "God, names of," *IDB*, II, 409-411.

Baltzer, Klaus. *The Covenant Formulary in Old Testament, Jewish, and Early Christian Writings*. Trans. David E. Green (Philadelphia: Fortress Press, 1971).

Barrett, C.K. *The Gospel According to St. John: An Introduction with Commentary and Notes on the Greek Text.* 2nd ed. (Philadelphia: The Westminster Press, 1978).

——*The Gospel of John & Judaism.* Trans. D.M. Smith (Philadelphia: Fortress Press, 1975).

Beasley-Murray, George R. *John*. Gen. eds. David A. Hubbard, Glenn W. Barker. "Word Biblical Commentary," Vol. XXXVI (Waco, TX: Word Books, 1987).

Bernard, J.H. *A Critical and Exegetical Commentary on the Gospel According to St. John.* Ed. A.H. McNeile. 2 vols., "The International Critical Commentary" (Edinburgh: T. & T. Clark, 1985).

Borsch, Frederick Houk. *The Son of Man in Myth and History.* "The New Testament Library" (London: SCM Press Ltd, 1967).

Bright, John. *A History of Israel.* 3rd ed. (London: SCM Press Ltd, 1984).

Brosnan, Brodie. *The Sacrifice of the New Law* (New York: Benzinger Brothers, 1926).

Brown, Raymond E., S.S. *Priest and Bishop: Biblical Reflections* (Paramus: Paulist Press, 1970).

——*The Gospel According to John.* 2 vols. Anchor Bible 29, 29 A (New York: Doubleday & Company, Inc., 1966).

——*Old Testament Reading Guide: The Book of Deuteronomy* (Collegeville, MN: The Liturgical Press: n.d.).

——*The Community of the Beloved Disciple: The Life, Loves, and Hates of an Individual Church in New Testament Times* (New York/ Ramsey/Toronto: Paulist Press, 1979).

——*The Gospel and Epistles of John: A Concise Commentary* (Collegeville, MN: The Liturgical Press, 1988).

——*An Introduction to the Gospel of John.* Ed. Francis J. Moloney, S.D.B. (New York: Doubleday, 2003).

Brown, Raymond E., Joseph A. Fitzmyer and Roland E. Murphy. Eds. *The Jerome Biblical Commentary*, 2 vols. (Englewood Cliffs, NJ: Prentice-Hall, Inc., 1968).

Bultmann, Rudolf. *The Gospel of John: A Commentary.* Trans. G.R. Beasley-Murray (Oxford: Basil Blackwell, 1971).

Buttrick, George Arthur, *et al.,* eds. *The Interpreter's Dictionary of the Bible: An Illustrated Encyclopedia*, 4 vols. and supplement (Nashville: Abingdon Press, 1962-1976).

Cancian, Domenico. *Nuovo Comandamento Nuova Alleanza: Eucaristia nell'interpretazione del capitolo 13 de Vangelo di Giovanni* (Collevalenza, Perugia: Edizione "L'Amore Misericordioso," 1978).

Casel, Odo. *The Mystery of Christian Worship.* Ed. Burkhard Neunheuser, O.S.B., A Herder & Herder Book (New York, The Crossroad Publishing Company, 1999).

Chenderlin, Fritz. *"Do This As My Memorial,"* The Semantic and Conceptual Background and Value of ἀνάμνησιν in 1 Corinthians 11:24-25, "Analecta Biblica, Investigationes Scientificae In Res Biblicas" 99 (Rome: Biblical Institute Press, 1982).

Clifford, Richard. *Deuteronomy with an Excursus on Covenant and Law.* Eds. Carroll Stuhlmueller and Martin McNamara. "Old Testament Message, A Biblical-Theological Commentary," Vol. IV (Wilmington, DE: Michael Glazier, Inc., 1982).

Craigie, Peter C. *The Book of Deuteronomy.* "The New International Commentary on the Old Testament" (Grand Rapids, MI: William B. Eerdmans Publishing Co., 1981).

Crane, Thomas F. *The Message of Saint John: The Spiritual Teaching of the Beloved Disciple* (Staten Island, NY: Alba House, 1980).

Culpepper, R. Alan. *Anatomy of the Fourth Gospel: A Study in Literary Design* (Philadelphia: Fortress Press, 1983).

Culpepper, R. Alan and C. Clinton Black. Eds. *Exploring the Gospel of John, In Honor of D. Moody Smith* (Louisville, KY: Westminster John Knox Press, 1996).

de Vaux, Roland. *Ancient Israel: Its Life and Institutions.* Trans. John McHugh (London: Darton, Longman & Todd, 1980).

de la Potterie, Ignace, S.J. *The Hour of Jesus: The Passion and the Resurrection of Jesus According to John* (New York: Alba House, 1984).

Dodd, C.H. *The Interpretation of the Fourth Gospel* (Cambridge: Cambridge University Press, 1980).

Donahue, John R. Ed. *Life In Abundance: Studies of John's Gospel in Tribute to Raymond E. Brown, S.S.* (Collegeville, MN: Liturgical Press, 2005).

Eichrodt, Walther. *Theology of the Old Testament.* Trans. John Baker. 2 vols. (London: SCM Press Ltd, 1983).

Ferland, Augustus, p.s.s. *Commentarius in Summam D. Thomae, De Sacramentis in Speciali, De Novissimis* (Montréal, Canada, Grand Séminaire, Faculté de Théologie, 1955).

Feuillet, Andre. *Johannine Studies* (Staten Island, NY: Alba House, 1964).

Gihr, Nicholas. *The Holy Sacrifice of the Mass, Dogmatically, Liturgically, and Ascetically Explained* (St. Louis, MO: B. Herder Book Co., 1953).

Good, E.M. "Peace," *IDB*, III, 704.

Gredt, Josephus, O.S.B. *Elementa Philosophiae Aristotelico-Thomisticae,* 9th ed., 2 vols. (Barcelona, Editorial Herder, 1951).

Grenier, Brian, C.F.C. *St. John's Gospel: A Self-directed Retreat* (Homebush, NSW 2140: St. Paul Publications, 1991).

Grenier, Henri. *Thomistic Philosophy.* Trans. J.P.E. O'Hanley. 4 vols. (Charlottetown, Canada: St. Dunstan's University, 1950).

Hahn, Scott W. Gen. ed. *Catholic Bible Dictionary* (New York: Doubleday, 2008).

——*Kinship by Covenant: A Canonical Approach to the Fulfillment of God's Saving Promises* (New Haven & London: Yale University Press, 2009).

Hayes, John H. and J. Maxwell Miller. Eds. *Israelite and Judean History* (London: SCM Press Ltd, 1984).

Heinisch, Paul. *Christ in Prophecy.* Trans. William G. Heidt (Collegeville, MN: The Liturgical Press, 1956).

Hillers, Delbert R. *Covenant: The History of a Biblical Idea.* Eds. George E. Owen *et al.* "Seminars in the History of Ideas" (Baltimore: The Johns Hopkins Press, 1969).

Horton, Michael. *God of Promise: Introducing Covenant Theology* (Grand Rapids, MI: Baker Books, 2006).

Journet, Charles. *La Messe, Présence du Sacrifice de la Croix.* 2d ed. "Textes et Études Théologiques" (Desclée De Brouwer, 1958).

Kasper, Walter. *Jesus the Christ* (New York: Paulist Press, 1977).

Kilmartin, E.J. "Eucharist (As Sacrifice)," *NCE*, V, pp. 611, 612.

Khamor, Levi. *The Revelation of the Son of Man* (Petersham, MA: St. Bede's Publications, 1989).

Koester, Craig R. *Symbolism in the Fourth Gospel: Meaning, Mystery, Community.* 2nd ed. (Minneapolis: Fortress Press, 2002).

Lacomara, Aelred, C.P. "Deuteronomy and the Farewell Discourse (Jn 13:31 - 16:35)," *CBQ*, 36, 1947, pp. 65-84.

Lampe, G.W.H. "Paraclete," *IDB*, III, p. 654.

Lawler, Michael G. *Symbol and Sacrament* (New York/Mahwah, NJ: Paulist Press, 1987).

Lepicier, Cardinal Alessio Enrico M. *In Che Cosa Consista L'Essenza del Sacrificio Eucaristico* (Roma: Officina Poligrafica Laziale, 1934-XII).

Lightfoot, R.H. *St. John's Gospel: A Commentary.* Ed. C.F. Evans (Oxford: Clarendon Press, 1983).

Lindars, Barnabas. *The Gospel of John.* Gen. ed. Matthew Black. "New Century Bible Commentary" (Grand Rapids, MI: Wm. B. Eerdmans Publishing Co., 1982).

Macy, Gary, *The Banquet's Wisdom: A Short History of the Theologies of the Lord's Supper* (New York, Mahwah, NJ: Paulist Press, 1992).

Marrow, Stanley B. *The Gospel of John: A Reading* (New York/Mahwah, NJ: Paulist Press, 1995).

Masure, Canon Eugene. *The Sacrifice of the Mystical Body* (London: Burns & Oates, 1954).

Mateos, J., J. Barreto, *et al. Il Vangelo di Giovanni, analisi linguistica e commento esegetico.* "Lettura del Nuovo Testamento" (Assisi: Cittadella Editrice, 1982).

——*Dizionario Teologico del Vangelo di Giovanni* (Assisi: Cittadella Editrice, 1982).

McCarthy, Dennis J., S.J. *Treaty And Covenant: A Study in Form in the Ancient Oriental Documents and in the Old Testament.* 2d ed. "Analecta Biblica, Investigationes Scientificae In Res Biblicas" 21 A. (Rome: Biblical Institute Press, 1978).

——*Old Testament Covenant, A Survey of Current Opinions* (Richmond, VA: John Knox Press).

——"Notes on the Love of God in Deuteronomy and the Father-Son Relationship Between Yahweh and Israel," *CBQ*, 27, 1965, p. 147.

McKenzie, S.J., John L. *Dictionary of the Bible* (New York: Macmillan Publishing Co., Inc., 1977).

——"Holy," *DOB*, p. 365.

McPolin, James, S.J. *John.* "New Testament Message," VI (Dublin: Veritas Publications, 1984).

Mendenhall, G. "Covenant," *IDB*, I, pp. 714-723; "Election," *IDB*, II, pp. 76, 77, 79.

Minge, J. *Patrologiae Cursus Completus*, Series Latina, 221 vols. (Paris, 1844-1864).

Moloney, Francis J., S.D.B. *The Johannine Son of Man.* 2d ed. "Biblioteca di Scienze Religiose," Vol. 14 (Roma: Libreria Ateneo Salesiano, 1978).

——"A Sacramental Reading of John 13:1-38," *CBQ*, 53, 1991, pp. 237-256.

——*The Gospel of John.* Ed. Daniel J. Harrington. Sacra Pagina Series, Vol. 4 (Collegeville, MN: A Michael Glazien Book, The Liturgical Press, 1998).

Morris, Leon. *The Gospel According to John: The English Text with Introduction, Exposition and Notes.* "The New International Commentary on the New Testament" (Grand Rapids, MI: Wm. B. Eerdmans Publishing Co., 1979).

Moulton, Harold K. Ed. *The Analytical Greek Lexicon Revised* (Grand Rapids, MI: Zondervan Publishing House, 1978).

Muilenburg, J. "Holiness," *IDB*, II, 617.

Napier, B.D. "Prophet," *IDB*, III, p. 913.

Nichols, Aidan, O.P. *The Holy Eucharist: From the New Testament to Pope John Paul II* (Dublin: Veritas 1991).

Nolli, Gianfranco. *Evangelo Secondo Giovanni, Testo Greco, Neovolgata Latina, Analisi Filologica, Traduzione Italiana* (Città del Vaticano: Libreria Editrice Vaticana, 1987).

O'Grady, John F. *According to John: The Witness of the Beloved Disciple* (New York/Mahwah, NJ: Paulist Press, 1999).

Olaguer, Jr., Dr. Edouardo P. *Born from Above: A Commentary on John's Gospel* (Worcester, MA: Ambassador Books, Inc., 1998).

Orchard, Bernard, *et al.,* eds. *A Catholic Commentary on Holy Scripture* (New York: Thomas Nelson & Sons, 1953).

Ott, Ludwig. *Fundamentals of Catholic Dogma.* English ed. James Canon Bastible. Trans. Patrick Lynch. 6th ed. (St. Louis, MO: B. Herder Book Co., 1964).

Panimolle, Salvatore Alberto. *Lettura Pastorale del Vangelo di Giovanni.* 3rd ed., 3 vols. (Bologna: Edizioni Dehoniae Bologna, 1988).

Pinto, Evarist. *Jesus the Son and Giver of Life in the Fourth Gospel* (Rome: Pontificia Universitas Urbaniana, 1981).

Prat, Ferdinand. *Jesus Christ: His Life, His Teaching, and His Work.* Gen. ed. Joseph Husslein. Trans. John J. Heenan. 2 vols. "Science and Culture Series" (Milwaukee: Bruce Publishing Co., 1951).

Pritchard, James B. Ed. *Ancient Near Eastern Texts Relating to the Old Testament,* 3rd ed. with supplement (Princeton, NJ: Princeton University Press, 1969).

Quast, Kevin. *Reading the Gospel of John: An Introduction.* Revised edition (New York/Mahwah, NJ: Paulist Press, 1991).

Ravasi, Gian Franco. *Il Vangelo di Giovanni* (Bologna: Edizioni Dehoniane Bologna, 1990).

Ray, Stephen K. *St. John's Gospel: A Bible Study Guide and Commentary* (San Francisco: Ignatius Press, 2002).

Riemann, P. A. "Mosaic Covenant," *IDB*, Suppl., p. 195.

Robinson, John A.T. *The Priority of John.* Ed. J.F. Coakley (London: SCM Press Ltd, 1985).

Roschini, Gabriele M., O.S.M. *L'Essenza del Sacrificio Eucaristico* (Roma: Officina Tipografica Romana Buono Stampe, 1936).

Sanders, J.N. and Mastin, B.A. *A Commentary on the Gospel According to St. John.* "Black's New Testament Commentaries" (London: Adam & Charles Black, 1977).

Schmaus, Michael. *Dogma. The Church as Sacrament,* Vol. V (London: Sheed and Ward, 1990).

Schnackenburg, Rudolf. *The Gospel According to St. John.* 3 vols. (New York: Crossroad, 1982).

Senior, Donald, C.R. *The Passion of Jesus in the Gospel of John.* The Passion Series, Vol. 4 (Collegeville, MN: The Liturgical Press, 1991).

Sloyan, Gerard S. *What Are They Saying About John?* Revised edition (New York/Mahwah, NJ: Paulist Press, 2006).

Smith, Canon George D. *The Teaching of the Catholic Church* (London: Burns & Oates, 1956).

Taylor, Michael J. *John, The Different Gospel: A Reflective Commentary* (New York: Alba House, 1983).

Vagaggini, Cyprian, O.S.B. *Theological Dimensions of the Liturgy.* Trans. Leonard J. Doyle and W.A. Jurgens. 4th ed. (Collegeville, MN: The Liturgical Press, 1976).

von Balthasar, Hans Urs. *The Glory of the Lord: A Theological Aesthetics,* Vol. VII. Theology: The New Covenant. Trans. Brian McNeil C.R.V., ed. John Riches (San Francisco: Ignatius Press, 1989).

von Rad, Gerhard. *Old Testament Theology.* Trans. D.M.G. Stalker. 2 vols. (London: SCM Press Ltd, 1982-1985).

——*Deuteronomy, A Commentary.* Trans. Dorothea Barton. "Old Testament Library" (London: SCM Press Ltd, 1979).

von Speyr, Adrienne. *The Farewell Discourses, Meditations on John 13-17.* Trans E.A. Nelson (San Francisco: Ignatius Press, 1987).

Weinfeld, M. "Covenant, Davidic," *IDB*, Suppl., 190, 191.

Wengier, Francis J. *The Eucharist-Sacrifice* (Milwaukee: Bruce Publishing Company, 1955).

Wijngaards, John, **M.H.M.** *The Gospel of John and His Letters.* "Message of Biblical Spirituality," Vol. XI (Wilmington, DE: Michael Glazier, 1986).

Zerwick, Maximilian. *Biblical Greek Illustrated by Examples.* Second ed. (Rome: Scripta Pontificii Instituti Biblici, 1983).

Index

God 3, 4, 6, 7, 10, 12, 14, 15, 17, 20, 21, 23-35, 38, 39, 44, 47, 53, 57, 58, 59, 61, 62, 65, 67, 73-75, 77, 80, 82, 85, 87-135, 137, 138, 139, 141, 142-144, 146-149, 151-153, 157, 159, 161

Great King 78, 79, 81, 82, 84, 85, 88, 91, 99, 102, 103, 106, 119, 133, 135, 146

H

Hesed 13, 24, 96

Historical 31, 45, 56, 57, 59-61, 63, 64, 66, 77, 81, 102, 103, 110, 116

Historical Prologue 81, 102, 103, 110, 116

History 12, 58, 81, 89, 103, 108

Holy 5, 18, 28, 30, 34, 41, 53, 56-58, 65-67, 93, 103, 104, 111, 112, 117, 118, 130, 131, 144, 155, 156, 159, 161, 162

Holy Spirit 30, 34, 58, 67, 104, 111, 130, 131, 144

Hour, the 3, 10, 29, 33, 37, 40, 44, 49, 91, 137

House 4, 23, 31, 127-129, 138, 152, 158, 159, 161, 163

Hypostatic 14, 21, 35, 47, 104

I

Infidelity 12, 80, 98, 108, 119, 121, 123, 152

Investiture 72, 75, 76, 84, 85, 88, 90, 91, 95, 97, 100-102, 105, 118, 123, 138

Ireland 65

Israel 11, 12, 14, 15, 17, 24-28, 30, 31, 33, 34, 44-46, 65, 73-75, 77-80, 82, 84-86, 92, 93-103, 105, 106, 109-112, 114, 117, 118, 120, 122, 124, 129-135, 139, 141, 143, 145-147, 151, 152, 157, 158, 161

J

Jesus 2-5, 9-11, 13-17, 19, 21, 23-35, 37-41, 43-61, 63, 64, 66, 67, 71, 73-75, 77, 86-139, 143-149, 151-156, 159, 160, 162

Joshua 77, 79, 120

Judas 9, 16, 41, 44, 45, 47, 90, 107, 108, 121, 154

Judgment 3, 12, 18, 29, 30, 32, 37, 38, 41, 49, 50, 75, 93, 117, 119, 124, 138, 139, 152

K

Kilmartin, E.J. 53, 56, 57, 160

King 6, 12, 18, 24-32, 34, 39, 47, 65, 74, 75, 78, 79, 81, 82, 84-86, 88-91, 96, 97, 99-103, 106, 109, 112, 118-120, 122, 133, 135, 138, 146, 147, 151, 154

Kingship 25, 27, 30, 74, 75, 84, 85, 102

Kinship 12, 13, 15, 82, 143, 159

Knock 65

L

Land 14, 23, 80, 122, 124, 129

Lepicier, Alessio Enrico M. Cardinal, O.S.M. 54, 55, 60, 160

Level 19, 89, 143

Life 84-86, 124, 152, 154, 157-159, 162

eternal 4, 23, 25, 29, 30, 32, 88, 94-96, 99-102, 105, 111, 114, 118, 123, 124-130, 144, 145, 152

Loisy, Alfred 18, 19

Lord 9, 10, 13-17, 19, 21, 30, 31, 49, 53, 55, 59-62, 64-67, 74, 75, 101, 102, 115, 118, 119, 121, 123, 125, 127, 128, 131, 137, 138, 153-156, 163

R

Refusal 15, 26, 119, 123, 152
Relationship 11-13, 15, 21, 24, 38, 39,
    46, 54, 56, 61, 62, 67, 75, 78-83,
    90, 92-101, 106, 108-112,
    114-118, 124, 125, 127, 130,
    133, 135, 136, 138, 139, 141,
    142, 144, 148, 152, 161
Report of covenant-making 69 ff.
Ritual 10, 12, 19, 57, 79, 80
Role 27, 34, 43, 47, 50, 52, 64, 66, 75,
    88, 89, 107, 117, 118, 130, 131,
    145, 146
Royal 23-25, 27, 28, 30-32, 34, 72, 73,
    75, 76, 78, 79, 81, 84, 85, 88-91,
    94, 95, 97-103, 105, 111, 114,
    118-120, 122-126, 128, 129,
    132, 133, 138, 139, 143, 144,
    146, 147, 151
    Provision Clause 85, 100-102,
    111, 118, 124, 126, 128, 129,
    138, 144
Royal Enthronement 132

S

Sacrament 57, 63, 64, 148, 160, 162
Sacrifice 4, 5, 19, 35, 53-61, 63-67,
    112, 113, 156, 157, 159, 160,
    163
    absolute 64
    complete 53-55, 59, 61
    elements of 64
    relative 63, 64
Schnackenburg, Rudolf 2, 5, 32, 41,
    44, 73, 102, 118, 145, 162
Servant 26, 30, 31, 33, 74, 82, 109
Service 4, 15, 17, 81, 83, 90, 102, 115,
    118, 130, 142, 146, 147
Setting 10, 13, 30, 43, 44, 45, 47, 48,
    71-73, 77, 85, 90, 101, 102, 121
Sign 10, 11, 39, 64
Son of God 14, 15, 23, 24, 27, 29, 31,
    32, 35, 39, 74, 75, 91, 94, 95,
    104, 110, 125, 144, 147, 151

Son of Man 25, 26, 30, 31, 37, 48, 50,
    157, 160, 161
Sovereign 25, 29, 34, 38, 47, 81, 82,
    98-100, 102, 114, 115, 142
Spirit 20, 26, 30, 34, 40, 49-52, 58, 67,
    74, 87, 94, 96, 104, 110-113,
    116-120, 125, 126, 130-133,
    144-146
    communication of 49-51
    Holy 30, 34, 58, 67, 104, 111,
    130, 131, 144
    of truth 50, 94, 116-118, 120,
    125, 131, 133, 145
Spoken 6, 14, 15, 17, 25, 26, 50, 59,
    74, 94, 95, 98, 100, 102, 114,
    130, 132-134, 139, 145, 156
St. Faustina 55
Statement of Relationship 81, 82, 97,
    98, 135
Status 23, 25, 27, 30-33, 43, 89
Stipulation 82, 97, 106-110, 113-115,
    121, 126, 128, 134, 142
Stipulation Clause 82, 97, 106-108,
    121, 126, 142
Suzerain 75, 78, 79, 81-83, 85, 88, 89,
    92, 96, 97, 101, 102, 119, 122,
    128, 135, 139
Symbolic 4, 5, 15, 19, 52, 79, 80, 142,
    143
Synoptic Last Supper Accounts 61

T

Titulary 81, 91
Titulary Clause 81, 91
Tradition 5, 16, 47, 48, 72, 76, 79, 84,
    85, 90, 91, 97, 100, 102, 106,
    108, 115, 118, 120, 122, 126,
    127, 135, 137, 141-143
Treaty 11-13, 19, 71, 72, 75-86, 88,
    89, 91, 92, 101-103, 106-108,
    113-116, 119, 120, 122, 126-129,
    135, 139, 141-143, 146, 151, 160
True vine 16, 27, 28, 34, 98, 99, 111,
    123, 124, 130, 134-136, 139,
    147, 148

About the Author

Msgr. Anthony A. La Femina, a native of New Haven, Connecticut, was ordained a priest in 1961 and is incardinated in the Diocese of Venice in Florida. He obtained a Licentiate in Sacred Theology and a Doctorate in Canon Law. Previous to his appointment to Rome, he had parochial, chancery and tribunal positions in the Diocese of St-Jerome (Quebec) and was an Advocate in the Tribunal of the Archdiocese of Montreal, Canada. In the Vatican he served as an official of the Roman Curia for 26 years. Following this he was occupied with Eucharistic evangelization in the Diocese of Charleston, South Carolina. Monsignor is a recognized iconographer; some of his icons are presented with this study.